POSTCARD HISTORY SERIES

New Philadelphia

IN VINTAGE POSTCARDS

(*cover*) The square of downtown New Philadelphia featured a "Welcome to Our City" sign on top of the Alexander Building and a banner displaying "Welcome Bill" during the Benevolent Protective Order of Elks (BPOE) celebration *circa* 1915.

POSTCARD HISTORY SERIES

New Philadelphia
IN VINTAGE POSTCARDS

Erin L. VanFossen

ARCADIA
PUBLISHING

ISBN 978-0-7385-3288-2

Published by Arcadia Publishing
Charleston, South Carolina

Printed in the United States of America

Library of Congress Catalog Card Number: 2004105602

For all general information contact Arcadia Publishing at:
Telephone 843-853-2070
Fax 843-853-0044
E-mail sales@arcadiapublishing.com
For customer service and orders:
Toll-Free 1-888-313-2665

Visit us on the Internet at www.arcadiapublishing.com

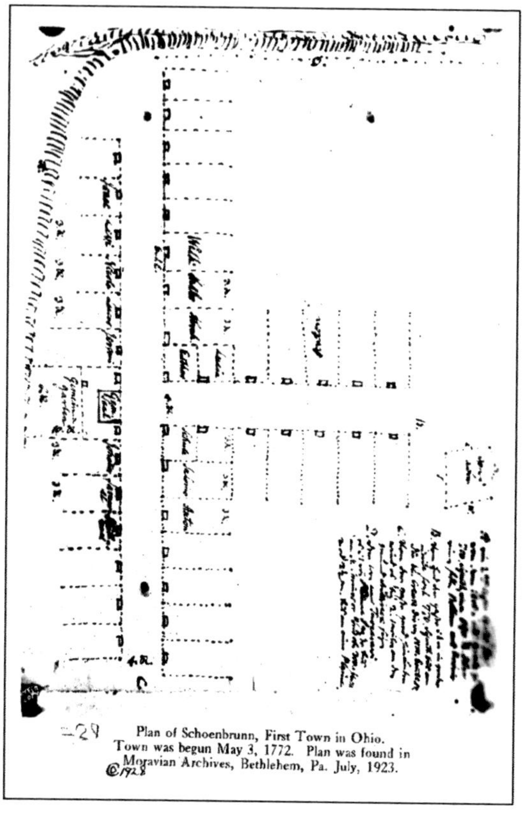

Schoenbrunn Village, the first town in Ohio, was begun May 3, 1772. This plan of the Village was found in the Moravian Archives in Bethlehem, Pennsylvania, in July 1923.

Contents

ACKNOWLEDGMENTS

This book would not be possible without the wonderful postcard collections of Mr. Richard H. Rausch II of 1038 College Drive SE, New Philadelphia, Ohio, and Mrs. Dorothy Mehok of 314 Orchard Street, Uhrichsville, Ohio. Their collections show a lifetime of history and a love for their communities.

My sincere thanks go to Debbie Courtright, Susi Cox, Joe Bonamico, George Laurence, Sandy Cox, the City of New Philadelphia Bicentennial Committee, the *Daily Times*, the *Times Reporter*, the Tuscarawas County Historical Society, and Mr. Fred Miller for their valuable input and talents.

New Philadelphia—My Home Town

The story of my home town
Is one man's dream come true,
John Knisely had a vision
And the strength to see it through.
On horizons of a forest land—
He saw a city rise.
And my home town was born that day—
Through a dreamer's eyes.

On a sweet summer evening
You can hear a trumpet in the land—
The story will remind you
To live in peace with fellow man.
From the trails at Schoenbrunn Village—
To the gates at Tuscora Park—
It's a place we love and call our home
And carry in our hearts.

No matter who you are,
No matter where you've been. . .
It's always good to find yourself—
Back home again.
I've been everywhere—
Traveled all around.
And I'm so glad that this town—
Is my home town.

As you can see, my home town
Has come a long, long way
With those who have gone before us
To make it what it is today,
We've built a home.
We've built a life
Where others showed the way—
And it's still a place where dreamers dream—
That's why I'm glad to say.

No matter who you are,
No matter where you've been. . .
It's always good to find yourself—
Back home again.
I've been everywhere—
Traveled all around,
And I'm so glad that this town—
Is my home town.

Every stop along the way has a story to be told,
And every generation has a heritage to hold.

–Susi Cox

FOREWORD

On October 26, 1903, the New Philadelphia *Daily Reporter* began printing plans for the Centennial Celebration, "Whereas, the year 1904 will mark the first centenary of the founding of this town of New Philadelphia, by its pioneer citizen John Knisely. Therefore, be it resolved by the council of the city of New Philadelphia, Ohio, that we hereby formally direct the general attention of our citizens, to an event of so much moment and interest, and that we commend its fit and worthy celebration to their care and favor. It is hoped that our citizens will take this matter up in time, and hold a celebration worthy the men who stood the hardships of the pioneer times, in order to found a town, which is now one of the prettiest little cities in the state of Ohio. In a matter of this kind, which appeals so strongly to the heart and mind of the citizen, it seems that a formal announcement is all that is necessary. All certainly have enough civic pride to take the time to attend (a public meeting) and to give opinion as the best method to be pursued. One of the most enthusiastic meetings ever held in this city convened...for the purpose of making arrangements to celebrate our centennial in a fitting manner." By January 1904, a *Daily Times* letter to the editor from "many citizens" opposed the committee's program of celebration, questioning efforts to raise $8,000–$10,000 dollars for it. On January 6, the committee submitted a proposal for the Centennial Celebration program to include: a memorial service in all county churches; museum and decoration day; school children's day and Schoenbrunn day; Tuscarawas County enlisted soldiers' reunion; and businessmen's day and an industrial parade with a grand fireworks display.

By February, the finance committee reported difficulty in raising funds, and by March, the *Daily Times* reported, "The centennial commission met in the mayor's office to decide whether the centennial should be or whether it should not be. J.C. Joss attended and said he would not be afraid to say in public what he thought. He said there was so much going on this year, that it would be wise to postpone the celebration for a year. A motion was made and passed. The reasons given by the members for the killing of the celebration was that all the enthusiasm had died out and that the people now wanted a library. It does certainly seem strange that a town having so many public-spirited people should let a thing like this die. Surely enough money could be raised by subscription to erect a monument at Schoenbrunn, but even that seems to be out of the question. However, as a matter of fact, the library agitation has been the cause of the demise of the centennial and the businessmen could not afford to contribute to both. Let us hope that our posterity in 2004 will have enough patriotism to have a bi-centennial that will fairly make the shades of their departed ancestors howl with envy."

September 25, 2002, the City of New Philadelphia held the first bicentennial-planning meeting. Mayor Greg Erb, current Mayor Ron Brodzinski, and council had the foresight to put funds aside each year in anticipation of this great event. George Laurence was elected chairman, and he designed the bicentennial logo, which incorporates the Johnson (Burry) Building, the Spillman carousel, the Tuscarawas County Courthouse, and the Union Flag with 15 stars, which flew over America in October of 1804. The yearlong festivities began at "Main Street At Midnight" with the lighting of the "Welcome To Our City" sign, once again placed on top of the Anderson Building. Commemorative plates were produced bearing the logo, and a plate auction was held at the grand opening of the refurbished Elks building, now the John Knisely Centre. A Bicentennial Ball and silent auction was held at R and S Party Center on February 7, 2004. Committee members marched in numerous parades during 2003–2004 carrying the bicentennial banner, a bicentennial wedding was held for Larry Lowdermilk and Jessica Butler with Mayor Ron Brodzinski officiating, downtown merchants revived the "Lucky Barrel," and a bicentennial tab was produced. The Tuscarawas County Public Library held Oral History Day on March 13th with local historians Fred Miller, Harry Robb, Art Cicconetti, Wayne Jackson, Mildred Pearch, and Ella Slough, and New Philadelphia City Schools engaged their third grade classes in a cityscape project to reflect the beginnings of New Philadelphia. Greg Scott painted a mural on the Johnson building, providing a glimpse into the streets of the early 1900s, and bicentennial banners bearing the logo were hung at the four main streets leading to the New Philadelphia Square. The Heritage Homes society hosted a walking tour of some of the city's oldest and finest homes, and stone signs were erected at Washington Square and Franklin Square. Both the Coin Club and the Stamp Club produced special coins and stamped envelopes to honor the event.

WTUZ Radio and Main Street New Philadelphia's Art on the Square sponsored a contest for a song to celebrate New Philadelphia's bicentennial, requiring references to John Knisely, the founder of New Philadelphia; Schoenbrunn Village, the first settlement; and *Trumpet in the Land*, the dramatization of our area's history. Susanna Massey Cox wrote "New Philadelphia—My Home Town" with her brother Ben Massey performing a variety of musical instruments and singing background harmony.

Other planned events include a fly-in at Harry Clever Field, and a time capsule with city mementos to be placed in the John Knisely Centre. Merchant Market Days are planned downtown during October, and a Founder's Day Celebration will take place at the Fair Avenue Cemetery at the gravesite of John Knisely. The yearlong celebration will end October 24, 2004, with a double-sided Ohio Historical Plaque hung to mark the first school and first church in Ohio at Schoenbrunn Village. The finale will be a countywide church service for all denominations held at Schoenbrunn. As our centennial predecessors hoped, our posterity in 2004 had enough patriotism to "make the shades of our departed ancestors howl with envy."

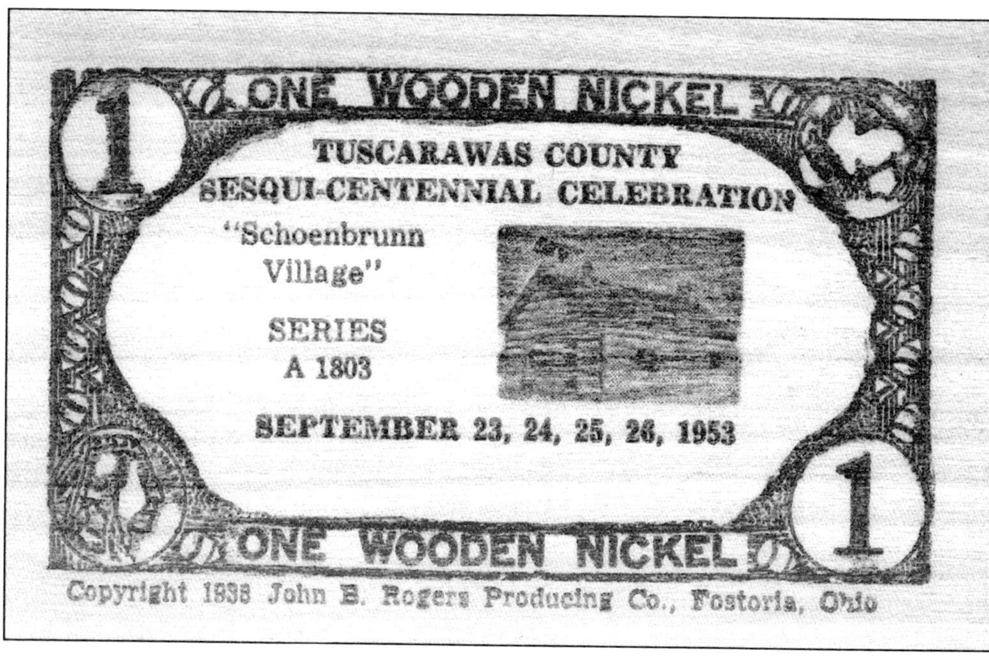

One

Schoenbrunn Village

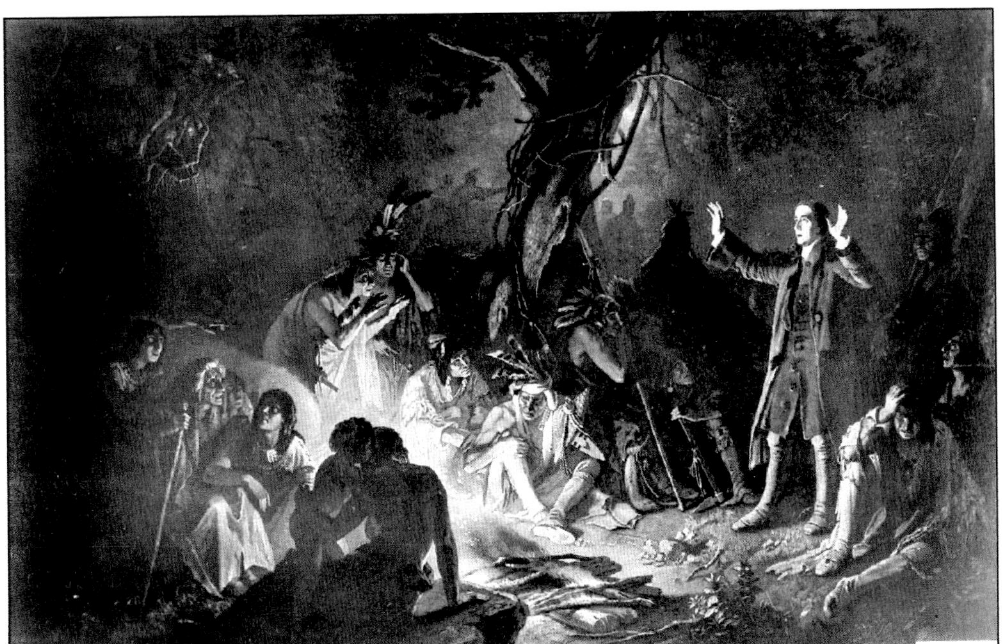

This painting, titled *The Power of the Gospel*, shows David Zeisberger preaching to the Native Americans. Zeisberger was granted a section of land about a quarter of a mile to the east of the future Lockport by the Delaware Indians. The land was to be used for the establishment of a community with the intention of educating the Native Americans about Christianity.

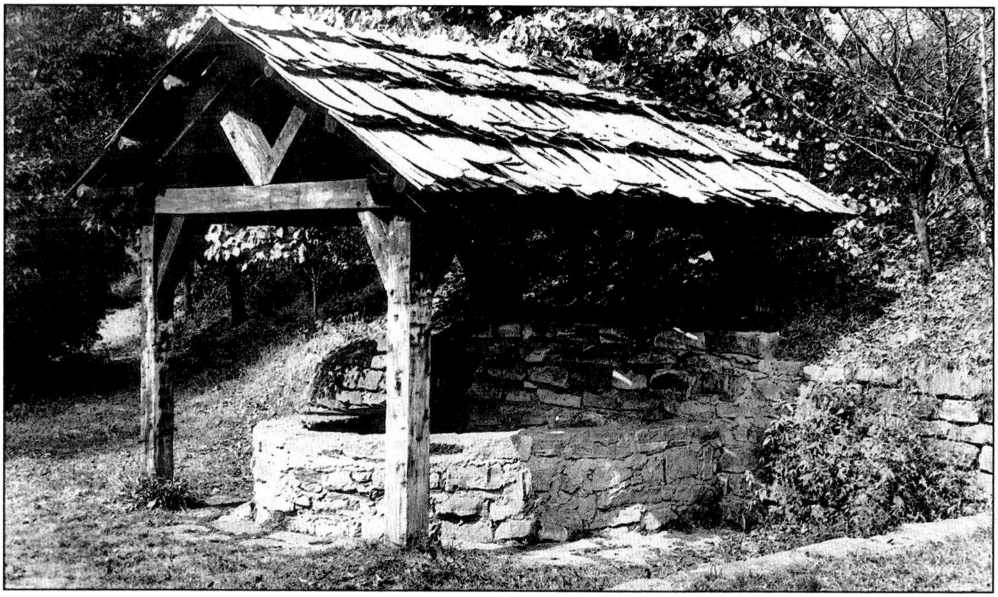

In 1772, Schoenbrunn, or "Welhik Thuppeek," meaning "beautiful spring," was established on the western bank of the Tuscarawas (Old Town) River by Moravian missionary David Zeisberger, who traveled from Bethlehem, Pennsylvania, to set up a Christian colony.

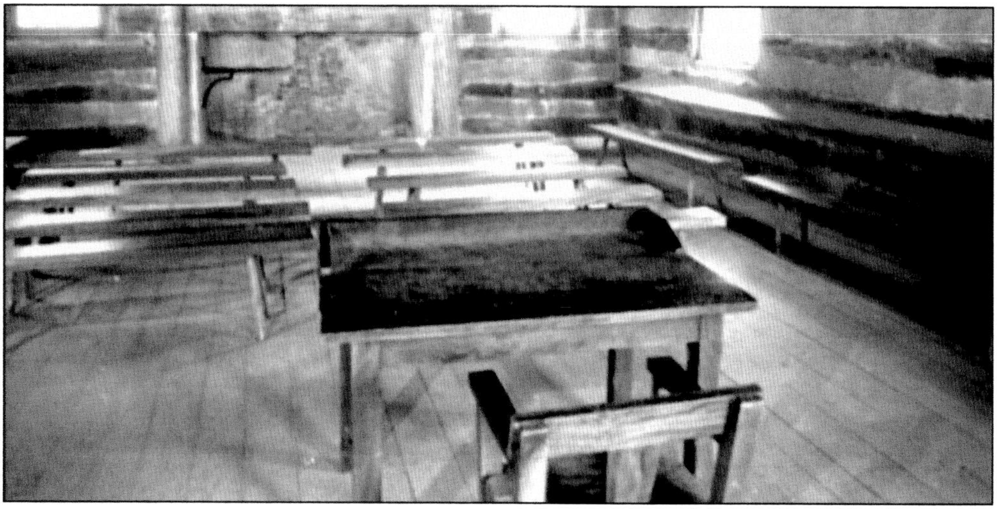

Ohio's first school and first church were built here. After only one year of teaching, Zeisberger and Schoenbrunn's Christian Native Americans organized the first temperance society west of the Allegheny Mountains and the first peace society west of Pittsburgh. By 1775, the settlement included 60 log cabins and the homes of 414 people, mostly Native Americans. Travelers were surprised by the Native Americans' industriousness and refinement of lifestyle. Foods at the mission included bread, meat, butter, milk, tea, coffee, and chocolate along with fruits and vegetables. They cleared hundreds of acres of land to farm and raised cattle, hogs, and poultry. Many Native Americans and travelers experienced famine outside of the mission. The site of starving travelers and Native Americans walking into the village was almost a daily occurrence. Some suggest that the refined lifestyle and ample food sources may have been the cause of so many Christian converts at the mission rather than the spiritual offerings.

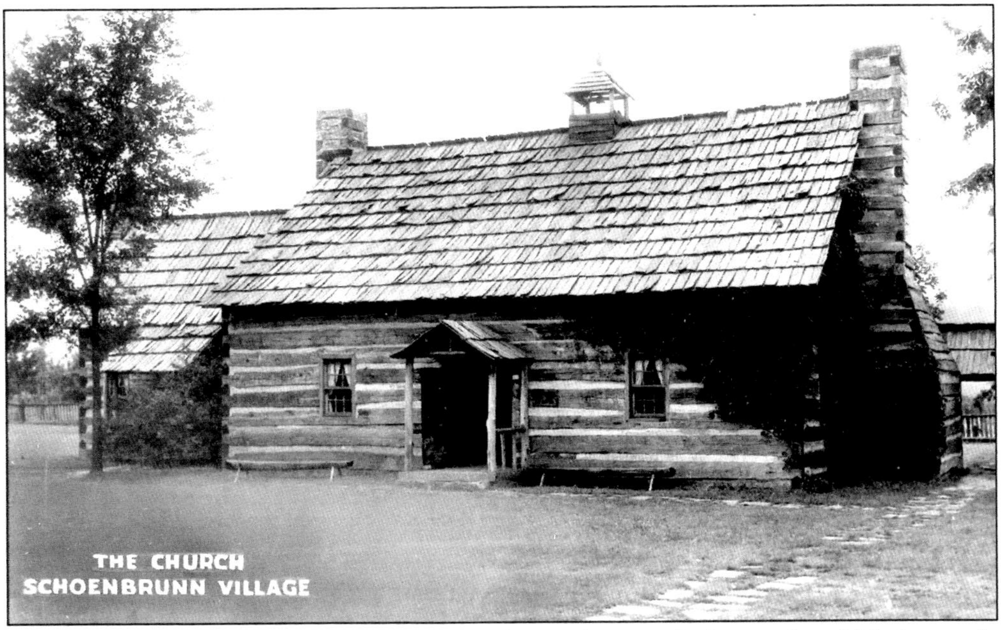

The Moravian Council from Bethlehem, Pennsylvania, drew up the laws under which the people lived. The mission dwellers were required to obey the teachers and to live amongst one another peacefully. All new Christian converts were placed on a probationary status for one year before they were allowed to become a member. No one could leave the mission even for hunting without first informing the teachers. No members could contract debt with traders or agree to sell goods for traders without the permission of council. No intoxicating drink was permitted. (This may have been the first prohibition law in Ohio). Anyone wishing to fight in a war was prohibited. Just as in today's society, anyone accepting stolen goods would be punished. The punishment resulted in the recipient being sent away from the mission. These rules were the first civil code in Ohio.

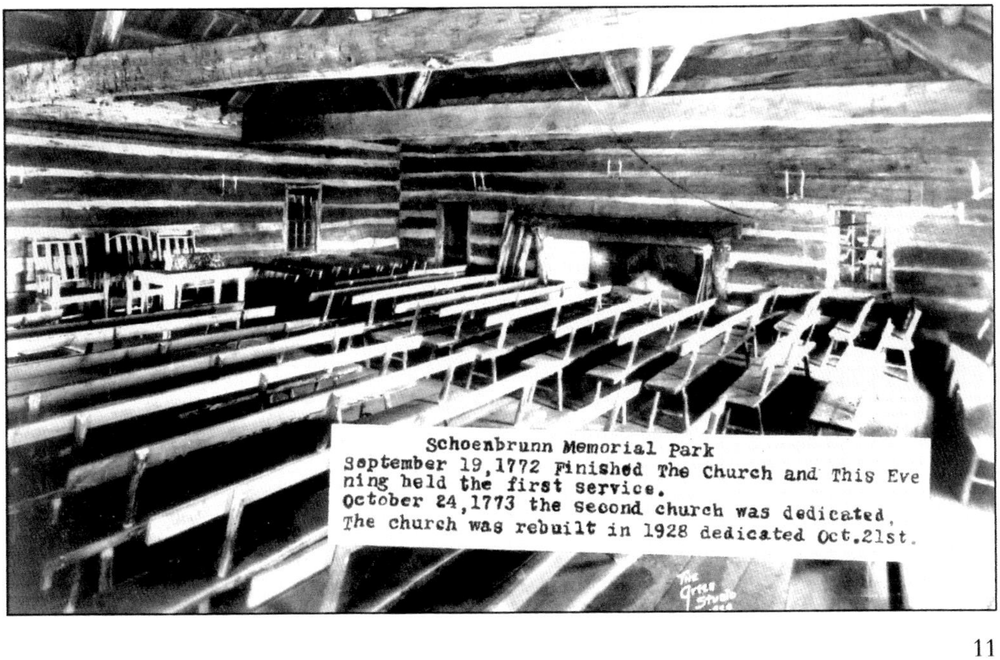

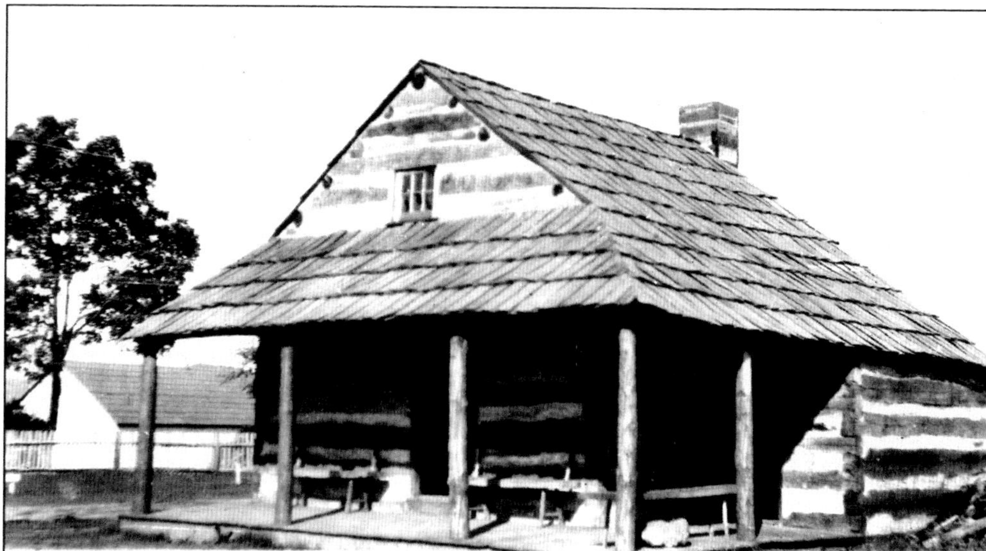

Cabin of John Joseph Schebosh Ass't. Missionary
Schoenbrunn Memorial State Park, New Philadelphia, Ohio.

Schoenbrunn inhabitants would feed, clothe, and shelter anyone in need. Their Moravian beliefs prohibited them from fighting. Therefore, they remained neutral pacifists between the British and Americans. Suspicions of the settlers were abundant between all factions. The inhabitants were perceived as spies and were forced by the British Army to relocate to Sandusky in 1777. The villagers burned Schoenbrunn church to the ground to prevent its desecration. Hostile Native Americans burned the remainder of Schoenbrunn Village. On March 8, 1782, the American militia massacred 96 Native Americans at the Gnadenhutten mission. The Tuscarawas Valley remained uninhabited for 16 years. Zeisberger did not return until 1798, when he settled the Goshen Mission west of the river about four miles below New Philadelphia.

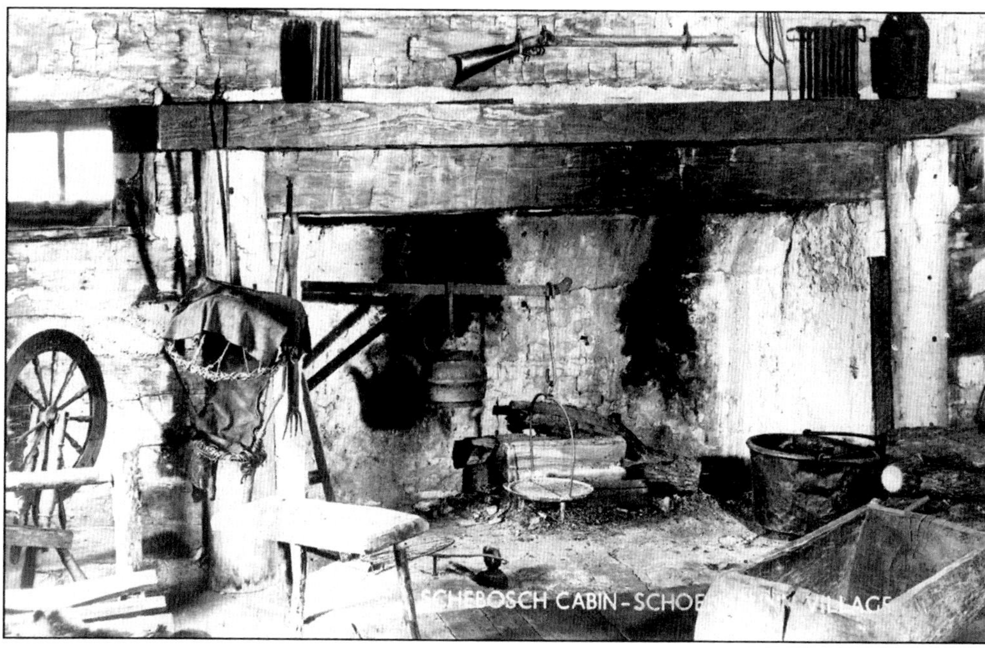

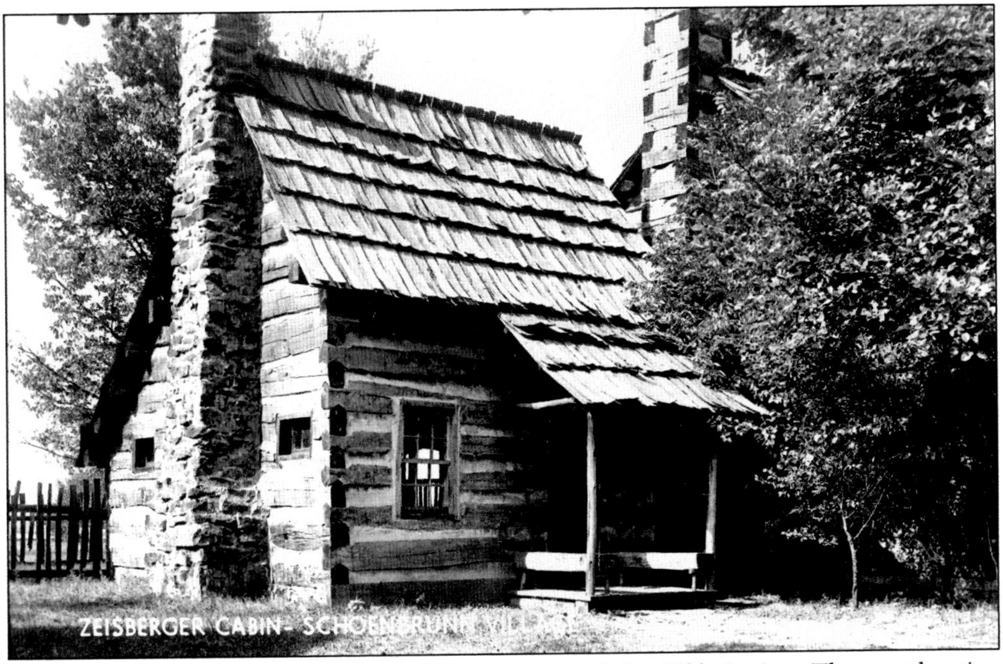

In 1812, John Jacobs deeded Schoenbrunn Spring to the Union Bible Society. The exact location of the original Schoenbrunn Village was unknown for 146 years. In 1922, the Tuscarawas County Historical Society was organized. The Society discovered long-lost maps at Bethlehem, Pennsylvania, in 1923.

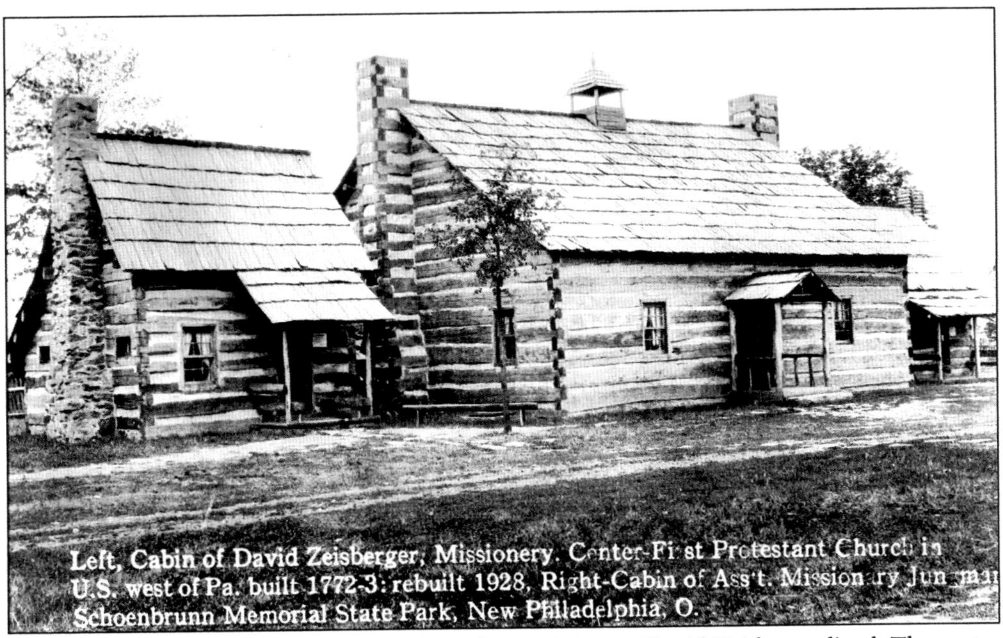

The left cabin is a reproduction of the cabin where missionary David Zeisberger lived. The center cabin is the first Protestant Church in the United States west of Pennsylvania. The church was built in 1772–1773 and rebuilt in 1928. The right cabin is a reproduction of where the assistant missionary Jungmann lived.

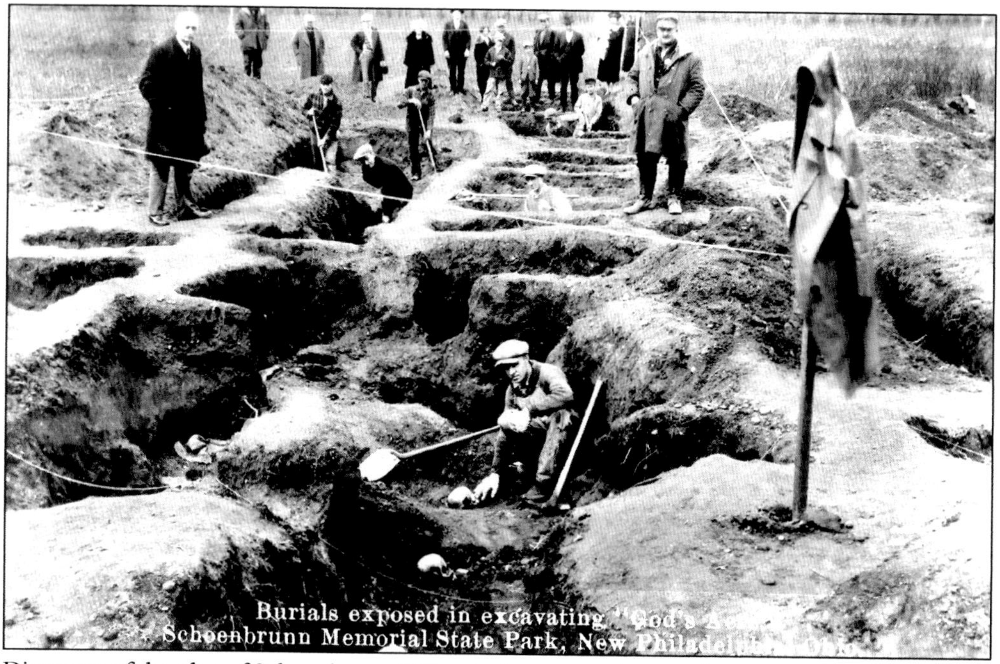

Discovery of the plan of Schoenbrunn Village led to excavations at the present site of the village. The Tuscarawas County Historical Society purchased the first 28 acres of Schoenbrunn from Emmet Myer.

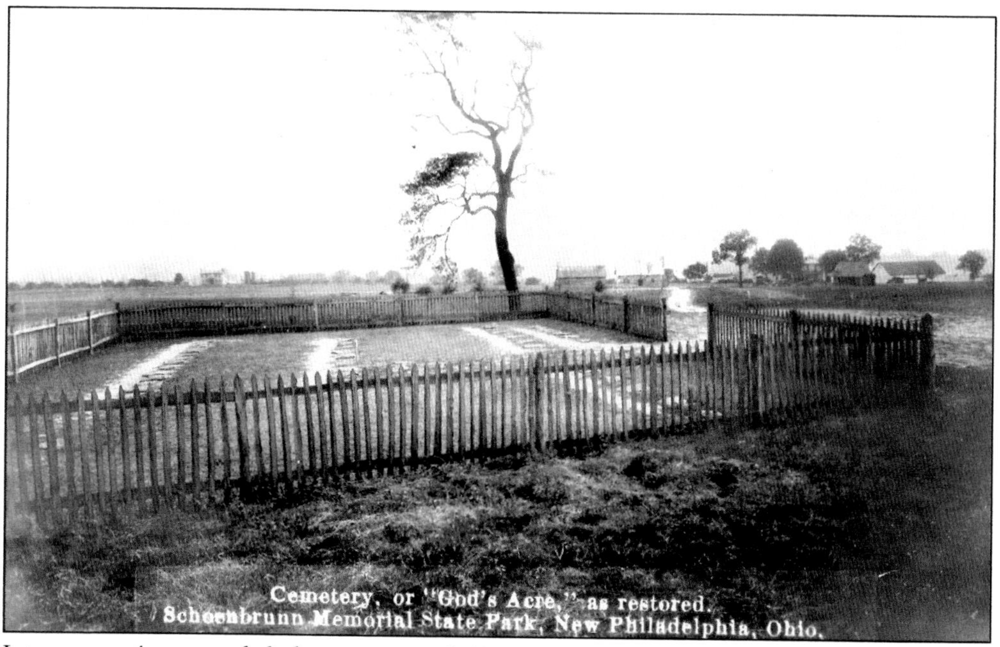

Later excavations revealed the contents of 44 graves in what was known as "God's Acre." The Schoenbrunn tract of land encompasses 4,000 acres. God's Acre was the burial ground of Schoenbrunn Village where inhabitants of the village who died between 1772–1777 are interred.

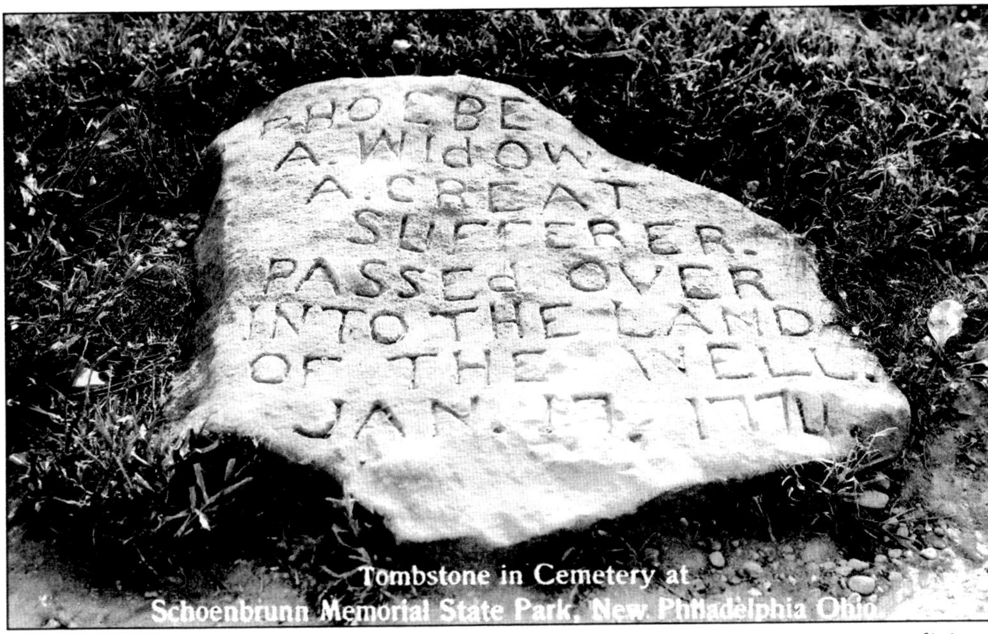

This tombstone marks the burial site of Phoebe. The people of Schoenbrunn were very religious. Note on the tombstone that Phoebe was remembered as a great sufferer.

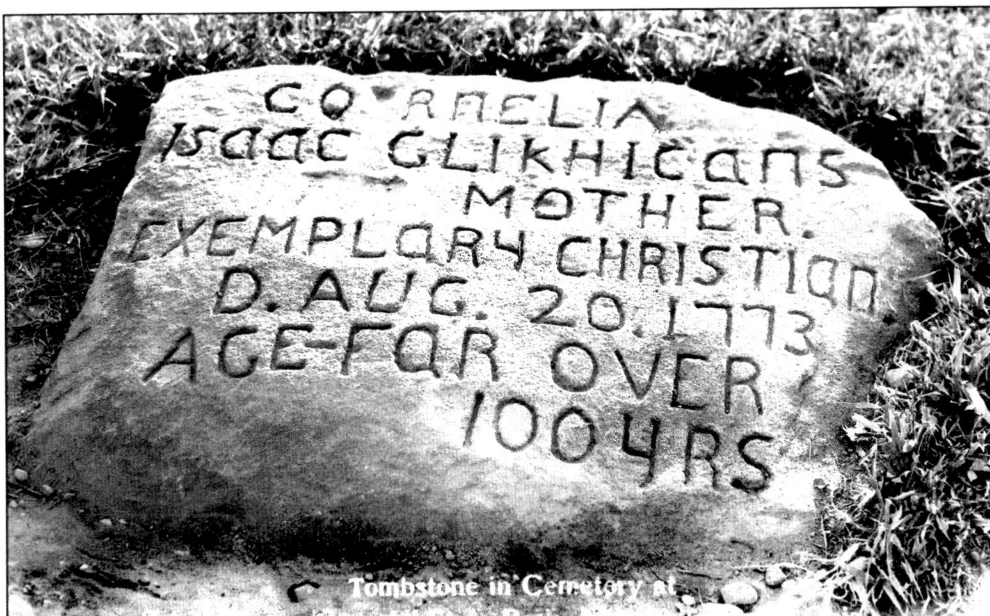

The tombstone of Cornelia Isaac Clikhicans (actual spelling is "Clikhikans") is inscribed with the remembrance of her as a mother and an exemplary Christian. Most astounding is the fact that Cornelia lived well beyond 100 years of age. Cornelia was the mother of Isaac who was buried at Gnadenhutten.

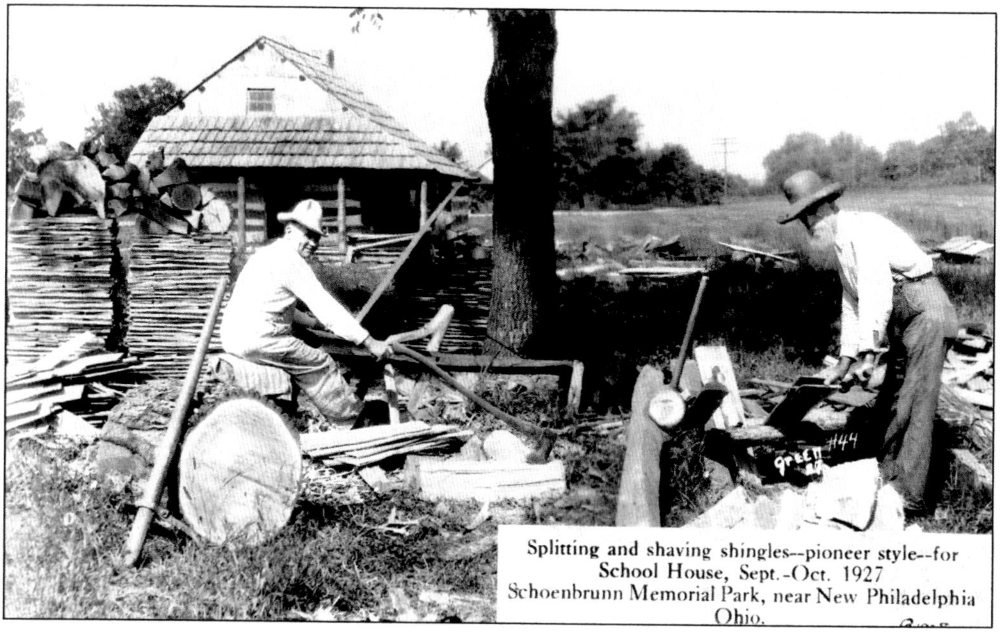

Craftsmen and volunteers worked diligently to recreate the Village of Schoenbrunn. These gentlemen are splitting and shaving shingles for the reconstruction of the School House in September 1927. The Ohio State Archaeological and Historical Society and the Ohio Legislature cooperated in building a village of 17 authentic cabins surrounded by a rustic picket fence. The log cabins were built out of rough-hewn logs with mud and clay chinking. Even the Moravian furniture was duplicated.

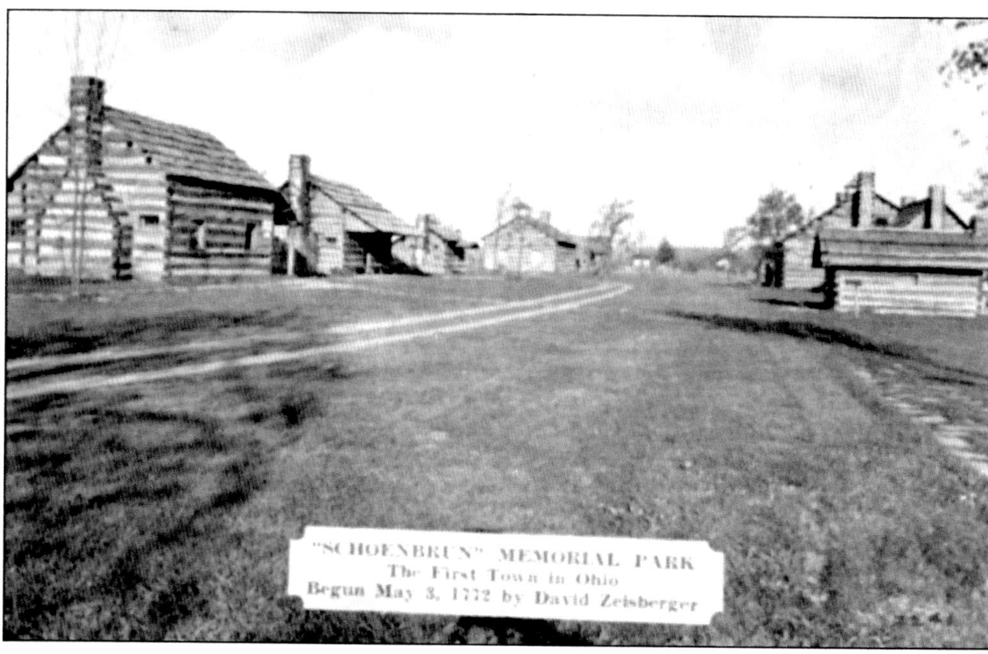

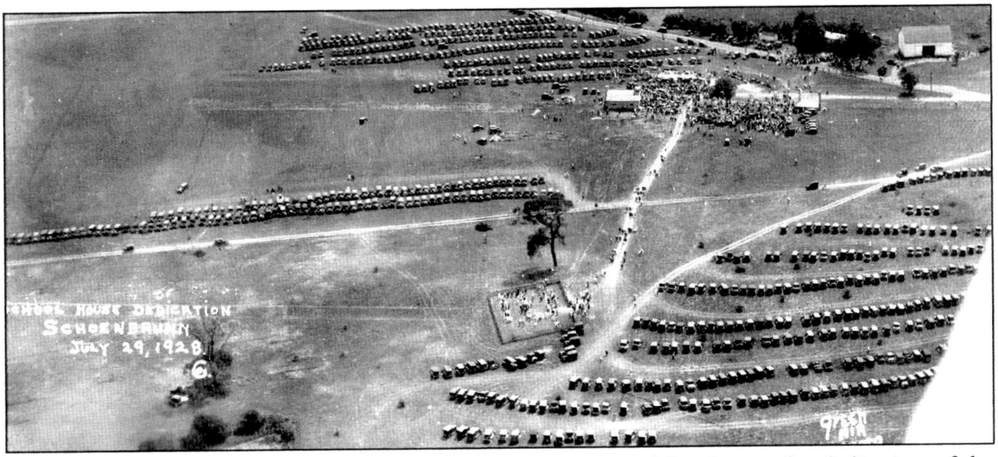

This aerial view shows a large crowd drawing for the great celebration at the dedication of the reconstructed Schoenbrunn Village School House on July 29, 1928.

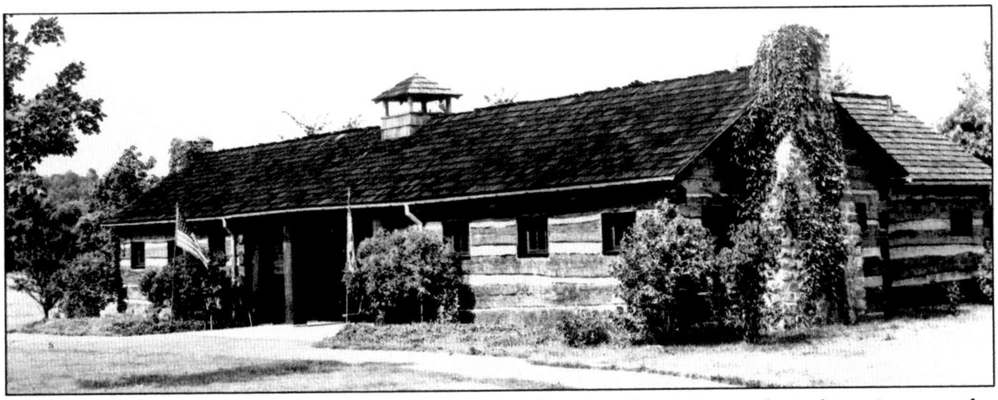

The Schoenbrunn Trading Post and Museum exhibit the chronology of pre-historic man, the movement of historic Native Americans into Ohio, and the growth of the Moravian Missions throughout the area. One room of the museum is devoted to the Missionaries' accomplishments at Schoenbrunn.

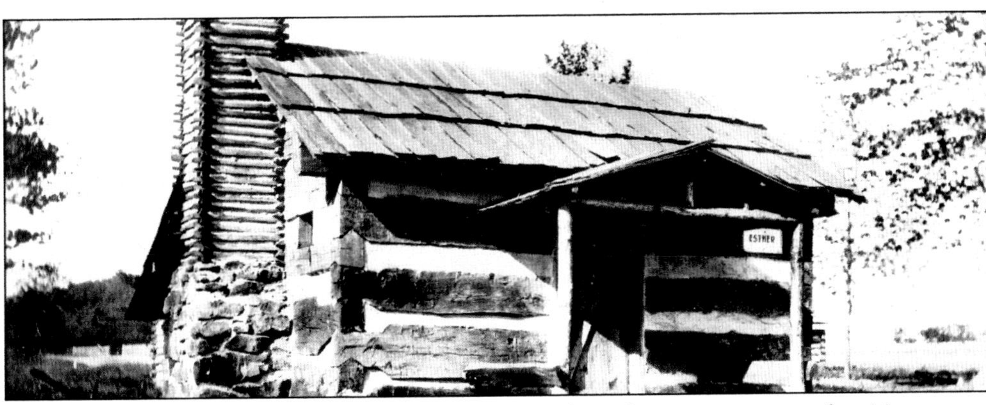

Schoenbrunn Village is now a State Memorial Park with gardens, a museum, and a visitor center. The traditional Moravian "Love Feast" is conducted at Easter sunrise in the restored village each year. The museum was dedicated in 1940.

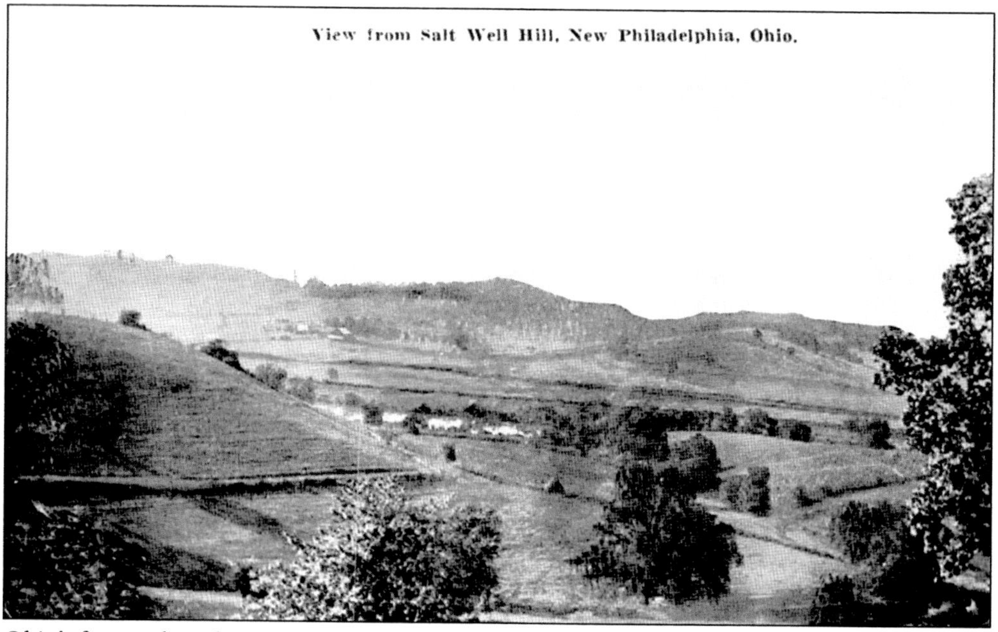

Ohio's first outdoor drama, *Trumpet in the Land*, began in 1968 at the Schoenbrunn Amphitheatre. This drama, set in the Moravian Missions of the Tuscarawas Valley from 1772 until 1782, portrays the development of a society where both white pioneers and Native Americans lived amongst each other in peace. The audience relives the arrival of David Zeisberger and his teaching of Christianity to the Native Americans and the anguish after the agitation of the American and British, as well as the complacency of the missions, leads to the Mission's final destruction.

Historical characters include David Zeisberger, a Moravian missionary who hoped to establish a peaceful Native American settlement along the fiery frontier; Simon Girty, a conniving border renegade who agitated hostilities and promoted war in the region; Captain Pipe, a young warrior chief whose hatred of all white men for the killing of his father added to the dangers facing the missionaries; and John Heckewelder, one of the first explorers of Ohio.

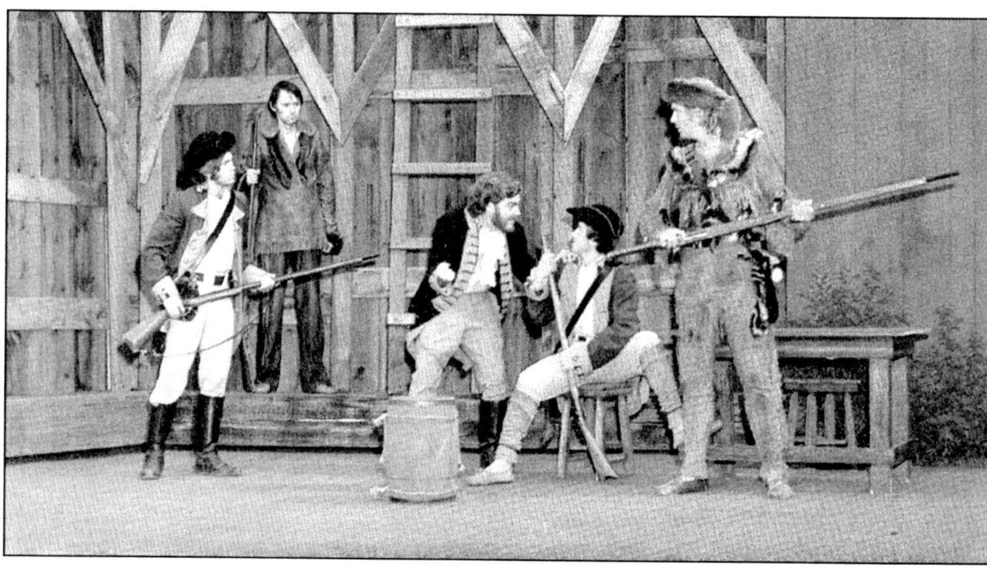

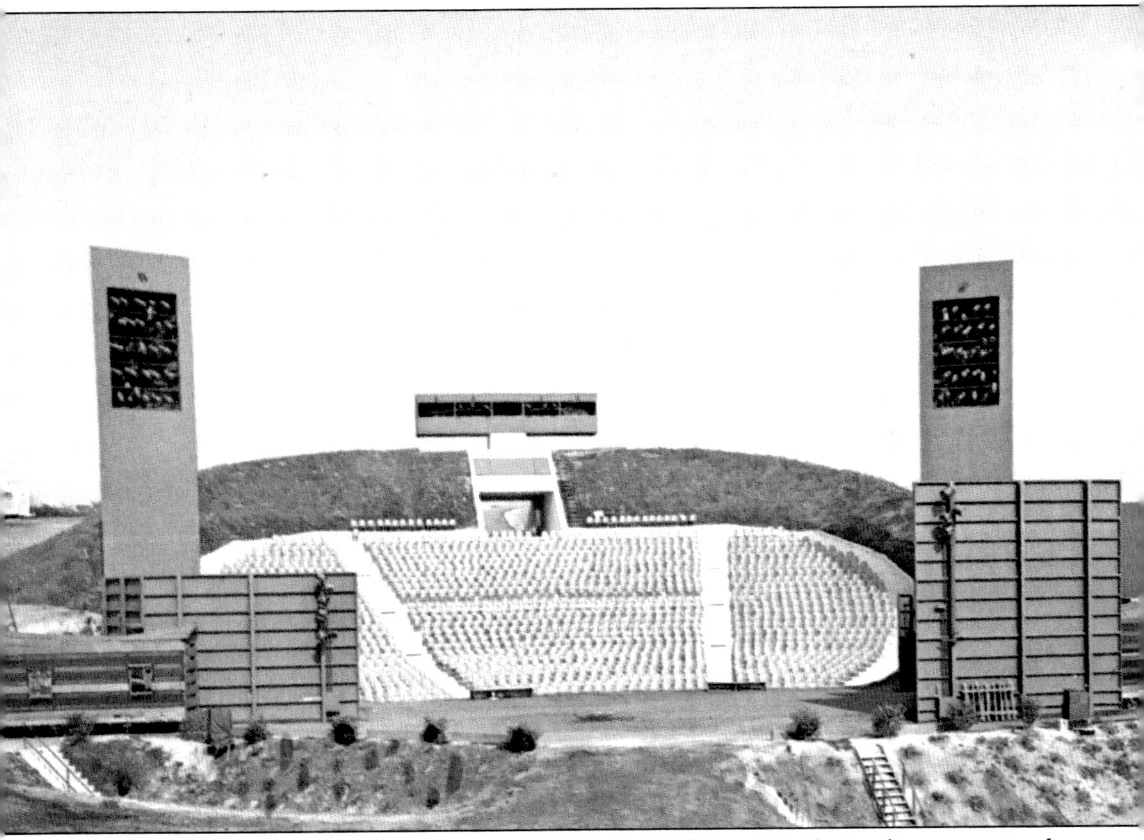

Written by Pulitzer prize-winning playwright Paul Green, *Trumpet in the Land* uses a cast and crew numbering over 70 people to bring this epic production to life. It combines professional actors, singers, and dancers and brilliant lighting, authentic looking costumes, battle pyrotechnics, and a state-of-the-art sound system for an outstanding evening of family entertainment. It has operated under the direction of Margaret Bonamico since 1971.

Also on stage each season at the Schoenbrunn Amphitheatre is *The White Savage*, the story of frontiersman Simon Girty.

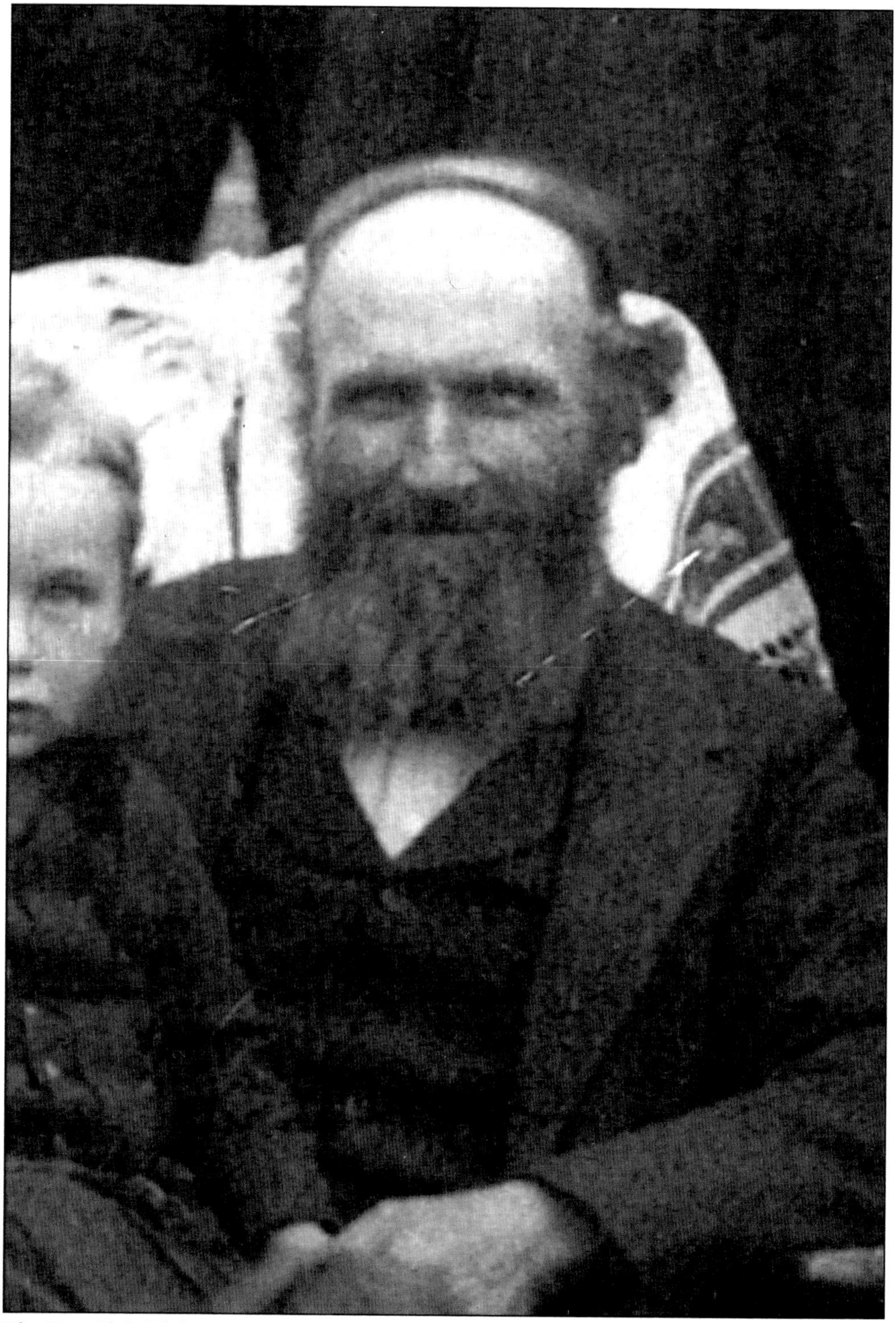

The New Philadelphia Bicentennial Committee believes this to be a photograph of John Knisely. It was provided by the descendents of Mr. Knisely.

Two

John Knisley
Founder of New Philadelphia

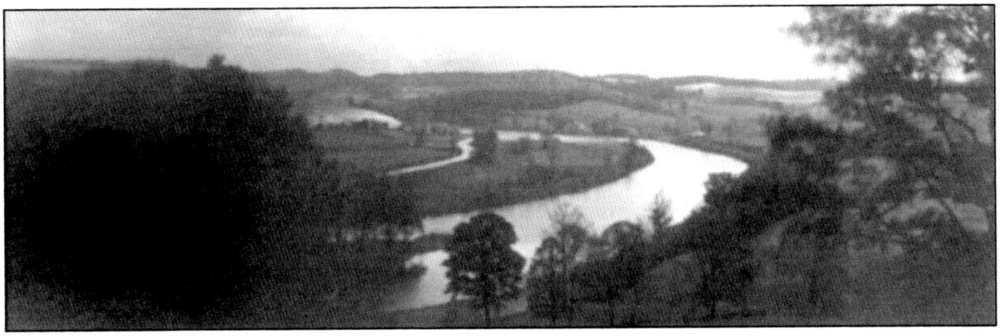

John Knisely was born in Lancaster County, Pennsylvania, on September 21, 1752. At age 20, he married Mary Miller. He and his wife had 10 children—six sons and four daughters. The children included Abraham, John, Samuel, David, Jacob Joseph, Sarah (Minnich), Elizabeth (Casebeer), Mary (Williams), and Susan (Strough). The family lived in York County, Pennsylvania, and later moved to Bedford County also in Pennsylvania.

Mr. Knisely operated a gristmill and inn and entertained traders, surveyors, and adventurers returning from the Northwest Territory. Here he heard the stories from the traders and travelers of the fertile and prosperous land beyond the mountains.

In the autumn of 1803, John Knisely and his son Samuel road west on horseback with rifles, an ax, a tomahawk, and a limited camping outfit to seek a new home where game was more plentiful. The trail led them across the Ohio River near present-day Steubenville and to the site of the Moravian mission at Schoenbrunn. The Knisely's were shown good deer hunting spots by the welcoming Native Americans. After exploring the area and surrounding country, John Knisely was greatly impressed with the beauty and natural advantages of the plains: the fertile river bottomlands, the fine timber, and the rich mineral resources of the Tuscarawas Valley.

Having decided to establish a town near Schoenbrunn, John left Samuel with the Native Americans while he returned to Pennsylvania to sell his farm. In early spring 1804, the Knisely family returned along with 33 pioneers, which he had convinced to accompany them. On October 23, 1804, Knisely met John Heckewelder at Gnadenhutten. Heckewelder, in addition to being the Moravian land agent, acted for other land proprietors in the East. In his capacity as land agent, he held the power of attorney from Godfrey Haga, a Philadelphia merchant who owned thousands of acres in Tuscarawas County (known as Muskingum County until March 1808), including New Philadelphia according to a patent signed by John Adams and dated March 28, 1800. With $5,454.33 of the proceeds from the sale of his Pennsylvania possessions (other accounts report $5,776), John Knisely bought 3,554 acres between present-day New Philadelphia and Dover, founding the City of New Philadelphia on October 23, 1804. He hired surveyor John Wells of Somerset County, Pennsylvania, to lay out New Philadelphia in a checkerboard fashion similar to Philadelphia. Many of the streets were even named after the streets of Philadelphia. He had three public squares laid out:

the present Public Square, Franklin Square (Upper Market Square) at the present junction of West High Avenue and Fourth Street, and Washington Square (Lower Market Square) at the junction of East High and Beaver Avenues. On May 22, 1813, the plat of this city was acknowledged before Judge Christian Deardorff. The plat included 558 lots, each 66 by 264 feet, marked by stakes, which provided enough space for a house, a stable, and a garden. The lots were situated along Broadway Street and High Avenue, which intersected at right angles to form the Public Square. Water, Front, High, Fair, and Ray Streets extended northwest. They were crossed at right angles by East, Second, Third, Broadway, Fifth, Sixth, West, Walnut, Mulberry, and Chestnut Streets.

Mr. Knisely did not build a cabin within the limits of town, but lived on a farm adjoining the town on the east, across Beaver Dam. His house was the stopping-place of all newcomers. Mr. Knisely took travelers to see his town and the site for the courthouse. Broadway and High Streets were the only thoroughfares for years. High Street was a mere footpath that wound through bushes and saplings to the next square, where a few trees had been cleared. Broadway was the only street that was partially cleared. John Hull, who accompanied Knisely from Pennsylvania, is said to have built the first house in New Philadelphia, but remained a resident for only a short time.

Mr. Knisely was determined to build up his town. Pioneers that came to the new county were given provisions and seed, and many times, John opened his own home to them for days and even weeks until they could build their cabins. He would frequently sign notes as security for them. Knisely gave the city land for the courthouse and public buildings. He also donated 100 town lots and 160 outlying acres to be sold by the county government. John Knisely also took an active interest in religion and education. He donated four lots to each of the following societies: the English Religious Society, the German Religious Society, the Moravian Religious Society, and the Fair Avenue Cemetery. One lot each was also donated for a German school house, an English school house, and a public defenders office for the county. Proceeds of the sales were designated by Knisely to be used to defray the expenses of the construction of the Court House and public buildings.

Tuscarawas County was created on March 15, 1808, and it was largely through Knisely's influence and donations that New Philadelphia was selected as the County Seat. Mr. Knisely called their attention to the fact that his town was the first white man's settlement in the county and offered to give land for government buildings, securing the honor over Dover. John Knisely objected, but the County Seat would be called "Knisely's Town" for his lifetime.

New Philadelphia was a stopping point for settlers traveling from the East. Taverns and lunchrooms prospered, and the town grew. In 1815, a Lutheran pastor arrived and with his arrival, the first church was established. Other early settlers of the village were Dr. Reverend Christian Espich, George W. Canfield (county clerk in 1818), Jacob Blickensderfer (county commissioner 1816–1819, associate judge 1829–1836 and 1850–1852, county auditor 1818–1820, and many other high offices), Philip Itzkin, the Peppers, Samuel Stough, and George Sluthour (a carpenter arriving in 1811). Samuel, Albert, Joshua, and John Pepper, brothers and bricklayers, constructed most of the early brick structures.

New Philadelphia was incorporated by an act of Legislature passed February 12, 1833, and the first election for officers was held on May 6: the first elected mayor was B.M. Atherton (then called "president"); Andrew Seaton, recorder; John Coventry, treasurer; Samuel W. Kenrick, marshal; and Francis D. Leonard, John W. Taylor, Peter Cribbs Sr., Thomas Sargent, and David Baltzly, Town Council.

John Knisely was endearingly referred to by all the townspeople as "Father Knisely." He died on December 15,1834, at the age of 84. His burial plot is located in the East Fair Street Cemetery, another of his donations to the city, where his tombstone simply states, "John Knisely, The Founder of New Philadelphia."

In 1995, the Ohio Historical Society placed a historical plaque at the site of the courthouse in honor of John Knisely. The mayor of the city at the time was David Knisely, a descendent of the founder of New Philadelphia.

Three

The Lateral Canal and the 1913 Flood

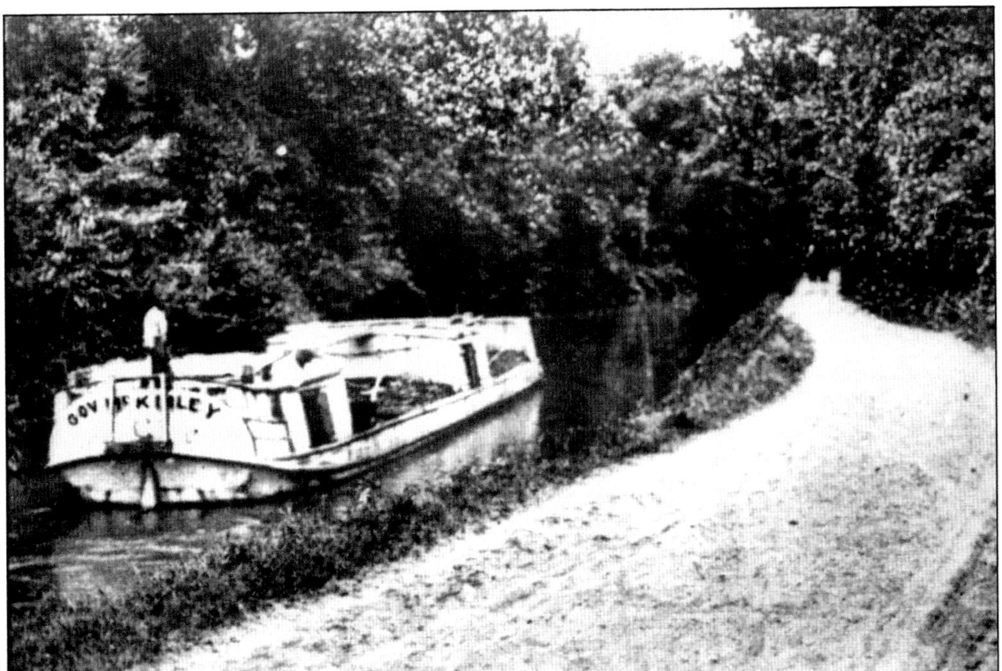

As early as 1765, George Washington surveyed the Ohio Territory, considering the Tuscarawas River as part of an all-water route from the Great Lakes to Chesapeake Bay. Early settlers built homes close to its banks hoping to prosper from the commerce created by the waterway, but the river became hazardous because of its shallow spots and rapids. A cross-state canal seemed to be the only solution for Ohioans. Several possible routes were surveyed before the route that was tentatively traced years before by Washington was chosen. The route for the canal entered Tuscarawas County at Bolivar, followed the river past Dover, and went south toward Newcomerstown.

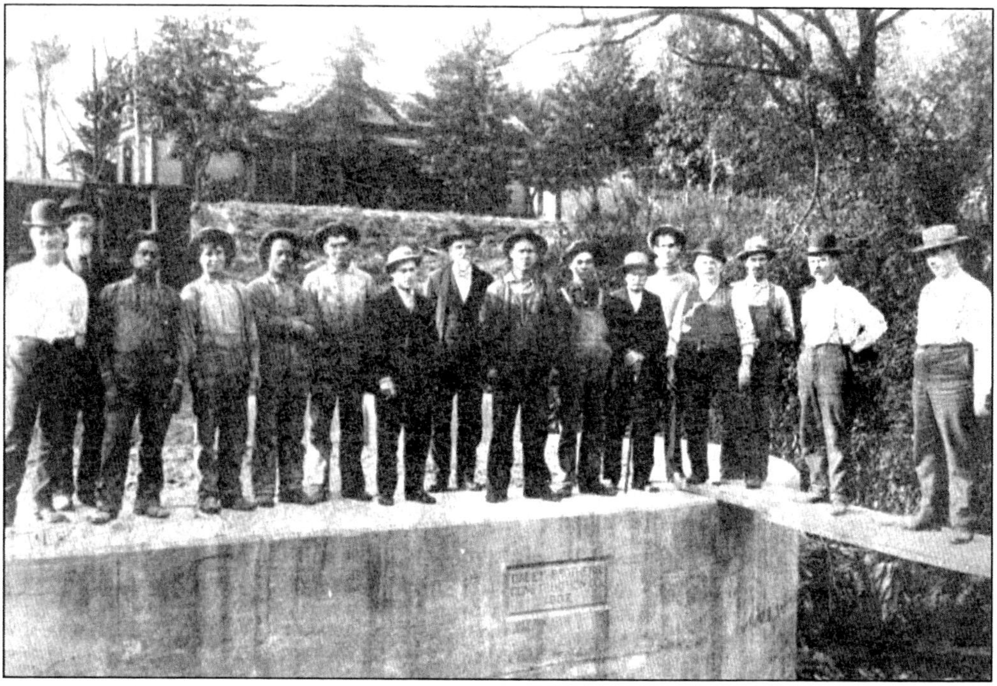

Abram Garfield (father of President James A. Garfield, who later was assassinated), one of many individual contractors, dug the canal by hand with the help of his son in one-half to one mile sections. The first canal boat to leave New Philadelphia in 1831 carried a cargo of coal to Cleveland.

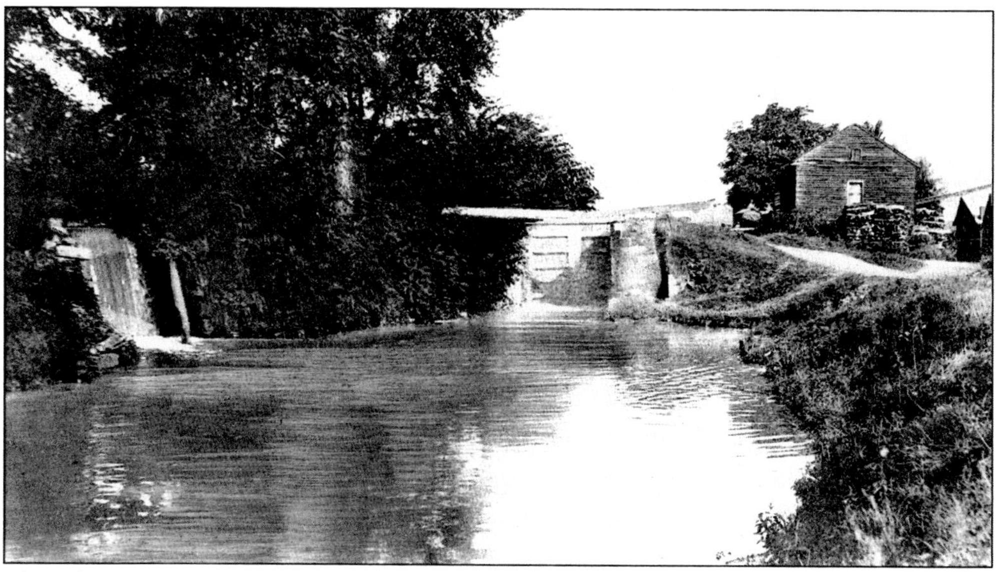

The Ohio-Erie Canal had bypassed New Philadelphia. A means of getting products to the markets was needed. The Lateral Canal Company incorporated on January 16, 1828, planning the construction of a two-mile long canal positioned along the north side of the Tuscarawas River on the south side of New Philadelphia. The hand labor involved in digging the Lateral Canal, known as "side-cut," would be at a considerable cost to the village, delaying the work.

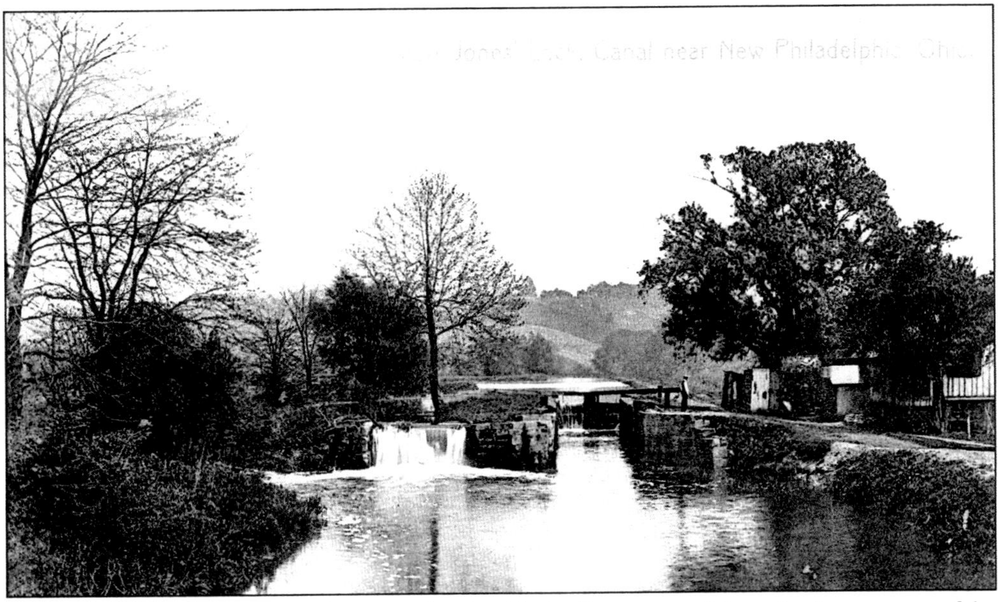

The Lateral Canal linked the Ohio-Erie Canal with the Tuscarawas River. At the entrance of the Lateral Canal, a short distance above the old Baker Mill Dam, a lock was constructed. From this entrance, boats were poled across the river and towed up the riverbank to the Sugar Creek Lock. The Lateral Canal placed New Philadelphia in a position of economic growth. The canal supplied access to the flourmill and waterpower for the woolen mill for 20 years.

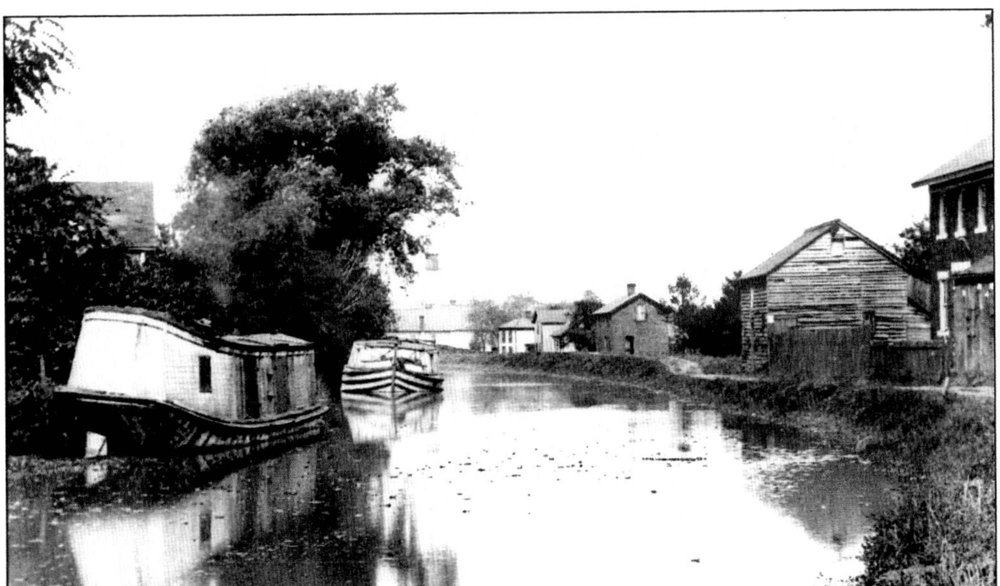

Blake's Mills, now a part of New Philadelphia's south side, was also called Lockport. Lock No. 13 along the Lateral Canal was located in Blake's Mills on the south side of the Tuscarawas River opposite New Philadelphia. It was a little German village of 300 people and was incorporated in 1883. The village contained one general store, two saloons, two blacksmith shops, a harness shop, a wagon shop, two butcher shops, an extensive limekiln, a large gristmill, a brewery, a paper mill, a grade school, and a Methodist Church.

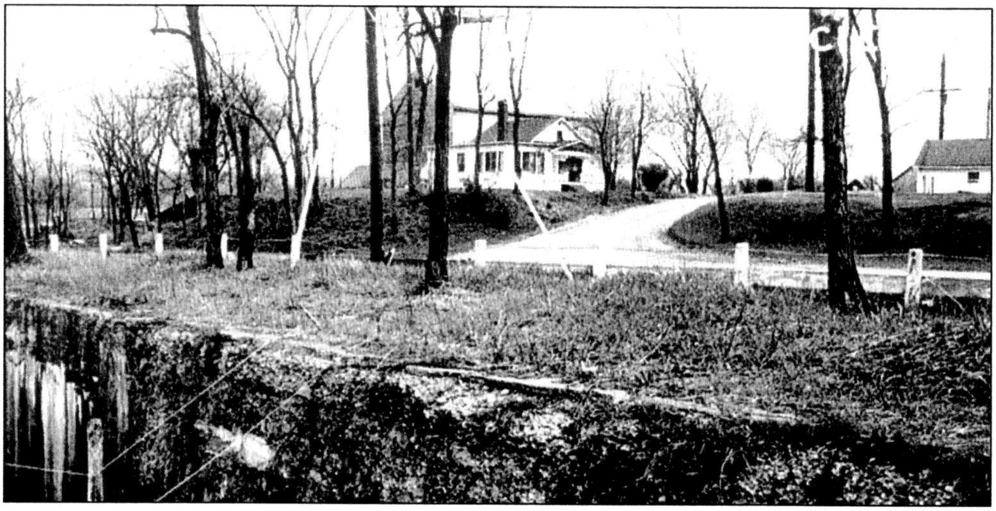

Frederick Shull and Gottlieb Fackler laid out Lockport on the south side of the Ohio Canal immediately above Lock No. 13 in 1829. The original plat included 69 lots. Dr. Espich, also a Lutheran minister, built the first house in Lockport. In 1830, an additional 40 lots were added north of the canal. The streets were Jackson, North Canal, Adams, Clay, and Ferry. Lots 110–121 were laid out on the south side of the canal. The streets in this section were First, Second, and Canal. In 1872, Lots 75–87 located on West Adams Street were vacated.

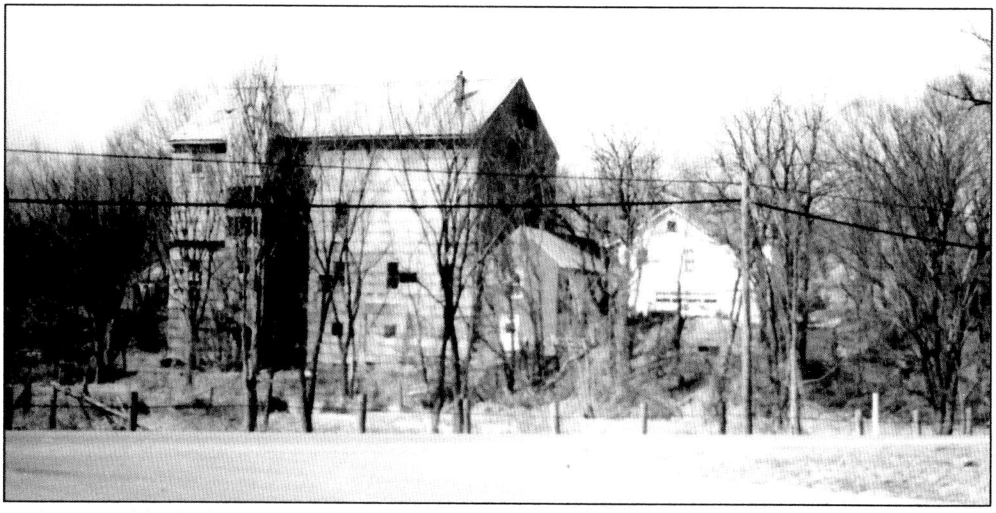

Walter M. Blake laid out Blakesfield in 1845 on land adjoining Lockport on the east. It comprised 42 lots, all of which were located between the canal and the river. Broadway was the main street, with 12 lots west of it and 30 lots east of it. In 1851, South Blakesfield was laid out south of the canal, adjoining Lockport. There were now 87 lots located on either side of Broadway Street.

In 1868, Samuel Howe made an addition to Blake's Mills (Lockport), consisting of 13 lots on the west side of "Oldtown Street," or Broadway, and south of and adjacent to the canal. In 1870, Jacob Darst made an addition of 26 lots south of the canal, on the east side of Broadway.

The advent of railroads in 1843 began the demise of the canal. It continued struggling on until the Flood of 1913 destroyed many of the locks. Only the outlines of the channel can be seen. In many communities, the canals are being renovated as walking trails and designated as historical sites.

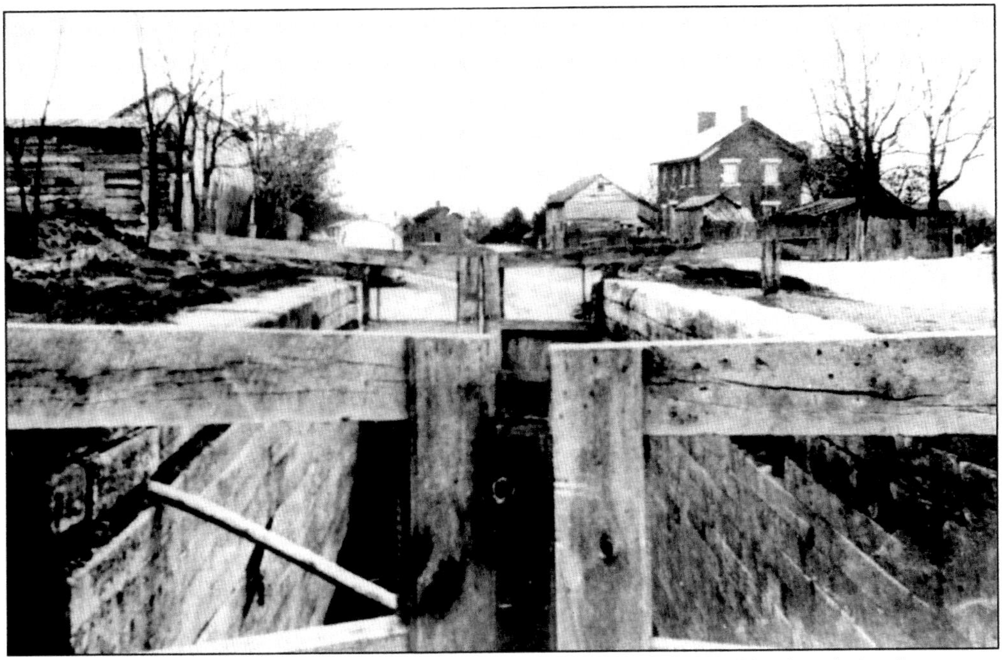

Lock No. 13 is seen here along State Route 416, near present-day Mark's Place hair salon.

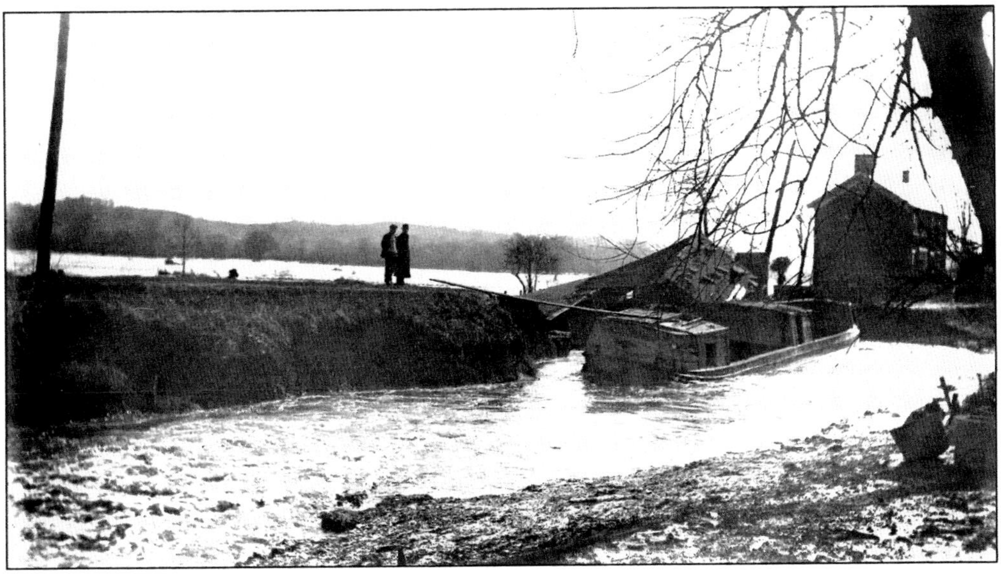

The 1913 Flood destroyed the lock house at Lock No. 13.

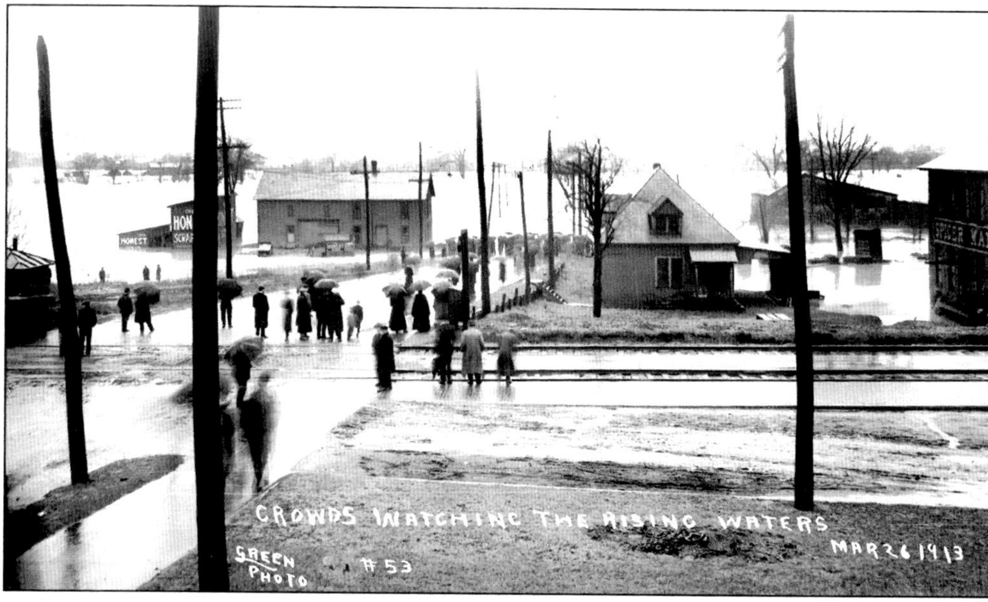

As the population swelled, floods became more frequent and more serious because of deforestation, intensive cultivation, and over-grazing. Levees built by communities proved ineffectual in coping with the problem. Floods in 1884, 1898, and 1907 emphasized the problem. Then came the big Flood of 1913. The rains began in the early morning of Easter Sunday, March 23, 1913. Old superstitions said rain on Easter Sunday would cause continuous rains on each of the next seven Sundays. Residents worried, but really felt the storm would pass. But the rain continued on Monday, Tuesday, and Wednesday.

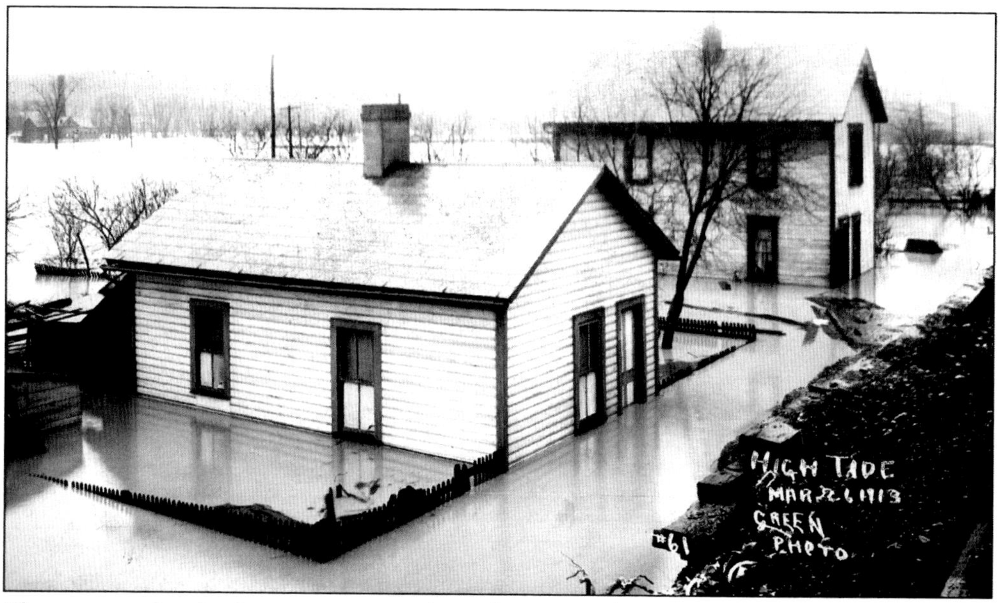

The property loss in the county was estimated at more than $1,000,000. On the evening of Wednesday, March 26, the bridge between New Philadelphia and the south side was swept away. There was no electrical power or drinking water, and there was a temporary milk and food shortage in the city.

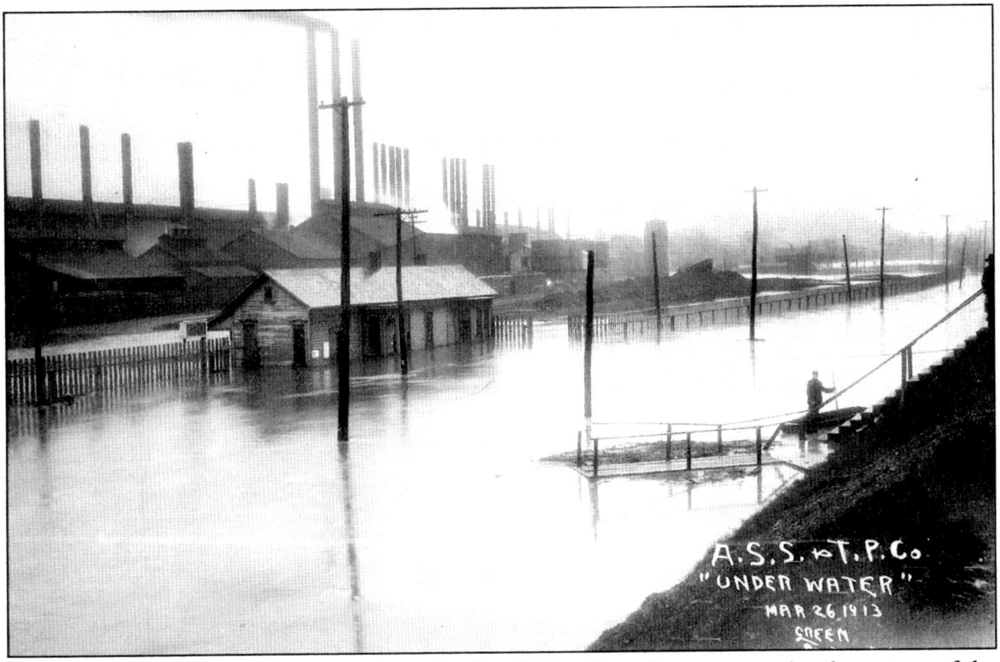

This photograph of the American Sheet Steel and Tin Plate Company under the waters of the 1913 flood was taken by photographer Wes Green on March 26, 1913.

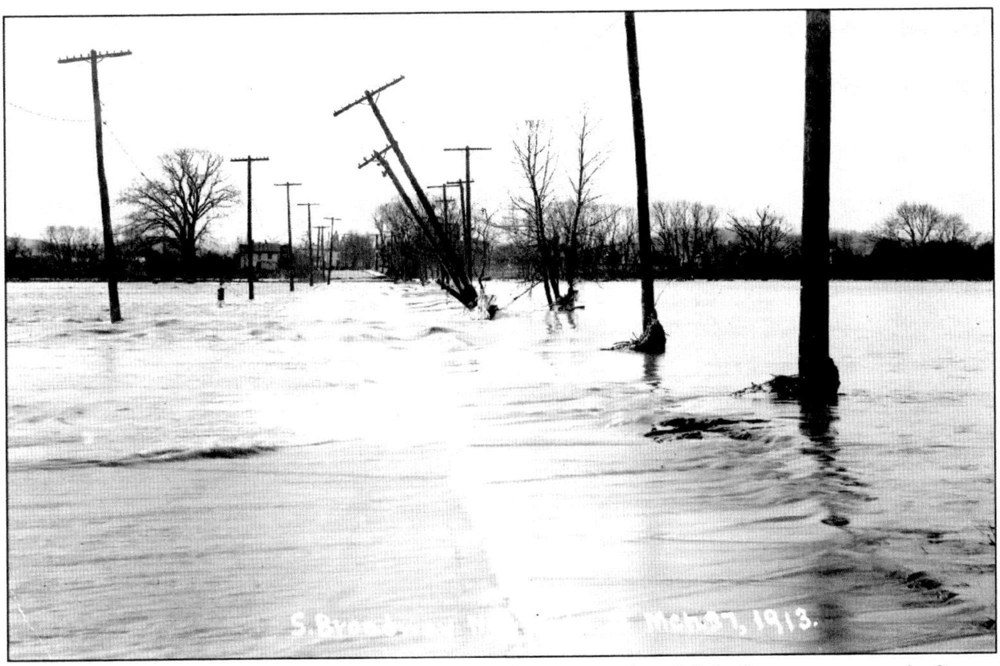

The waters rushed down the creeks, streams, and river carrying debris from upstream. At 3 a.m. on Thursday, March 27, the waters crested after more than 17 inches of rain had fallen. On March 17, 1913, the *Ohio Times and Democrat* stated: "It is estimated that the county will suffer a $3,000,000 loss in bridges alone . . . No word has been received from the south side of the city in the past 24 hours."

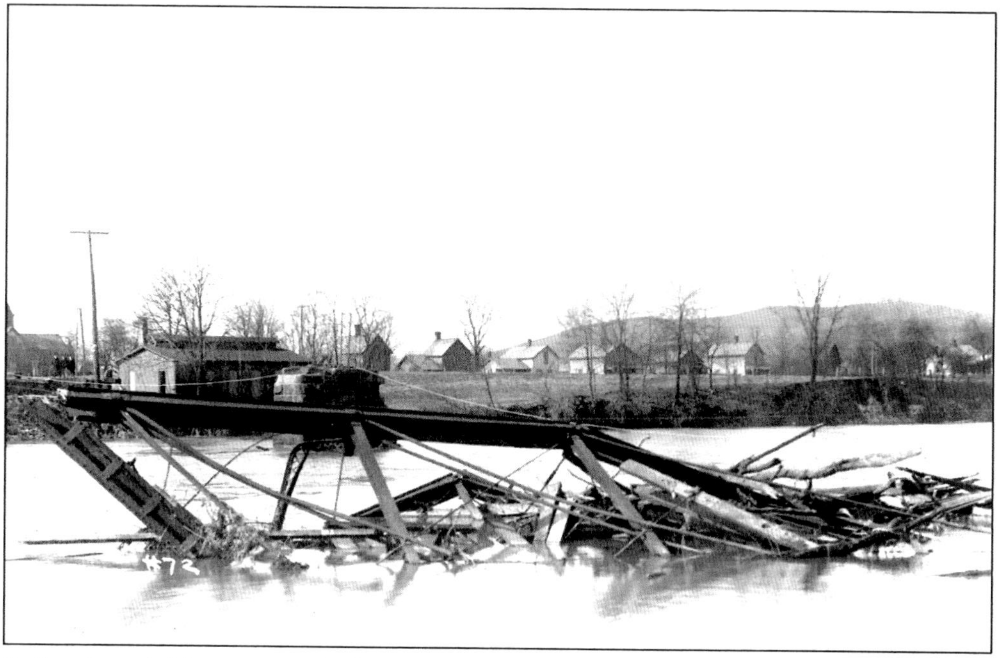

Railroads and bridges were washed out, requiring a heavy bond issue to be forced on the people. Debris from the South Side Bridge is seen in the background of this photograph.

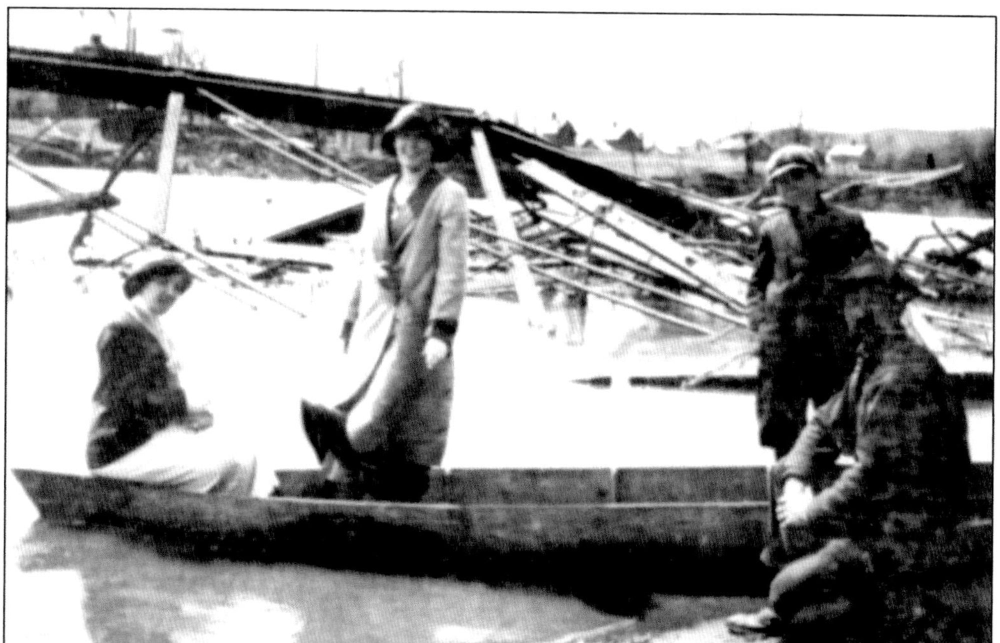

A ferry was maintained on the south side until a new bridge could be constructed. Boats and rafts were used to ferry people and goods across the Tuscarawas River between New Philadelphia and the south side by the use of towropes.

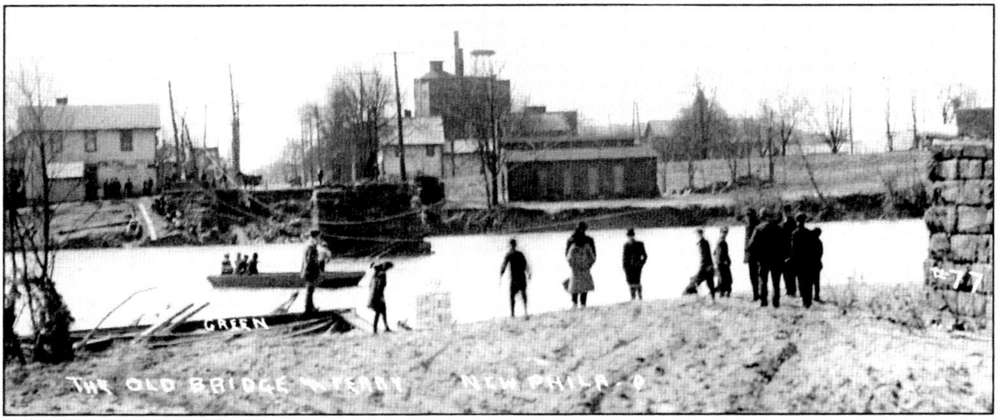

The ferry was the only means of getting from the south side to downtown New Philadelphia. Crowds would line up on both banks of the Tuscarawas River to wait their turn. Boats were in high demand to ferry people across.

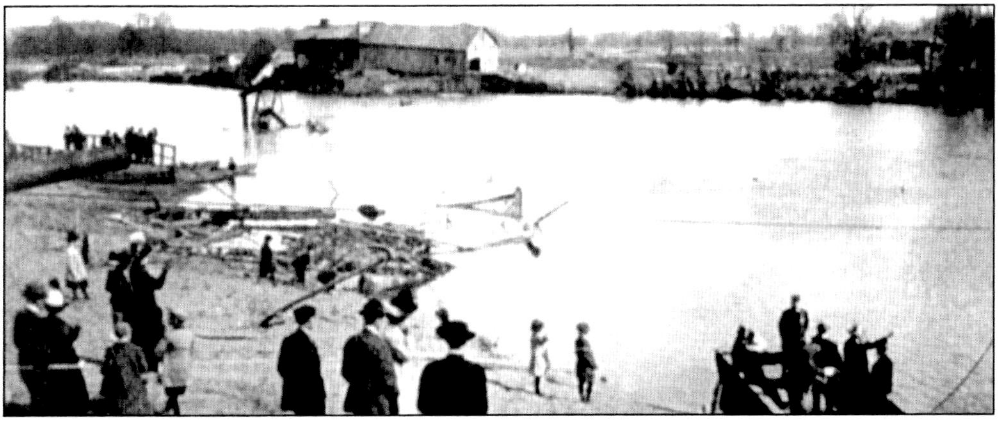

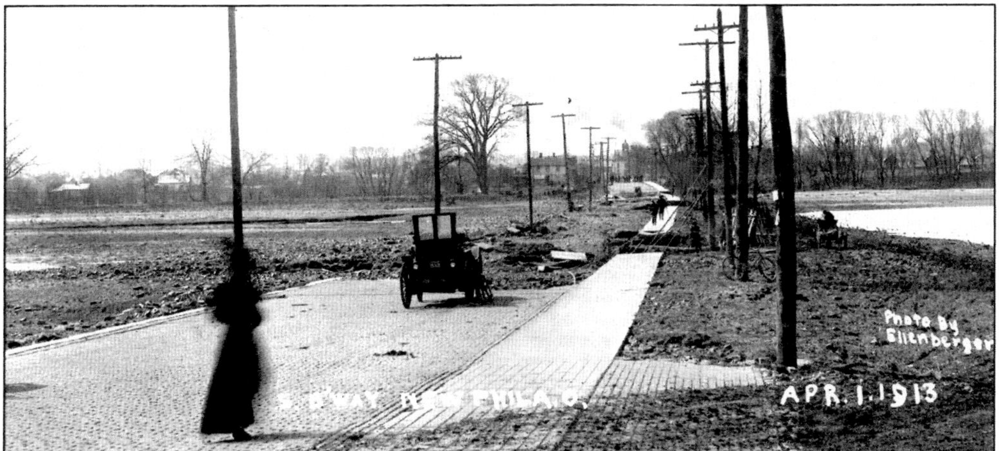

The water slowly receded leaving behind wide destruction. Residents returned to devastated homes, businesses, and bridges. Once the waters receded, destruction could be seen everywhere. Seen here is South Broadway Street, a brick roadway that had been washed away.

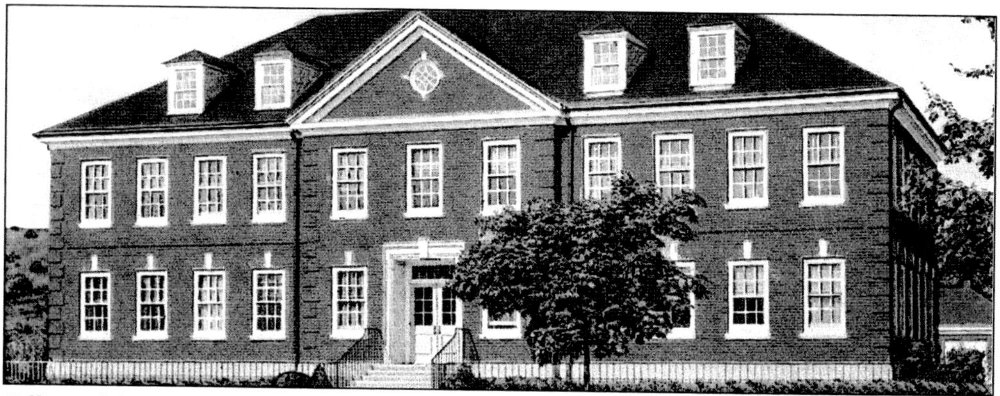

Offices of the Muskingum Watershed Conservancy District, 1235 Third Street NW, occupy an imposing two-story red brick building specially erected for this agency and designed by Charles Marr of Marr, Knapp, and Crawfis Architects in 1945.

The citizens of Ohio knew something had to be done about flooding, but no solution was taken for more than 15 years. Smaller floods continued, but in 1930, drought threatened Tuscarawas County as well as all of Ohio. Wells and springs were going dry, crops were failing, and even city water supplies were threatened. The communities urged the Ohio Department of Public Works (ODPW) to intervene. The ODPW conducted a survey of the Muskingum Valley to find a solution to water conservation, flood prevention, and betterment of existing navigation facilities. This resulted in the formation of the Muskingum-Tuscarawas Valley Improvement Association, including representatives of the 18 counties in the Muskingum Watershed. The study indicated that both flood control and water conservation were possible and that the benefits would greatly exceed the cost, but the survey indicated the sum of money necessary to complete such a project would be larger than the citizens could afford. In 1933, the Muskingum Watershed Conservancy District (MWCD), a local corporation, was created, patterned after an earlier, similar venture in southwestern Ohio, the Miami Valley Conservancy District. The name of Bryce Browning is almost synonymous with the MWCD. In late December of 1933, they sought aid from the federal government, and a grant of $22,590,000 from the Public Works Administration (PWA), supplemented by approximately $12,000,000 from the state and local districts, provided the funds for an extensive rehabilitation program in the Muskingum Valley. Other grants raised the total funds to $43,000,000. These grants were the first direct co-operative effort in the United States involving the federal, state, and local governments.

Soon after the grant was announced, actual work on the flood-control program began with headquarters in New Philadelphia at the former residence of Dr. E.B. Shanley at 205 North Broadway. In January 1935, construction began on the Dover, Beach City, Atwood, and Bolivar Dams in Tuscarawas County as well as 10 other dams in the district. The MWCD's water control project was dedicated on July 17, 1938, at the Bolivar Dam. Under authority of Congress, the U.S. Corps of Engineers assumed responsibility for the flood control operations on August 11, 1939. In development programs, the district planted trees, made general improvements to thousands of acres, and constructed major recreation facilities including state parks, beaches, lodges, vacation cottages and homes, golf courses, ski slopes, and campsites. Closely associated with these features was a system to retard soil-erosion.

An emphasis was placed on conservation. Extensive reforestation of eroded areas and barren slopes was undertaken by the Civilian Conservation Corps (CCC), formed at Schoenbrunn in April 1933, and other agencies. Landowners were urged to plant trees to prevent runoff of precious soils and damaging surface waters. Contour farming, crop rotation, and development of woodlands were done to restore the natural landscape. The MWCD now operates on income from its water and land facilities.

Four

SCHOOLS, CHURCHES, AND SECRET ORDERS

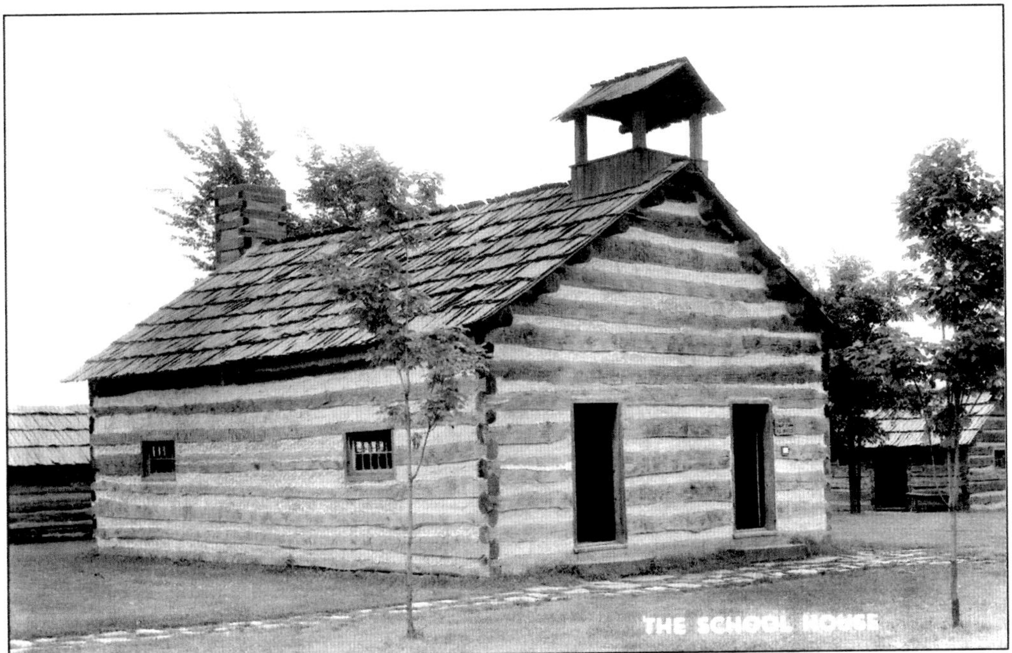

This is the reconstructed Schoenbrunn Village School House. The missionaries and Native Americans at Schoenbrunn Village began building the first log school house on December 22, 1772. According to an entry in the *Schoenbrunn Journal* on December 4, 1774, "School opened again, giving the children great joy. Brother David (Zeisberger) and Brother (John) Heckewelder divided the duty of conducting the school in the Indian language. As we have no books for the children, we must write some for the time being, a considerable task in itself, but it is worth the effort if the children learn anything." Zeisberger published the textbook, *Essay of a Delaware Indian and English Spelling Book for the Use of the Christian Indians on the Muskingum River*—probably the first book written in Ohio. It included Biblical selections such as the Lord's Prayer and the Ten Commandments. The curriculum at Schoenbrunn consisted of religious education, spelling, and singing. Hygiene may also have been included as the *Journal* mentioned the reference book *Something of the Bodily Care for Children.*

In 1805, several citizens pooled their funds to hire a teacher, secured available textbooks, and rented quarters for a school in the only unoccupied building in town—the jail. This arrangement worked as long as law enforcement did not have prisoners. The teacher was paid less than $15 per month and boarded with families of his pupils. A few years later, a hewed-log school house was built on a lot donated by John Knisely at the west end of Getzman lot 253. For many years, the school occupied four rooms above the market house, formerly lot 156, East High Street, the site of Wells' drug store.

The profession of teaching became a woman's career about 1830 when men entered factories and industry for better wages. Teachers were expected to be devout in character and to adhere to rules written and unwritten: they were not to be out after dark (8:00 p.m.); they were not to leave the city limits unless permission was granted by the board of education; they were to wear at least two petticoats and not wear bright colors; they were not to be seen in a carriage in the company of a man unless it was their brother or father; they were not to indulge in smoking or drinking alcohol; and they were to remain unmarried. (In 1945, women were recruited for national defense during the war, creating a shortage of teachers, and the board of education had to rescind the latter rule.) If a teacher was sick very long, they would find themselves relieved from their job. School curriculum included hunting and shooting, and the school term was three months.

In 1844, the fourth school opened in the old storeroom of the Overholt Store. New Philadelphia also proudly claimed two private schools: the New Philadelphia Male Academy and the New Philadelphia Female Seminary. A writing school was also held in the grand jury room of the courthouse by Mr. B.N. Kerr. By 1847, the school term had been lengthened to four months with schools in session five and a half days per week. In 1848, the school records show four schools, four teachers, and 310 youth attending, aged 4–21.

In 1850, District No. 1 in Goshen Township organized a school board and a special district for school purposes and purchased four lots from John and Lucinda English on which a two-story brick school house measuring 40 by 75 feet was erected. The school, New Philadelphia Union School, opened in the fall of 1850 and was divided into three grades teaching English, physiology, history, algebra, natural philosophy, and rhetoric. The school term was set at 50 weeks, five days per week. It was the only high school, so outlying students throughout the area paid tuition to attend. The site of the first hewed-log school house, along with another lot donated by John Knisely, fell under jurisdiction of the new school board and were sold. In the spring of 1858, four rooms were added to Union School, and in 1866, 14 rooms were added. On April 25, 1864, and again on March 12, 1872, the Union School was closed indefinitely because of smallpox, and then on February 28, 1877, the entire building was destroyed by fire. The same spring, the Legislature authorized the school board to erect a new school, Central High School.

Compulsory school attendance became law in Ohio in 1877. On September 9, 1900, New Philadelphia Public Schools opened with five school buildings and an enrollment of 1,267 students, and in 1919, the African-American school on West Front Avenue was abolished, and all children were permitted to enter the public schools in the district they resided.

Another school, Schoenbrunn School, a two-story brick Victorian-style building two miles southeast of the city held classes from 1878 to 1926, when a portion of Goshen Township School District No. 7 was annexed to the New Philadelphia Public Schools. The Dover-New Philadelphia Transit Company provided bus transportation for the students of the Schoenbrunn School to the Central High School in 1933. Schoenbrunn School closed in 1944 and became the site of the Schoenbrunn Grange. It was dismantled in 1960, and the school bell is now displayed at the site of the old school on the corner of University Drive and East High Street.

Sacred Heart Church opened its first parochial school in September 1908, holding classes in two rooms adjacent to the pastor's residence. In 1910, children returned to school in a new two-story building on Fair Avenue. In 1952, a cafeteria, kitchen, and four classrooms were added, and in January of 1963, a new Parish Hall was opened, housing a gymnasium and classrooms.

Other schools, on the outskirts of New Philadelphia, included: the Beaver Dam School (District 2) on State Route 39 (Beaver Avenue), operating from 1823–1939; the Henderson School (District 4) on County Road 89 (Henderson School Road), operating from 1890–1942; the Baltzley Valley School on County Road 69 (Baltzley Valley), closed in 1931; the Pleasant Valley School, or the Wallace School, on Township Road No. 314 (Pleasant Valley), closed in 1931; the Beidler School (District 8) on lot no. 40 of Schoenbrunn on State Route 416;

the Goshen Hill School (District 9) on Township Road 324 (Goshen Road), operating from 1900–1923; and the Goshen School, a consolidation of Goshen Hill School and Beidler School in 1923, on State Route 416, closed in the 1960s.

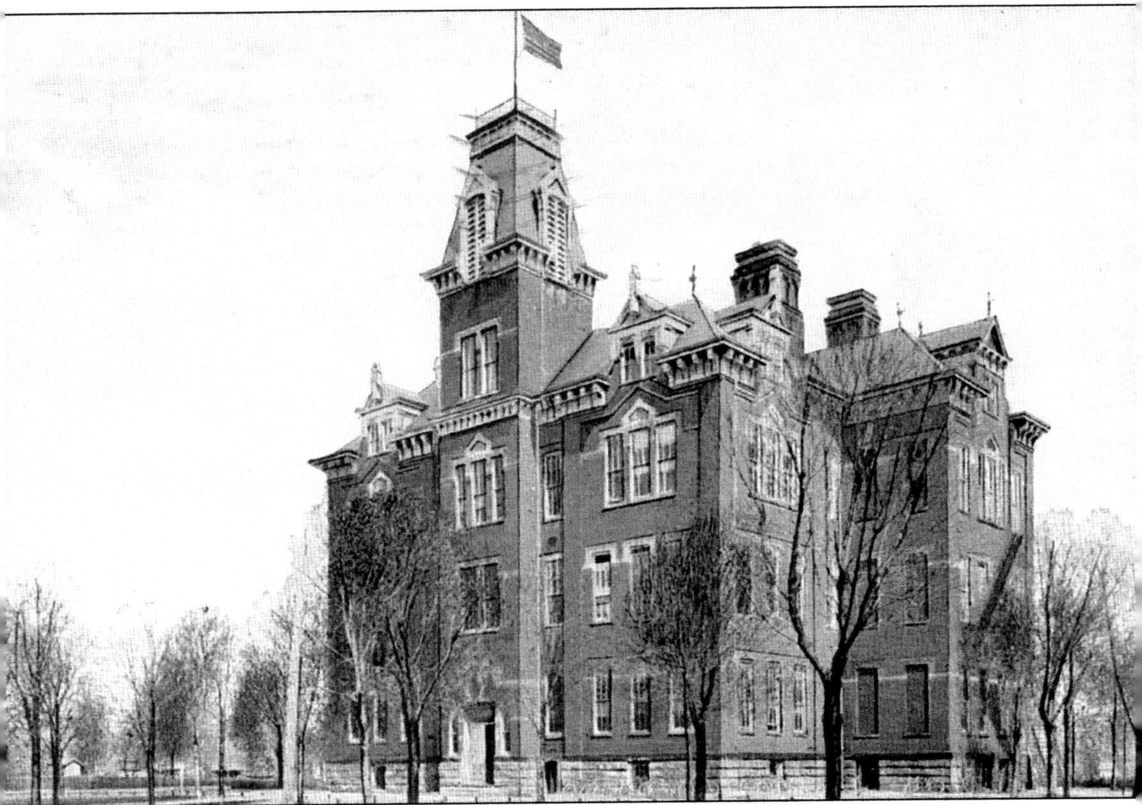

Central High School was completed in 1877 and had 18 rooms with 40 students per class. It was one of three secondary schools in the county at the time and was recognized as a top grade high school in Ohio and the North Central States Association. No diploma was issued to any student with less than an 80 percent average. Its graduates through 1908 were admitted to any college in those states without sitting for entrance exams.

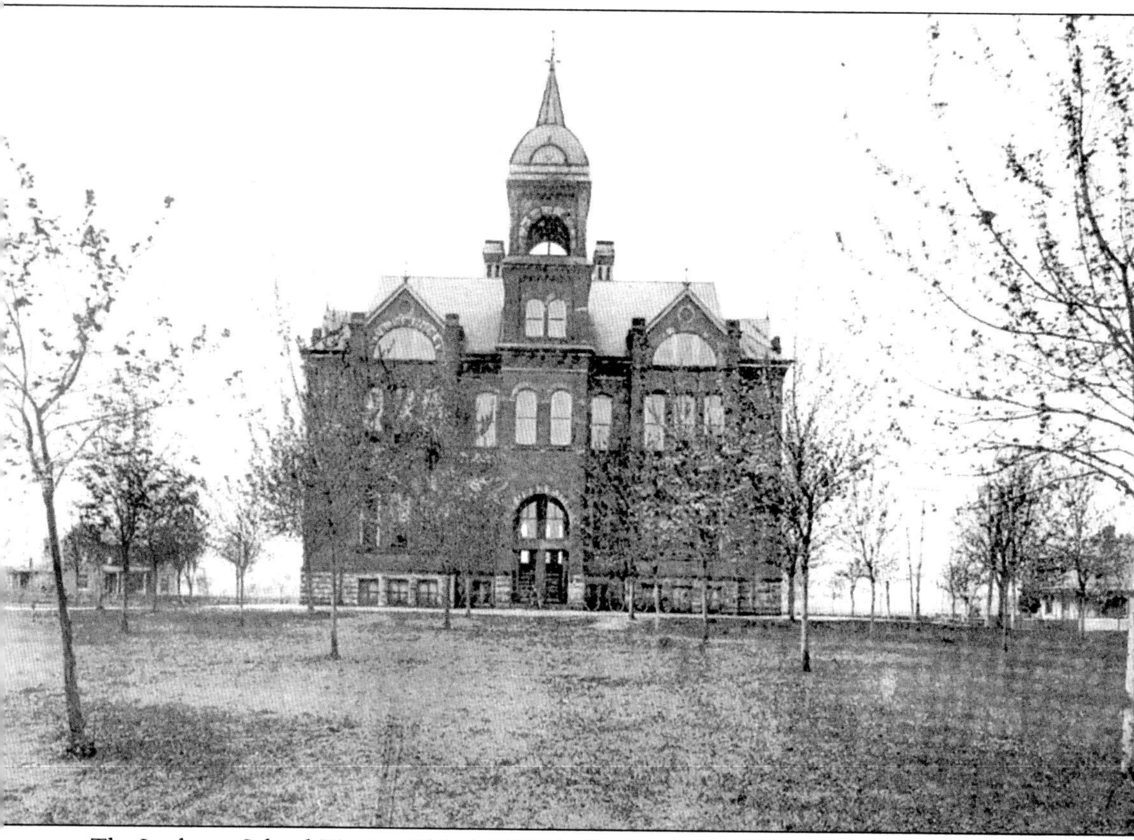

The Lockport School District (Blake's Mills) built a new school in 1892, but in 1899, Lockport became the south side of New Philadelphia. So in 1900, the Lockport School District was annexed into the New Philadelphia school system, and the school name was changed to South School.

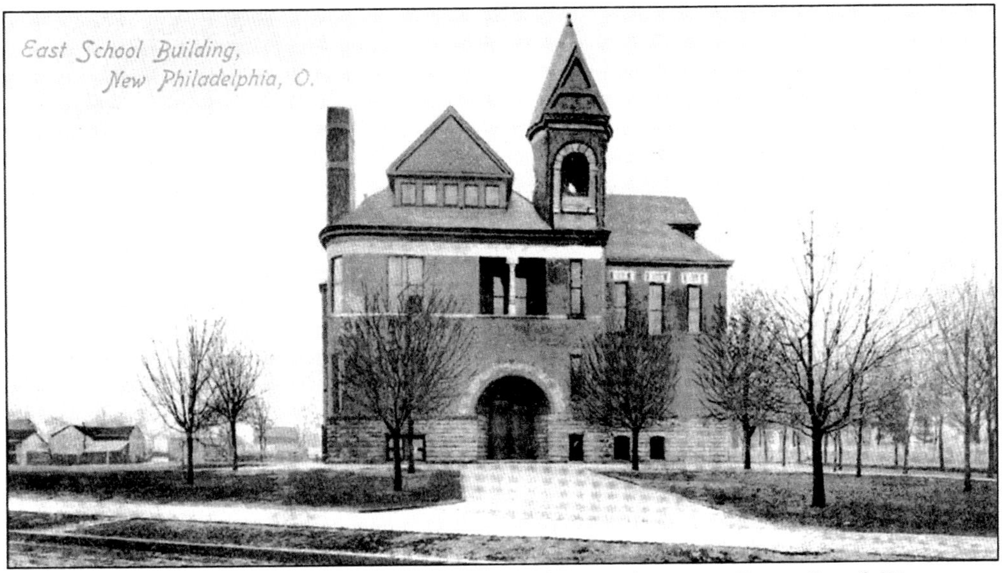

In 1890, four acres were bought on the west side of town adjacent to Dover Road (Tuscarawas Avenue) from Joseph Welty, the former superintendent, and a triangular-shaped parcel on the east end of Fair Avenue was purchased from the Doerschuk estate. Construction of the East and the West School buildings was undertaken simultaneously with West School having six rooms and East School having four.

By 1896, only four years after its construction, West School was over-crowded, and it was necessary to add two additional classrooms. In the same year, the three-year high school curriculum was expanded to four years due to the demands of colleges and universities, even though only 10 percent of all high school-aged youth attended secondary schools. By 1903, East was also brimming with students, and it added two additional classrooms in 1904.

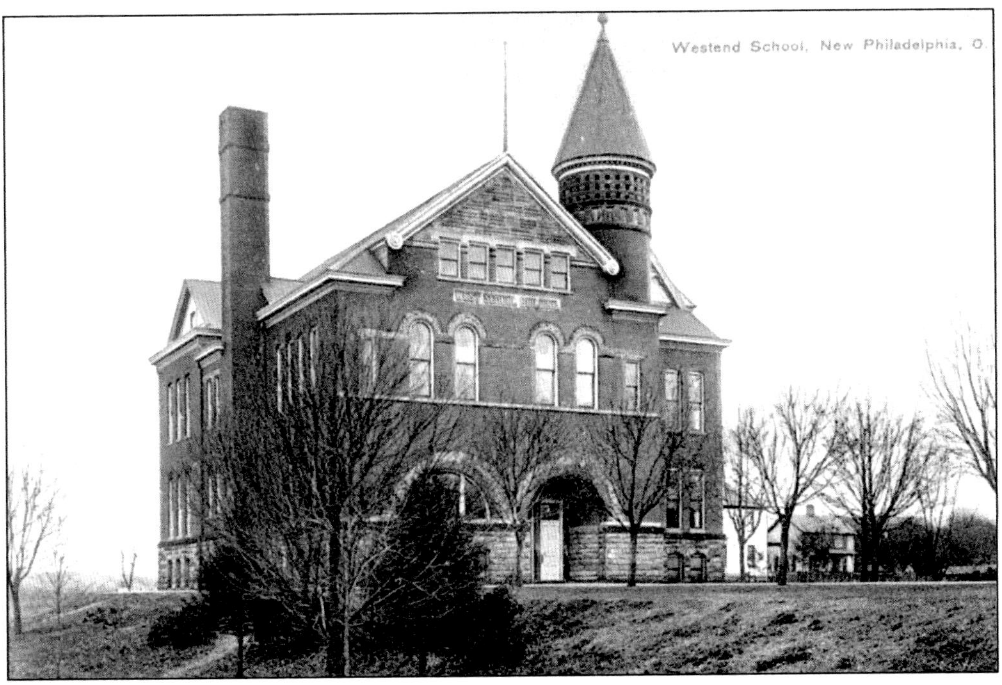

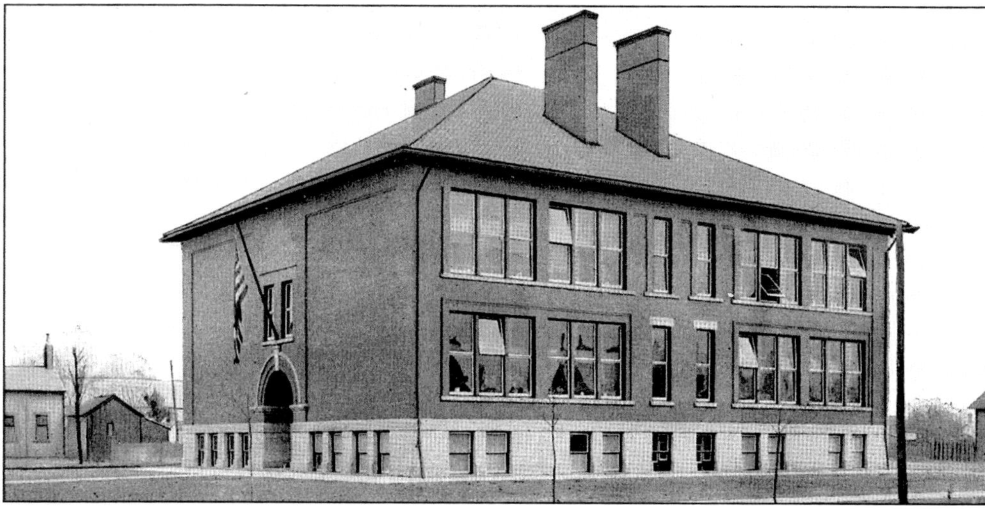

Front Avenue School was constructed in 1906. A dental clinic was actually set up in one of the Front School rooms in 1923 and served the district until 1950. In 1929, the school instituted an "Opportunity Room" for learning disabled children. They were taught the basics as well as woodworking, weaving, and other skilled handiwork.

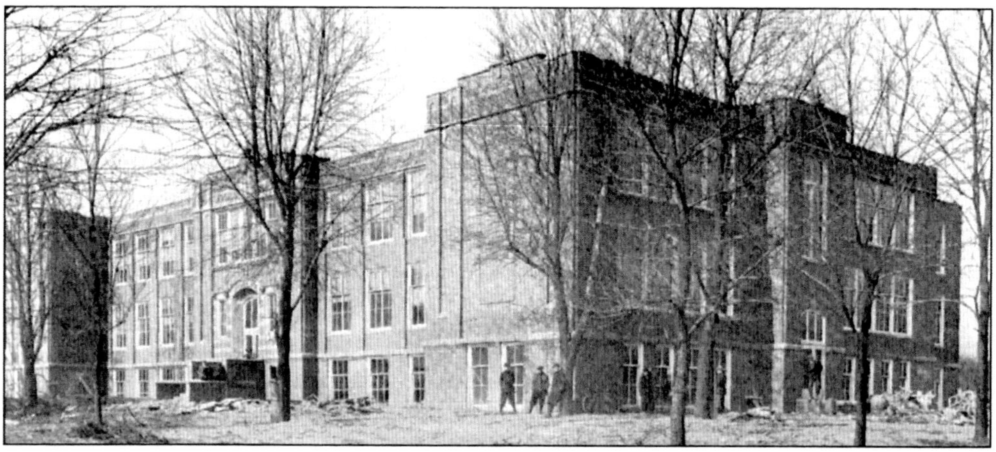

In April of 1913, an election was held for a new high school and elementary school, and in 1914, Central High School became Central Elementary School, and a new high school was built on the corner of Ray Avenue and Fourth Street. In 1915, new courses in domestic sciences, business, and manual training were considered non-degree, and students enrolled in these courses were not eligible to continue on to college. In domestic sciences, young women studied cooking, nutrition, and sewing. In 1917, military training became part of the curriculum for high school boys and continued until the end of World War I.

The New Philadelphia Athletic Association formed in 1919, and track, baseball, and co-ed basketball teams became prominent. Dancing was banned from 1917 until 1920, and with the decline and disappearance of competitive girls' sports, the institution of the high school cheerleader began. In 1931, a quarter of a credit was given for music classes, and the following year, the high school band fund was established, and Band Mothers was organized. In 1942, new courses were added to the high school curriculum: pre-flight aeronautics, emergency mathematics, physical fitness, girls' industrial arts, and vocational training for war workers (adult evening classes).

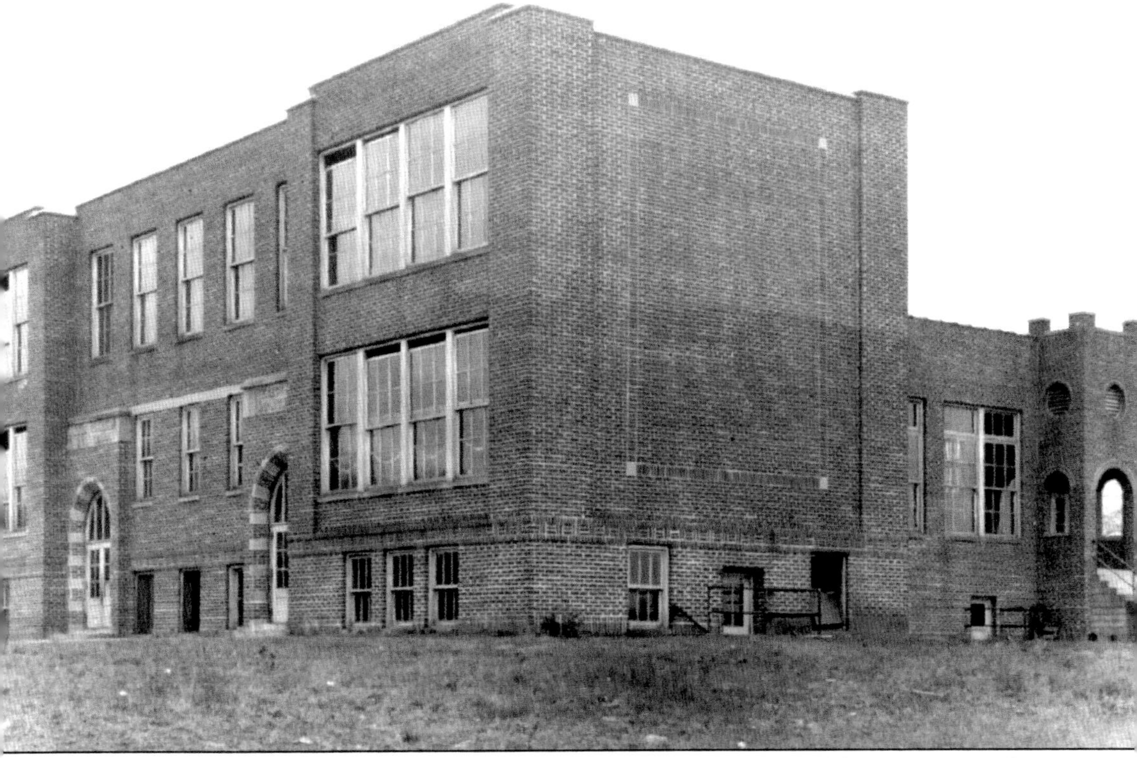

In 1914, Tuscarawas Avenue Grade School was constructed. In the 1914 *Delphian*, Superintendent Charles F. Limbach commented, "Fifty years ago the popular opinion was that the school was performing its full duty whenever it succeeded in teaching readin', ritin', and 'rithmetic. Of late years, the function of the school has been widening to such a degree that we are beginning to wonder where it will end. Whenever anything goes wrong in the life of the nation, the people look to the school for the remedy."

The school board established adult night school in 1918 because of pressure and demands from local industry. Partially funded by the American Sheet Steel and Tin Plate Company, these evening classes were open to any district adult resident, but were for the express purpose of giving the opportunity of learning English "to the foreigners of the city." Later, additions to the night classes included mining, mine engineering, and the retail grocery business.

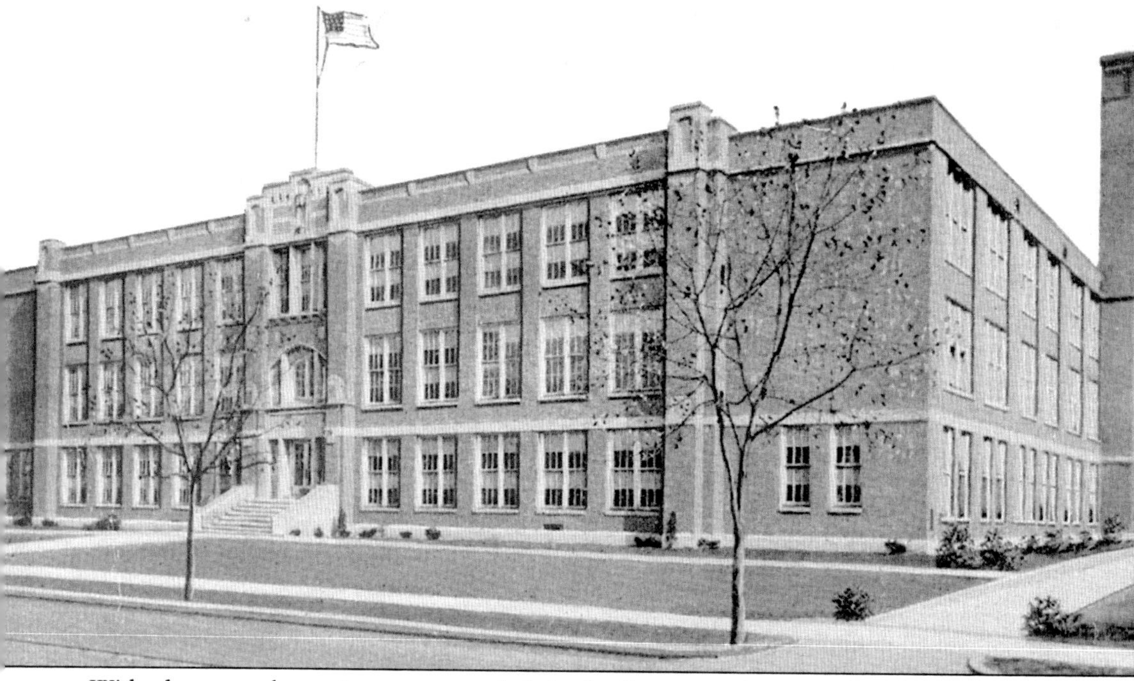

With classrooms becoming over crowded, land adjacent to the rear of the high school was purchased from the Bonnell, Wood, and Steinbaugh families to build the Joseph Welty Junior High School. It opened its doors on November 29, 1926, and all seventh and eighth graders from Central Elementary School transferred to the new Joseph Welty Junior High School, leaving only the first and second floors in use at Central Elementary. In 1943, a library was established at Welty Junior High School.

In 1934, the New Philadelphia School Board designated Central Elementary School as the John Knisely School. The dedication was held on December 12, 1934, the 100th anniversary of the founder's death, and a bronze tablet commemorating this occasion was affixed to the school's facade. Not long after, in 1940, the John Knisely School closed, and all elementary students were transferred to the South and Front buildings. On June 29, 1941, the cornerstone of the new Central Elementary building was laid—the John Knisely School name was dropped. The building was completed in 1942 consisting of 12 classrooms. The first kindergarten in the New Philadelphia school system began here.

The John Knisely School was torn down in 1942 when it did not meet state fire regulations. The only item scheduled to survive the destruction was the 1,450-pound school bell, which was to be placed in the new Central Elementary building for sentimental purposes—however, no one seems to know what happened to the bell. The bronze tablet bearing the inscription "The John Knisely School" was moved to the new school's custodian's room.

On June 1, 1952, dedication of the new East School was held. In the same year, schools were closed for one week because of a polio epidemic, and Quaker Stadium was named. Quaker Stadium was home to Football Hall of Fame Coaches Woody Hayes, Paul Hoerneman, Johnny Brickels, and Bill Kidd. Wayne Woodrow Hayes applied for the head coaching position in 1938 and was accepted. He stayed until 1941, when he enlisted in the United States Navy.

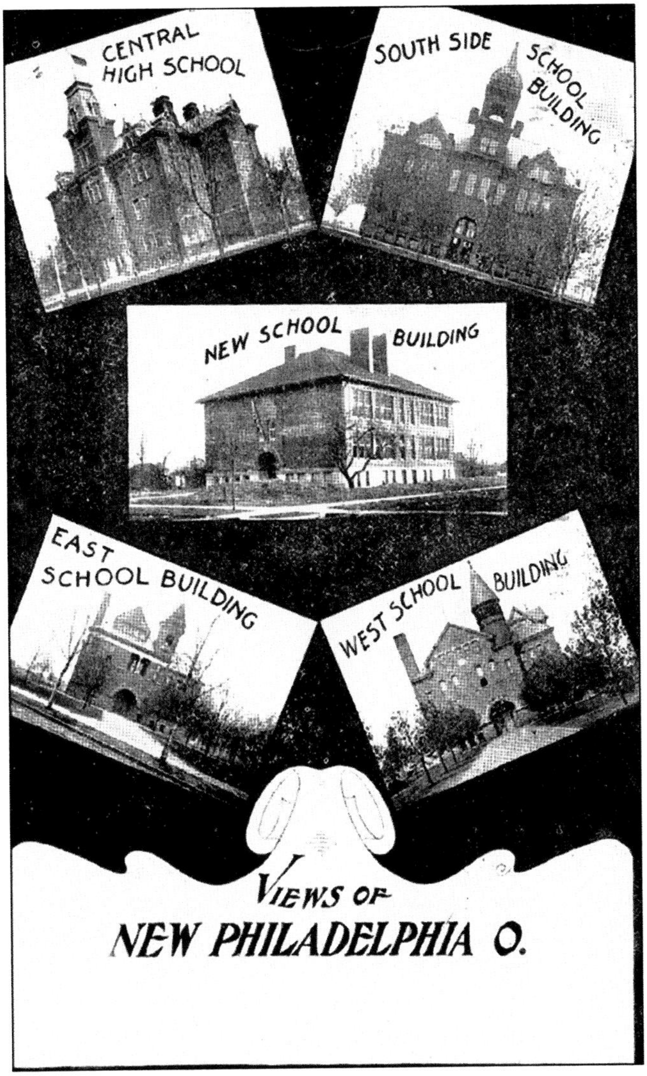

In 1955, New Philadelphia voters approved a new West School building. The cornerstone was laid on October 20, 1957. With the new school's completion, the old West building was demolished.

In 1957, many schools added classrooms and remodeled. Properties adjacent to the New High School on Ray Avenue were purchased for plans to construct a gymnasium and a vocational department. Through the efforts of Superintendent Leon Force, a grant of $150,000 was received from the Timken Foundation to complete and equip the new automotive and machine shops, as well as add the first PA system and landscaping. Another gift of $6,000, given by Mr. William Bichsel, as well as $4,000 raised by band parents, led to the construction of the first band shelter at the stadium. (The shelter was torn down in 2003, and a new structure was built by donated funds.)

York Elementary was annexed into the New Philadelphia School District in 1958 and Stone Creek School in 1964. Stone Creek was downsized to an elementary school and then closed at the end of the 1973–1974 school term. Tuscarawas Central Catholic High School was established in 1970 in a new building located on Third Street NE. A part of the Columbus Diocese, it is a chartered and accredited institution funded by parishioners, student tuition, and the diocese. The First Baptist Church of New Philadelphia founded the Indian Hills Christian School in 1973 on Fair Avenue NE. The school was moved to its present day location on Commercial Avenue SW in 1974. Also in 1974, the new South Side School was opened with an open classroom concept. Ronald Quillen demolished the old South Side School in the spring of 1977.

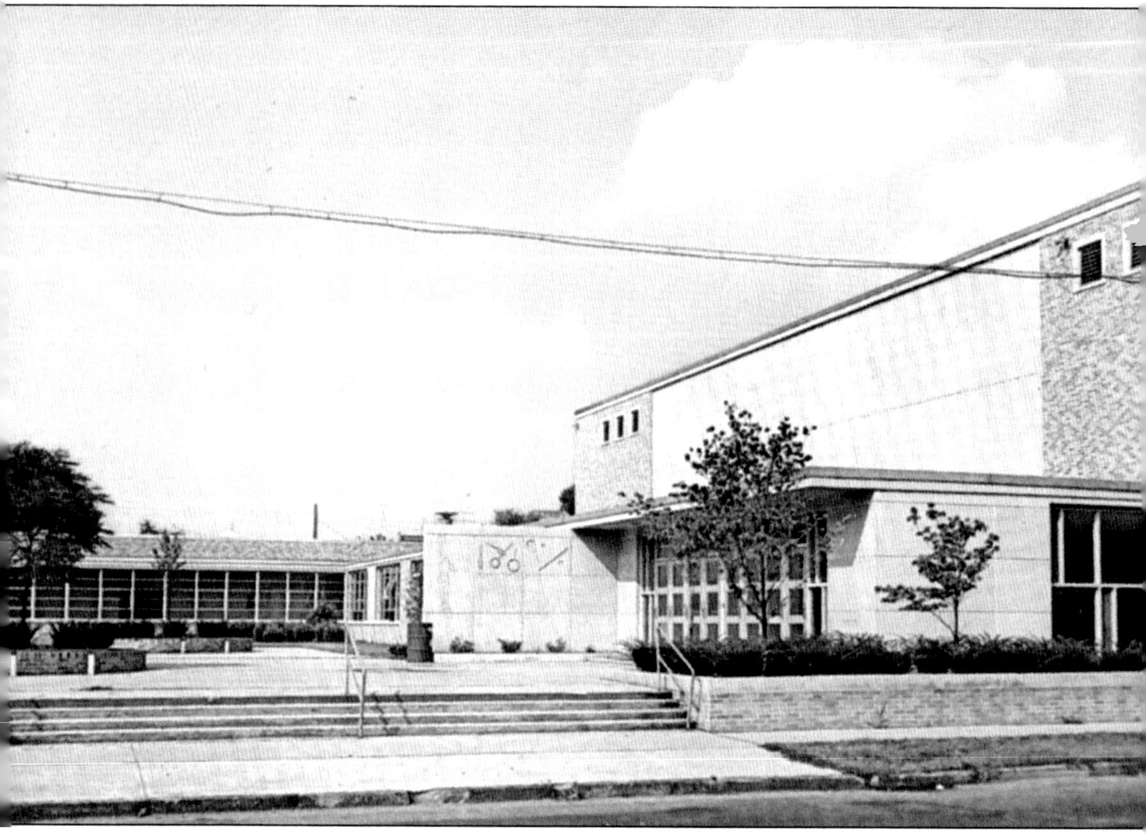

In October 1976, a fire partially gutted Front School. The school was restored and used for classrooms until 1980. In January 1981, it became the central office for administration. On March 4, 1990, a fire struck New Philadelphia High School. High School students finished the year at both Buckeye Career Center and Kent State University Tuscarawas, and Welty Junior High Students held classes in various churches. Students returned to the school on August 31, 1993.

In 1965, the Ohio Department of Education authorized planning districts for the construction of joint vocational schools throughout the state. Buckeye Career Center encompasses parts of eight counties and serves eleven school districts, including: Carrollton, Claymont, Conotton Valley, Dover, Garaway, East Holmes, Indian Valley, New Philadelphia, Newcomerstown, Strasburg, and Tuscarawas Valley. The dedication was held on August 15, 1976, and classes began on September 8, 1976. The Career Center offers 33 vocational training programs for 11th and 12th graders, as well as several programs off site. Kent State University Tuscarawas houses the Technology Preparation programs for both computers and engineering, and the equine program is held at Rockhaven Stables in Dover. Eight satellite programs are held at the home schools. Adult Education at the Center also began in 1976. Today, the program encompasses 10 consultants, 12 full-time career development programs, and over 200 part-time programs, serving over 4,000 adults each year. The Adult Education division operates classes at the Career Center, on a five-acre land lab, and at the Monroe Centre in the Buckeye School of Practical Nursing, which opened in July 2003.

Located on 170 acres in New Philadelphia, Kent State University Tuscarawas was built in the late 1960s and is recognized as one of the fastest growing campuses in the state. The campus is unique being owned by the county commissioners. The newest addition to the campus, the 50,000-square-foot Science and Advanced Technology Center is a testament to the campus' commitment to its students, local business, and the surrounding community. Each year more than 4,000 students attend Kent State University, Tuscarawas.

The Tuscarawas County Center for the Arts opened in November 2001 at 461 Robinson Drive SE (the former Liberty Seed Company). Lauren International CEO Dale Foland, a longtime supporter of the arts, provided the down payment and six months operating funds toward the center. The purpose of the center is to provide educational and cultural opportunities to encourage participation in and appreciation of the arts and cultural programs for residents of Tuscarawas and surrounding counties.

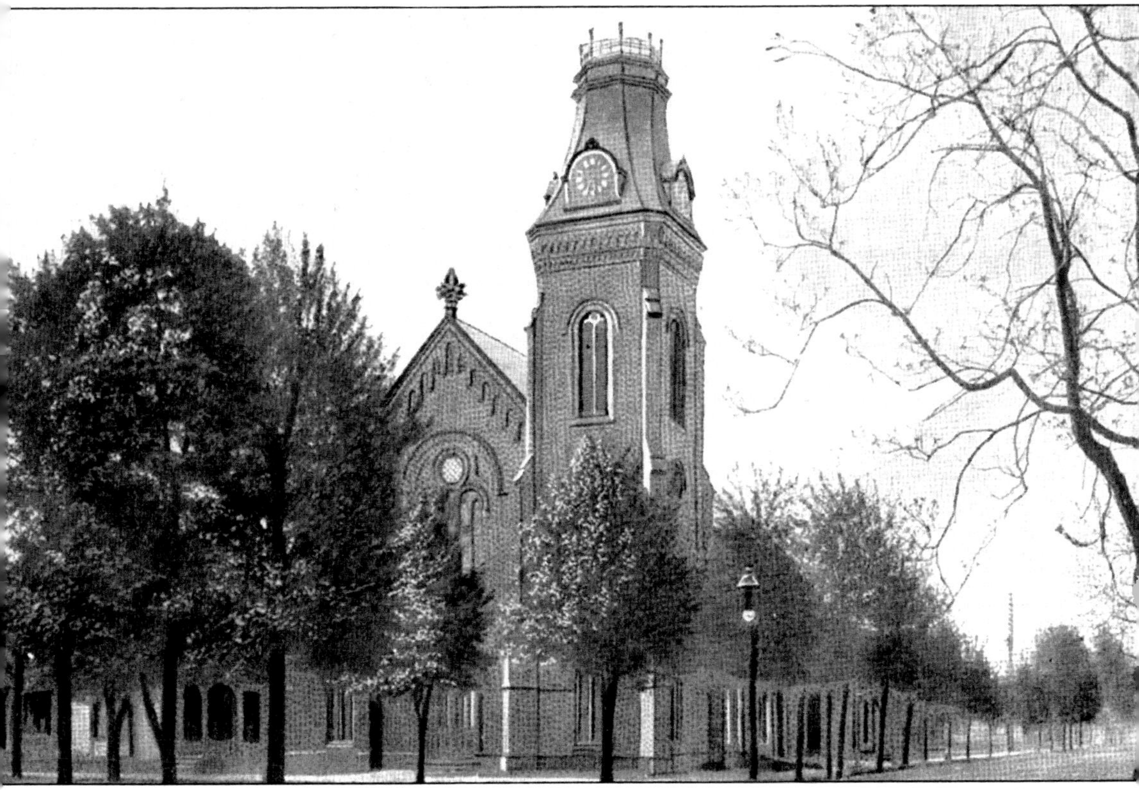

In 1808, Reverend Christian Espich, also a trained medical doctor, arrived. There were only four families here at the time. The Lutheran services were held in German in a log cabin. By 1811, the citizens of New Philadelphia held religious meetings in different homes, including the Knisely home. Services were held in the second story of the old log jail until about 1816. A few years later, the hewed-log school house, erected north of the courthouse, served for both a church and school. After the first brick courthouse was completed in 1819, services were held there for about 15 years.

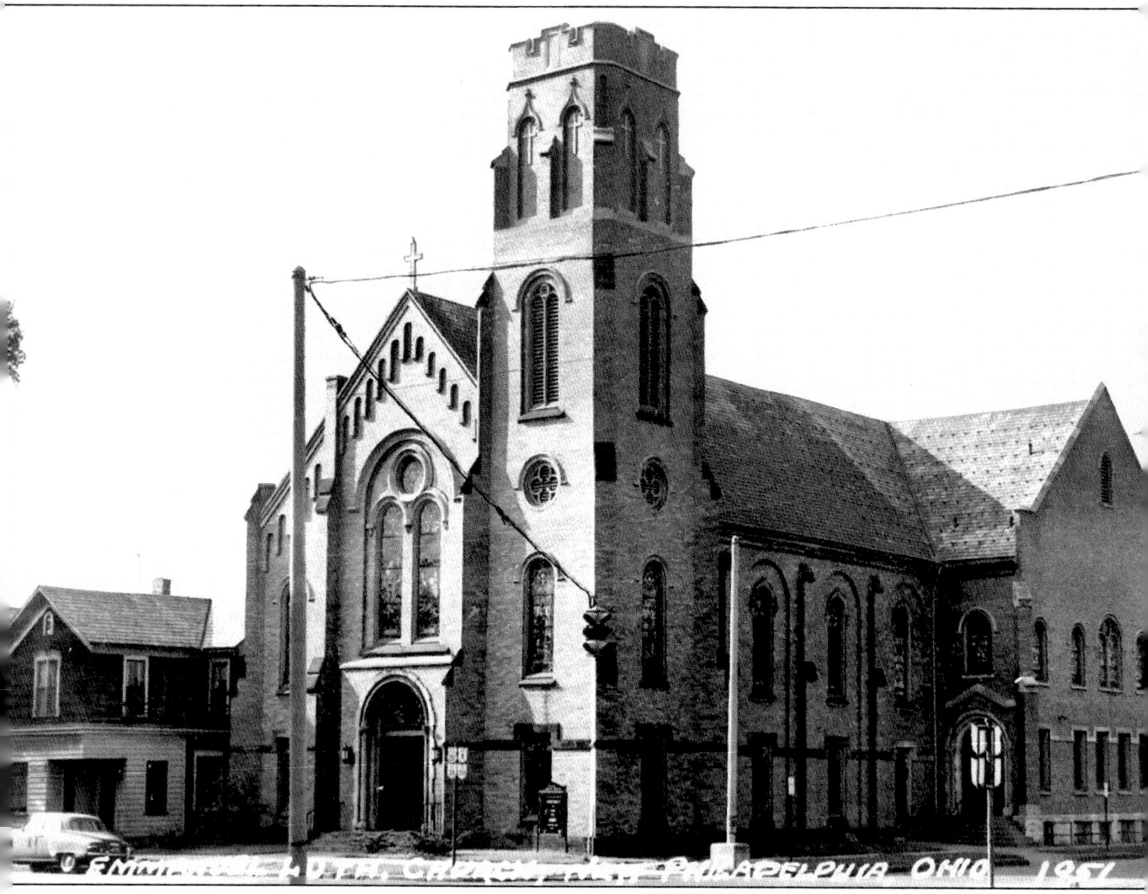

In 1834, the Lutheran Church was erected. Both Lutherans and Presbyterians occupied the structure on alternate Sundays. It was a one-story structure with a spire and bell and a seating capacity of 700. Reverend Greenwold presided here for twenty years. Sometime between 1860 and 1864 a parsonage was erected, and in 1871 a new brick church was constructed.

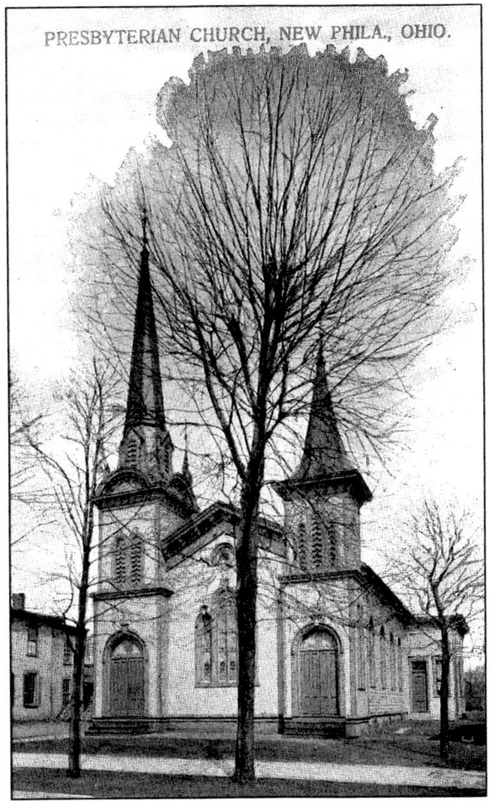

In the 1820s, the first Presbyterian minister who preached regularly at New Philadelphia was Reverend Jonathan Leslie. Services were held at the courthouse until a church was built in 1841 at its present site on a lot donated by Thomas Sargent. In 1856, the congregation divided into two branches, the Congregational Church and the Old School branch, but in 1864, the two groups reconciled. The church was remodeled in 1873 at a cost of $6,000.

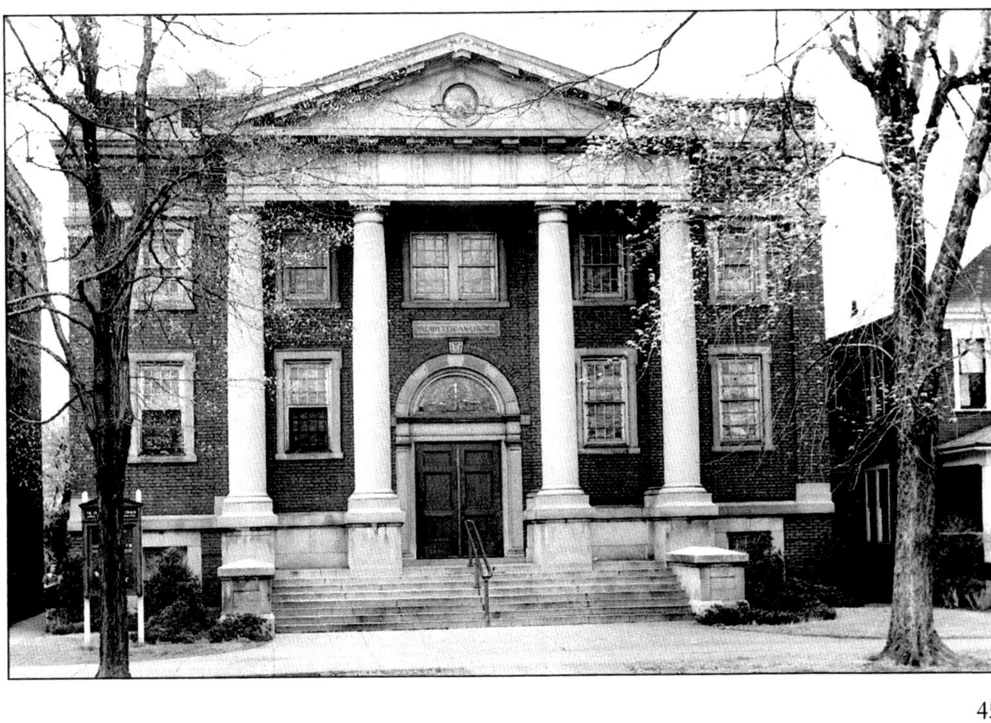

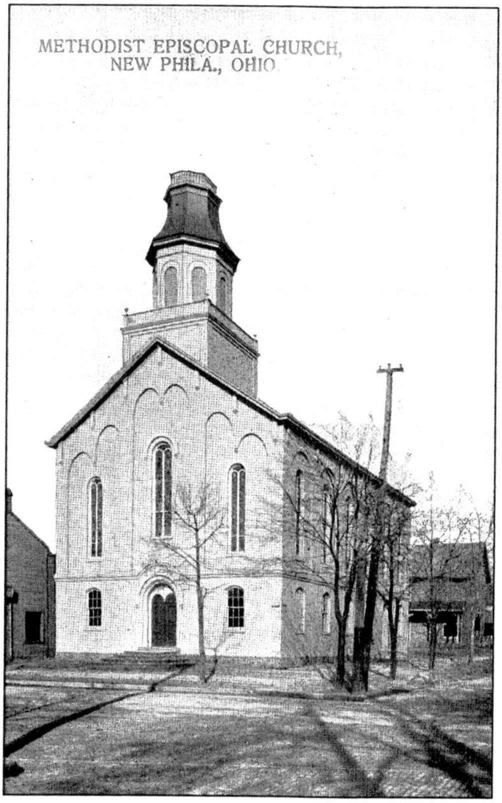

The First Methodist Society of New Philadelphia was organized in 1827 or 1828. They built their first church in 1841 for $950 on lot 117, West Front Avenue. A larger church was erected on the northwest corner of Fifth and High Streets, as well as a parsonage for about $20,000.

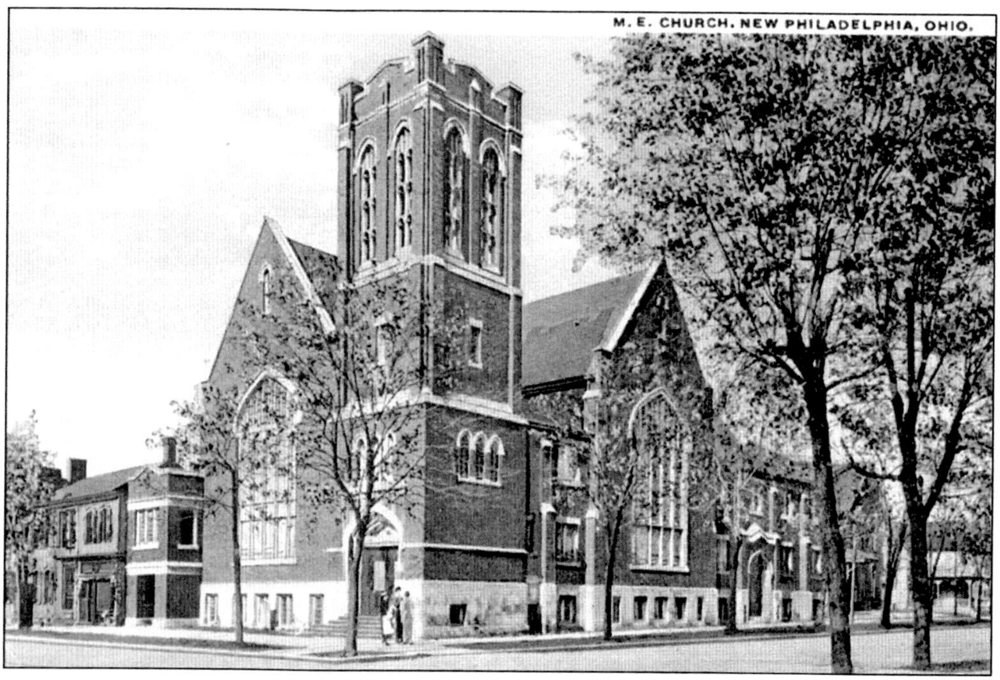

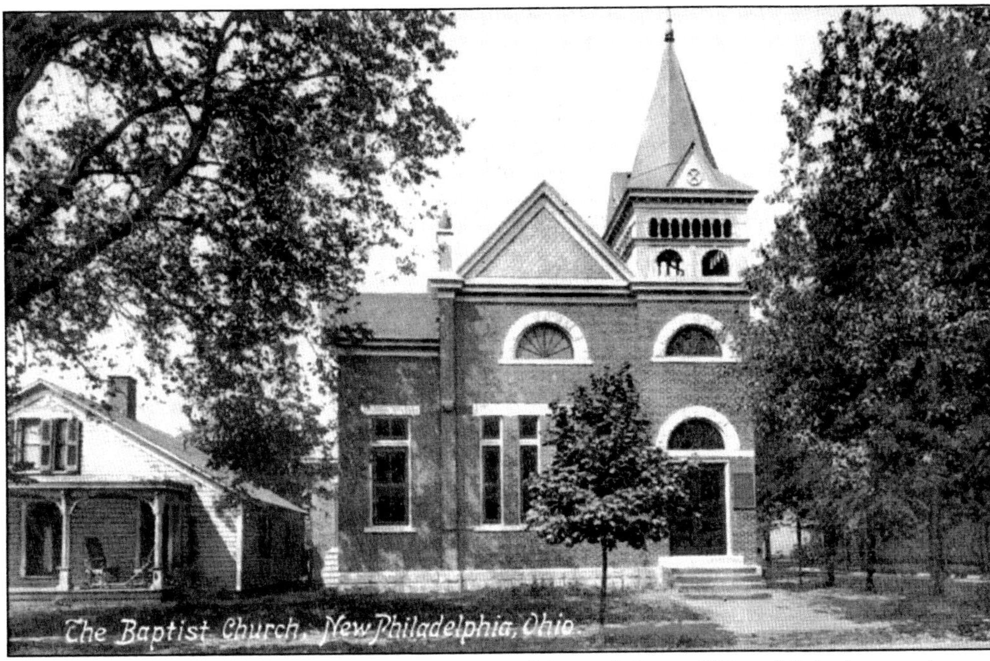

The old Baptist Church located on the corner of Second Street NE and Fair Avenue is now inhabited by the Tuscarawas County Child Enforcement Agency. The Church members built their new church on Commercial Avenue on the south side of New Philadelphia.

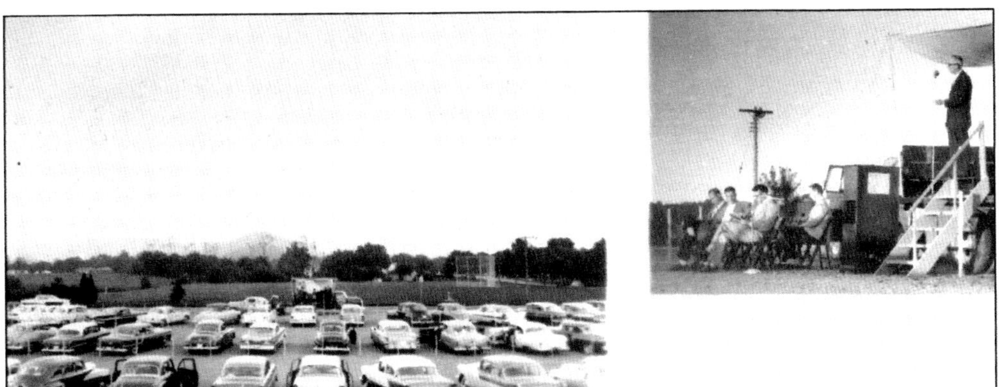

The First Regular Baptist Church was organized March 7, 1858. They built a brick church on lot 256 on the southwest corner of Fair and Third Streets.

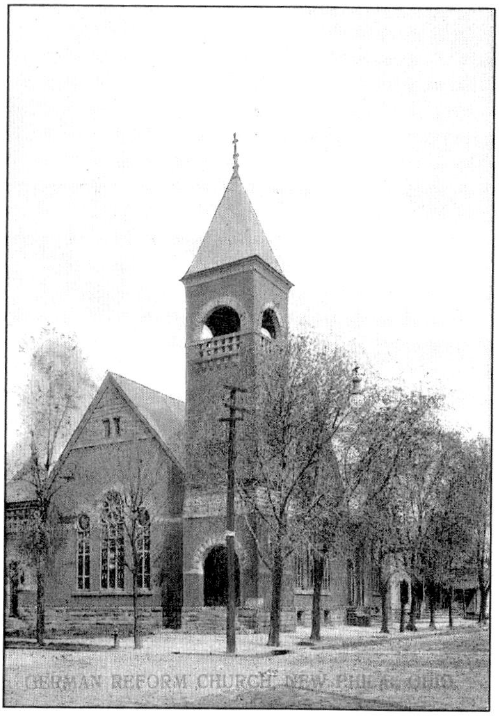

The German Reformed Church was organized in February 1859. The services were spoken in German and held in the English Lutheran Church. In 1861, a brick structure was erected on Second Street (today's Third NW) and Fair Street with a parsonage being built on Ray Street opposite the cemetery. In 1883, a new parsonage was constructed next to the church. The church split, and those leaving formed the German Rational Congregation built a frame church on East High Street, later sold to the United Brethren. Today the Otterbein Methodist Church is located on the site.

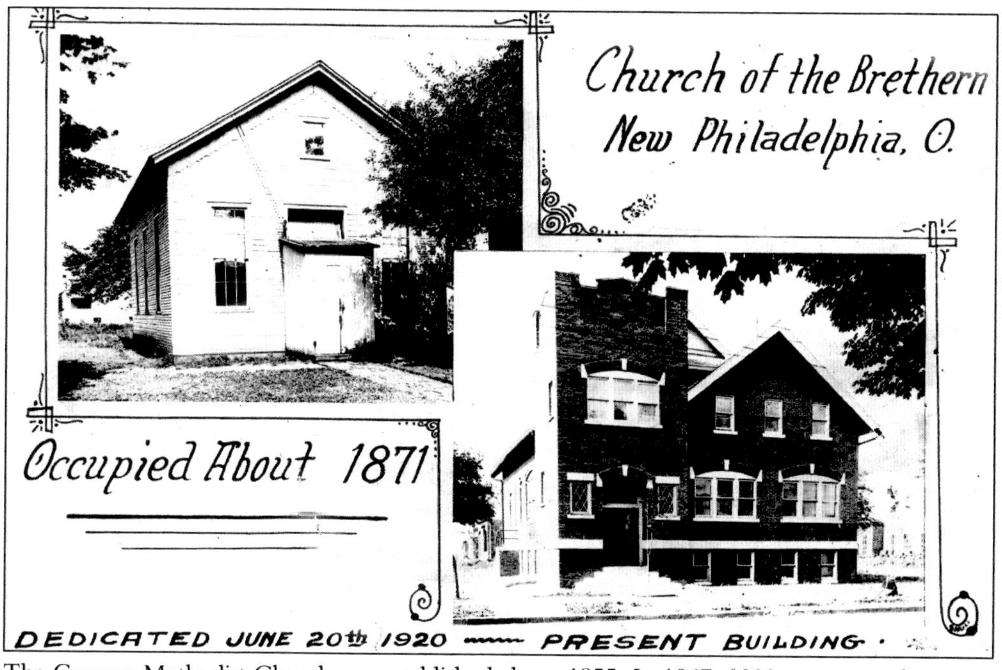

The German Methodist Church was established about 1855. In 1867, $900 was secured to erect a chapel on a lot donated by Mr. C.H. Mitchener in the Mitchener Addition southwest of New Philadelphia. The structure was completed in 1869, and the property was then deeded to the German Methodist Episcopal Conference, the United Brethren, and the German Baptists respectively.

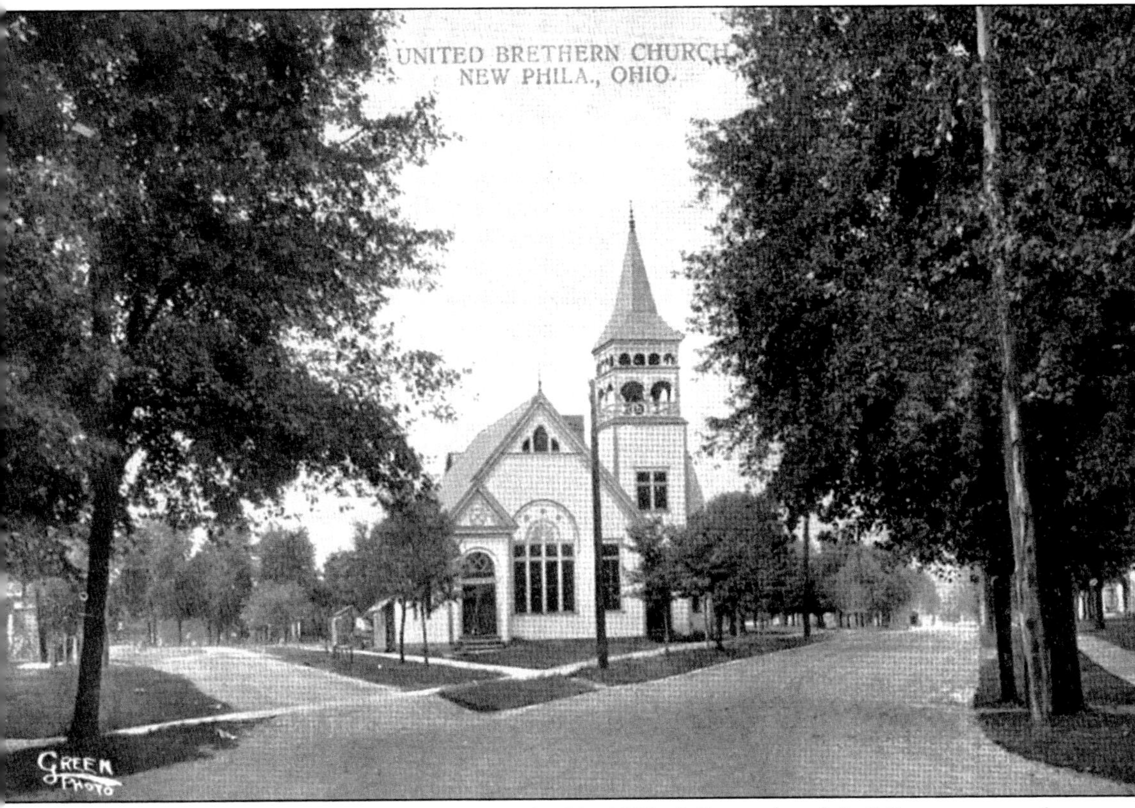

The United Brethren congregation was organized in 1875. A frame church building was erected on the corner of East Street and the Beaver Dam Road, a lot purchased from the German Universalists (also known as the German Rationalists).

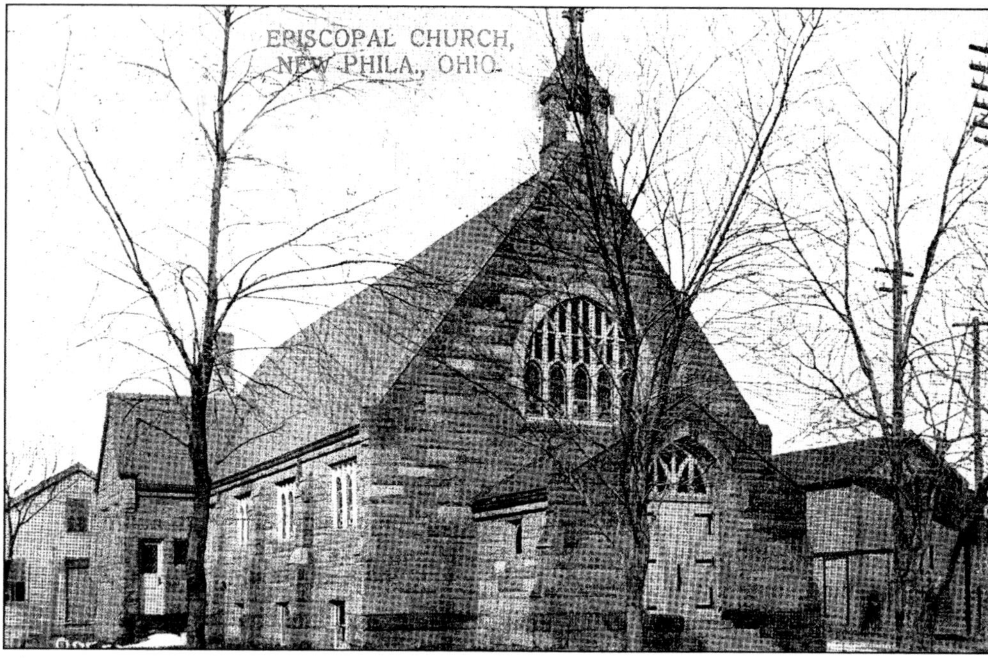

The Episcopal Church, also known as the Angelican Church of New Philadelphia or Church of England, is located on Third Street NW.

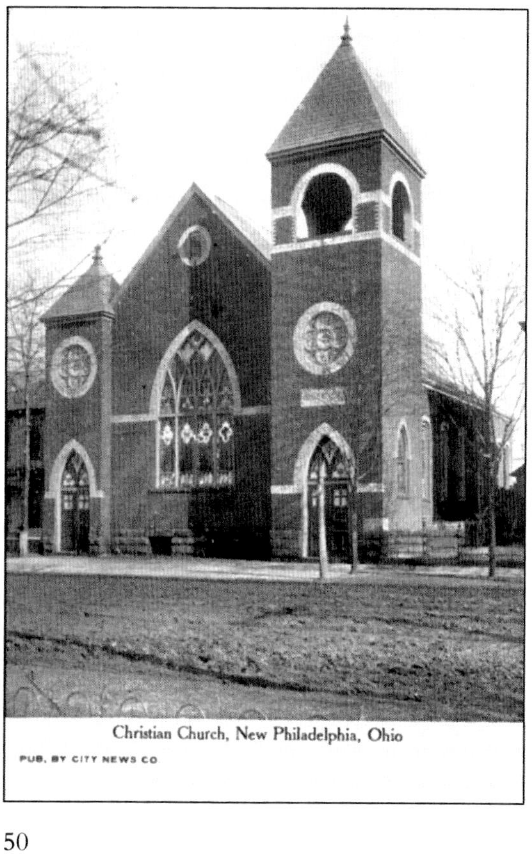

The Disciple Church, probably the oldest religious structure, was situated at the corner of High and Sixth Streets NW. It was erected in 1842 of brick. As others did, services had been held at the courthouse prior to the structure being built.

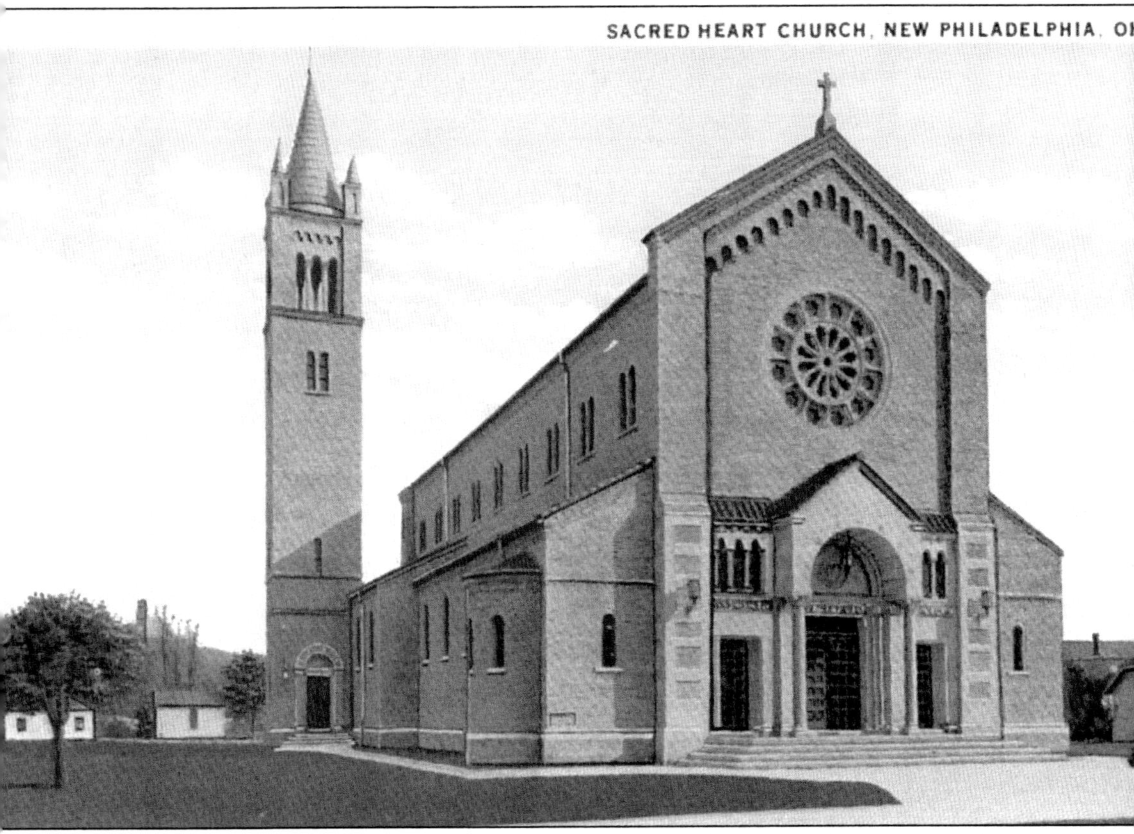

Sacred Heart Roman Catholic Church at the corner of Third Street and Fair Avenue NE in New Philadelphia was dedicated on June 9, 1895. It was designed in the Romanesque style with rounded arches and a bulky tower. It had a red tile roof and walls of buff brick trimmed with Indiana limestone. This church site later became Parish Hall, part of the Sacred Heart School. A new church was built beside this site on Third Street.

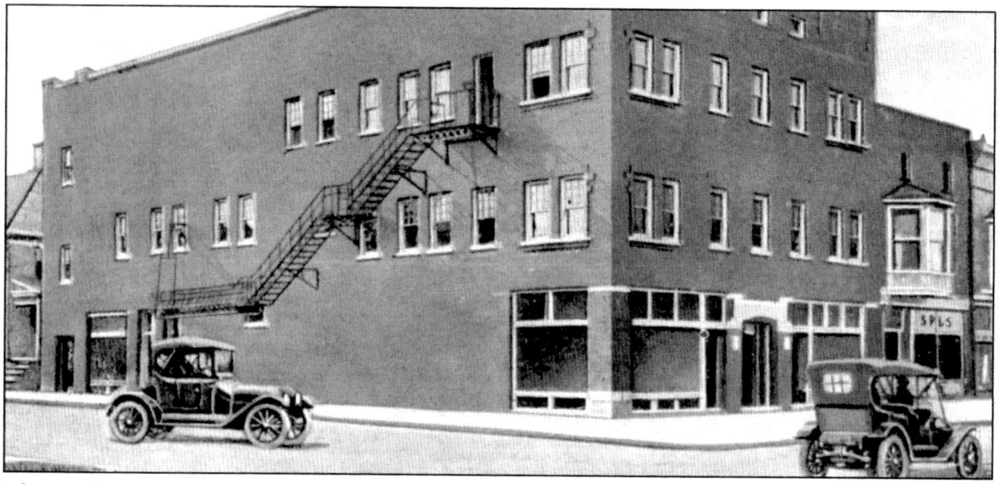

The Lodge of Freemasons, New Philadelphia Lodge No. 59, began in March of 1820. The masons surrendered their charter in 1828. Charted on December 21, 1821, the Free and Accepted Masons, Lodge No. 50 adjourned on February 16, 1826. Until the 1840s, it was extremely dangerous for a man to admit being a member of the masons. Lodge No. 50 never reorganized in New Philadelphia but did become a Masonic order in Dover. The New Philadelphia Lodge jewels were recovered from a Wayne County farmer where they had been left for safekeeping and were taken to Dover where they are still owned by Lodge No. 50. The laying of the cornerstone for the new Masonic Temple was held at the corner of West High Avenue and South Fifth Street (now Second Street NW) in May of 1915.

Mount Mariah Lodge No. 177 F and AM held its first meeting at the Lion Hotel on May 16, 1844, and a charter was granted in October 1849. In September 1853, the name was changed to New Philadelphia Lodge because another Moriah Lodge existed in the state. Their meetings were held in the Lion Hotel, which later became the W.T. Grant store.

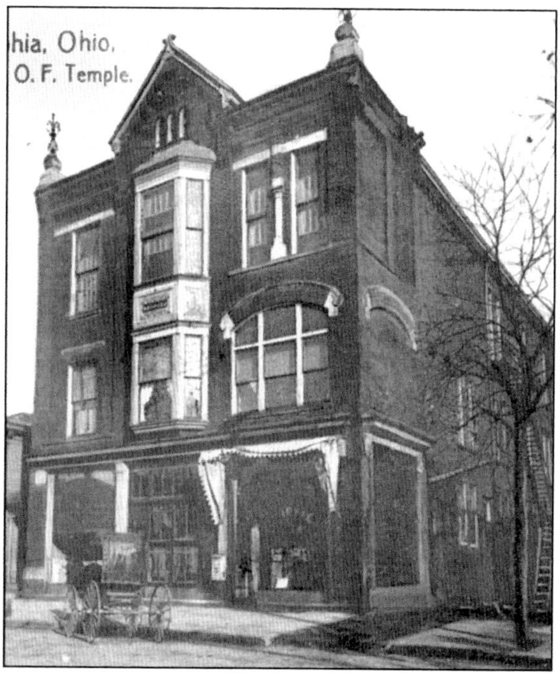

New Philadelphia Lodge No. 107 of the International Order of Odd Fellows (IOOF) was instituted April 4, 1848. In 1860, the size of the lodge was so great that it was necessary to organize a new lodge, Schoenbrunn Lodge.

Equity Lodge No. 73, Knights of Pythias was organized at New Philadelphia September 12, 1874, and Philos Council No. 390, Royal Arcanum was instituted October 2, 1879. The object of the association was beneficiary. The lodge met in the hall of the Knights of Pythias. They had purchased the Empire Hotel structure in 1912, but in 1969, sold the lodge to Williams Furniture Inc. It has since been demolished. The Tuscarawas Lodge of Amalgamated Association of Iron and Steel Workers was instituted April 14, 1833.

Five

Public Square and Events

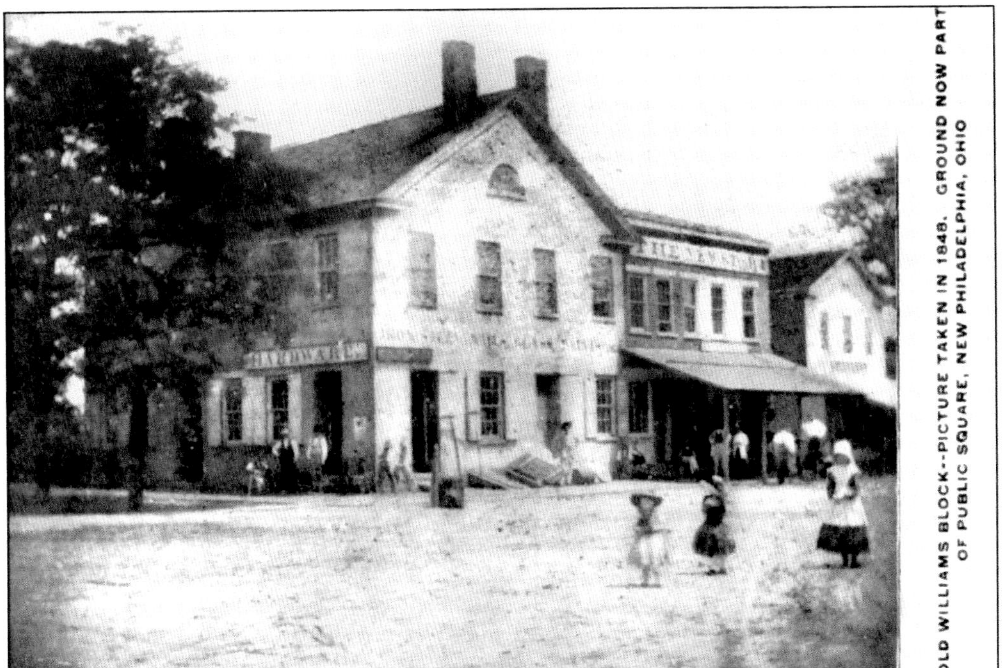

This photograph of Old Williams Block was taken in 1848. This area is now part of Public Square.

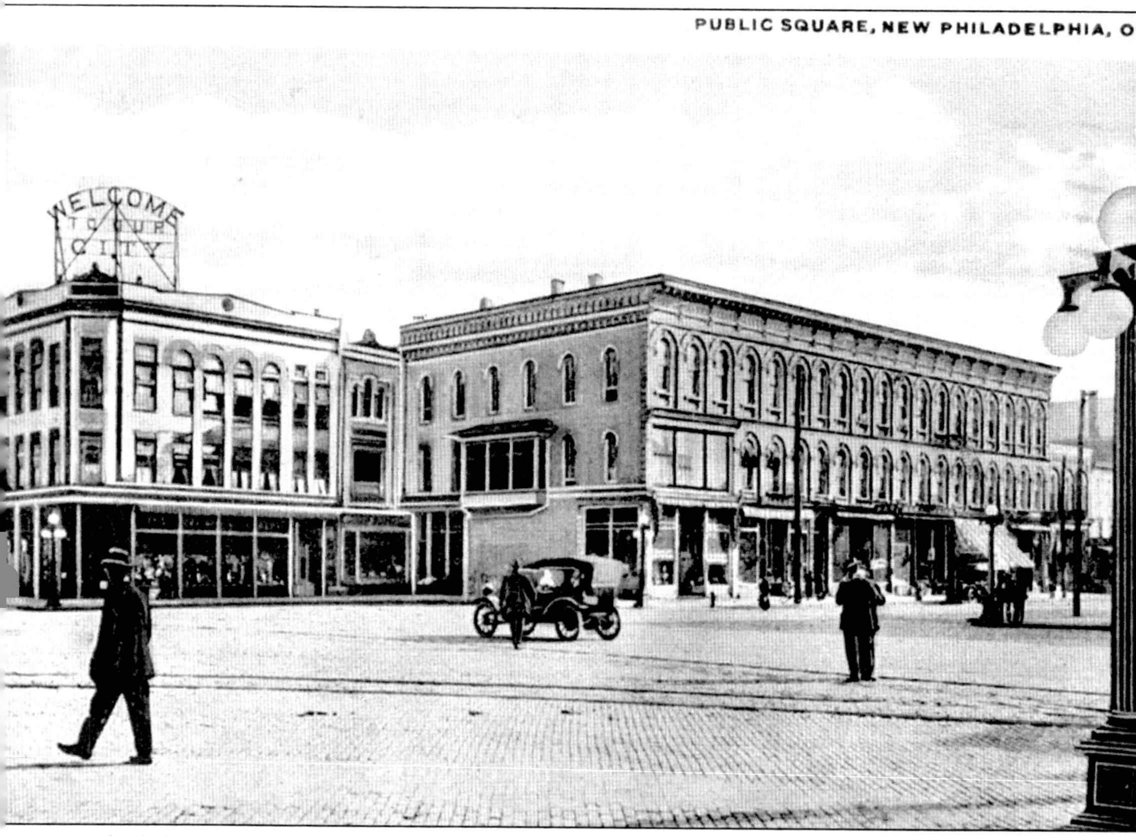

The lighting of the "Welcome to Our City" sign atop the Anderson building drew a large crowd on September 24, 1912, during a homecoming celebration. Several parades were held, and over 3,000 people gathered for the occasion. On Armistice Day, a lighted flag replaced the "to Our City" portion of the sign. The extra letters were taken down and stored on the third floor. The rest of the sign remained until 1936 when deterioration caused the sign to be torn down on July 28 by Elmer Kennedy.

The sign once again sits on top of the Alexander building, having been resurrected from remnants of the original sign and precise reconstruction of the missing parts by George Laurence. Laurence, chairman of the New Philadelphia's Bicentennial Committee and owner of Museum Acrylics in New Philadelphia, revitalized the sign for the city's bicentennial celebration.

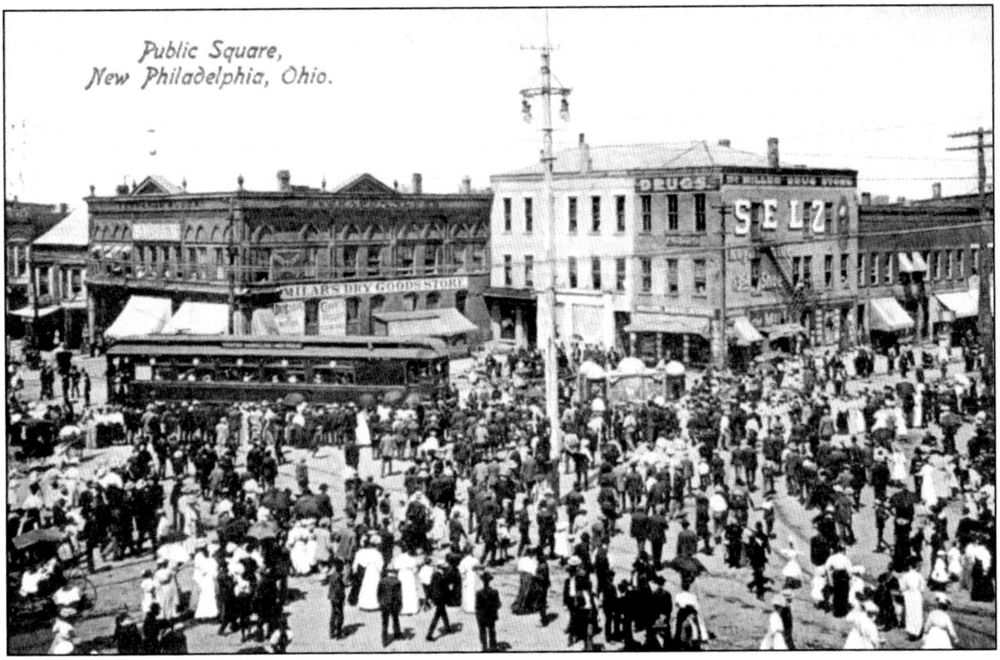

On August 23, 1877, there was a double parade—one for a circus in New Philadelphia and one in Dover on the same date. They passed each other on Tuscarawas Avenue. In 1895, the village was advanced to the status of city, and in 1898, Public Square was paved, providing the city's first paved street.

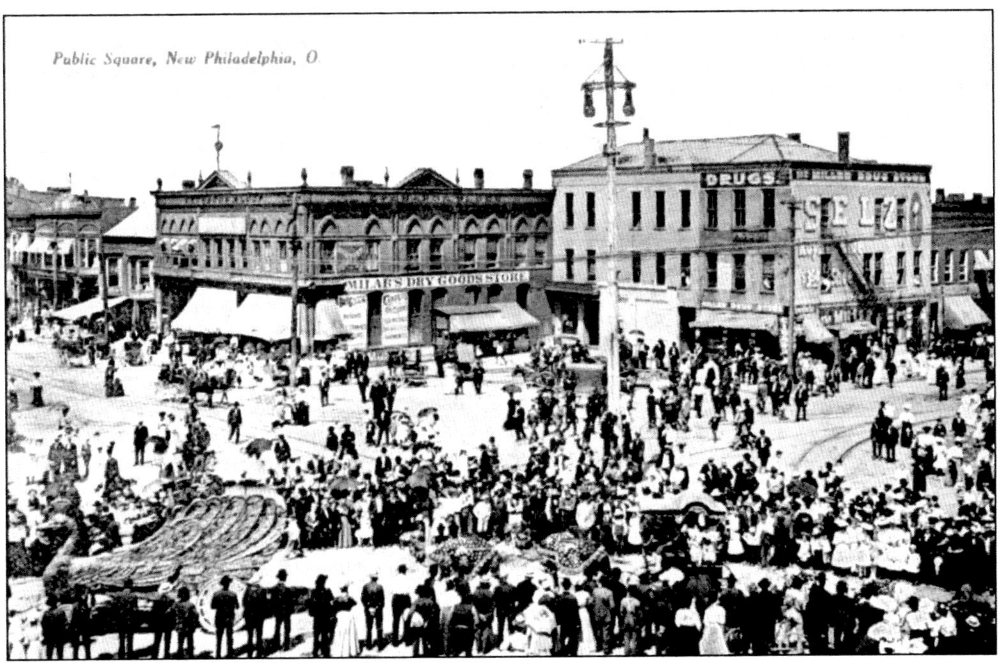

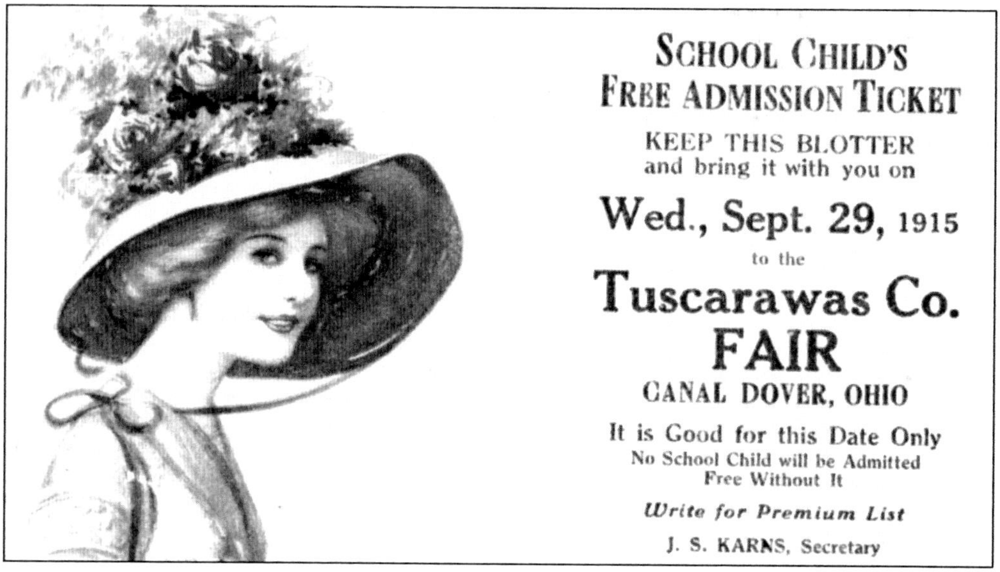

In August 1906, the first Tuscarawas County Chautauqua (similar to a county fair) was held at Reeves Grove in New Philadelphia. The program included concerts, lectures, plays, and other entertainment. The Chautauqua filled a summer need in those days when vacations, televisions, and radios were not prevalent. These events usually ran a week to ten days.

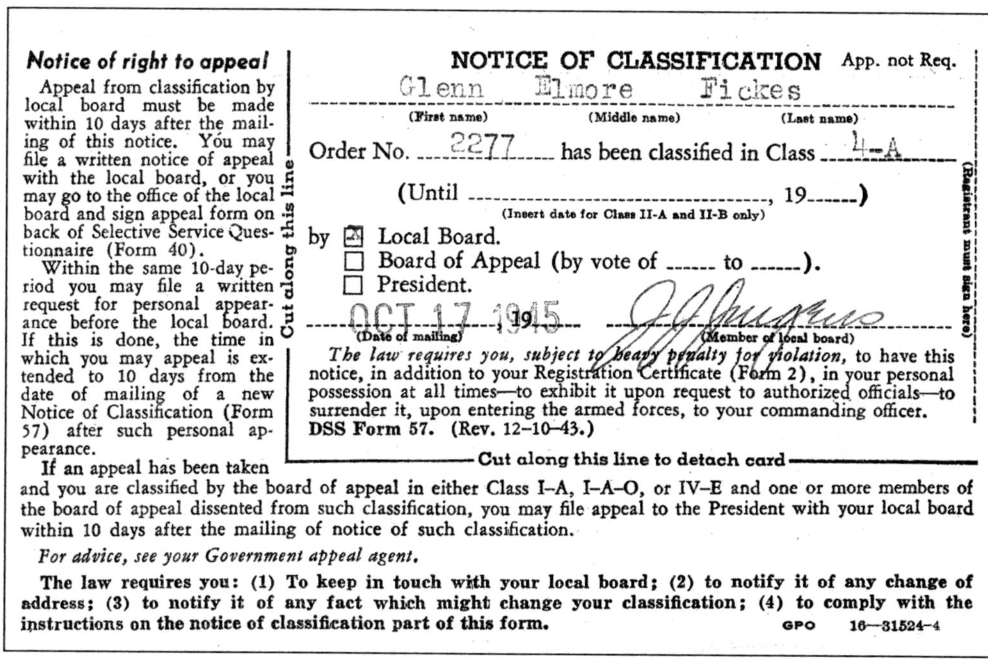

Notice of right to appeal

Appeal from classification by local board must be made within 10 days after the mailing of this notice. You may file a written notice of appeal with the local board, or you may go to the office of the local board and sign appeal form on back of Selective Service Questionnaire (Form 40).

Within the same 10-day period you may file a written request for personal appearance before the local board. If this is done, the time in which you may appeal is extended to 10 days from the date of mailing of a new Notice of Classification (Form 57) after such personal appearance.

If an appeal has been taken and you are classified by the board of appeal in either Class I–A, I–A–O, or IV–E and one or more members of the board of appeal dissented from such classification, you may file appeal to the President with your local board within 10 days after the mailing of notice of such classification.

For advice, see your Government appeal agent.

The law requires you: (1) To keep in touch with your local board; (2) to notify it of any change of address; (3) to notify it of any fact which might change your classification; (4) to comply with the instructions on the notice of classification part of this form. GPO 16—31524-4

Cut along this line

NOTICE OF CLASSIFICATION App. not Req.

Glenn Elmore Fickes
(First name) (Middle name) (Last name)

Order No. 2277 has been classified in Class 4-A

(Until ______, 19___)
(Insert date for Class II-A and II-B only)

by ☒ Local Board.
☐ Board of Appeal (by vote of ___ to ___).
☐ President.

OCT 17 1945 (Date of mailing) ______ (Member of local board)

The law requires you, subject to heavy penalty for violation, to have this notice, in addition to your Registration Certificate (Form 2), in your personal possession at all times—to exhibit it upon request to authorized officials—to surrender it, upon entering the armed forces, to your commanding officer.

DSS Form 57. (Rev. 12–10–43.)

(Registrant must sign here)

Cut along this line to detach card

The Selective Service peacetime draft again began operating in October 1940 requiring all males from 21 to 35 years of age on October 16th to register. The draft was again put into effect during the Korean War.

Six

Businesses

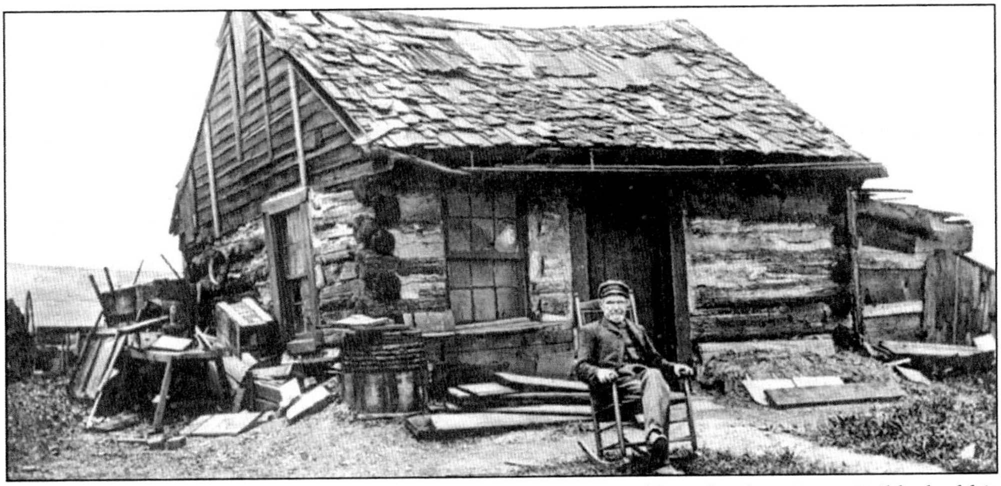

In the spring of 1808, the population of the town consisted of four families. Peter Cribbs had his cabin and potter-kiln on the east side of Broadway and Front. A paper mill was built south of the canal on Broadway in 1808 by the New Philadelphia Paper Manufacturing Company. Two years later, Judy, Knisely, and Company rebuilt it on the riverside. They produced 50 tons of straw wrapping paper per month, but it was forced to close after it emptied poisonous drainage in the river killing the fish. Gabriel Cryder, arriving with an assortment of goods that he had received in exchange for a house and lot in Pennsylvania, sold the goods to Peter Williams, who was then but 16 years of age. Peter Cribbs offered up half of his little cabin, and they rudely fit a storeroom in it—resulting in the first mercantile venture. Christian Stout, a carpenter, lived in a house on Water Street. He came from Washington County, Pennsylvania, and his son Joseph is said to have been the first child born in New Philadelphia in 1807. Also from Pennsylvania, Henry Laffer, Ohio surveyor, opened a tavern at his dwelling on lot 205, High Street during the War of 1812. Laffer was also sheriff of the county from 1810 to 1813. (He eventually left to found Sandyville.) William Albert succeeded Laffer and operated Albert's Tavern in 1814. The Alberts later built a large, brick hotel, the first three-story brick building in the village, on the site of the old building. Much later, it became the site of the Mathias and McFarland's store.

In the 1800s, taverns provided a resting place for weary travelers and supplied them with provisions and liquor. After New Philadelphia was designated as the County Seat, a steady stream of new settlers came. George Leininger was the first tavern keeper in Ohio, taking out a license on August 19, 1808. Mr. Leininger died soon after, but his widow, Margaret Leininger carried on the business at the southwest corner of Broadway and Front. It was here that the first courts were held. Abraham Shane opened a tavern in 1809, and Samuel Shrill paid for a tavern license in 1812 and 1813, as did Daniel Hummel in 1813, Christian Stout in 1814, and George Gray in 1816.

The Gray House, standing on the southeast corner of Broadway and Front, was used as the tavern for many years. During its prime, from 1836–1850, it was the leading tavern in town.

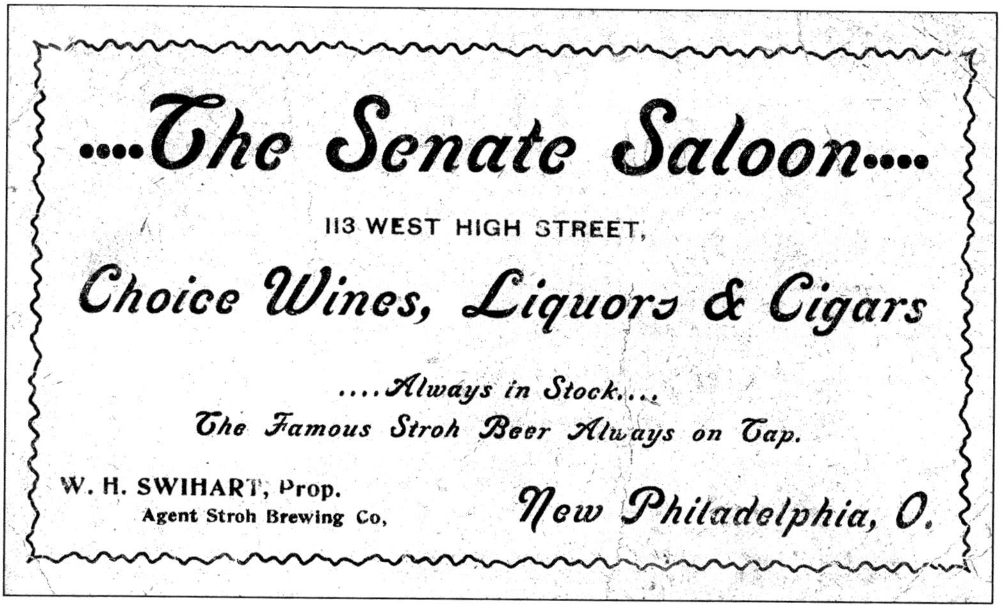

The first temperance society was formed in 1833 in New Philadelphia, long before the first big prohibition movement developed in the 1870s. The Crusaders worked through bands of women who would kneel in front of saloons and pray until the bar customers left. Sometimes they took up collections and bought the saloon's supply of liquor and dumped it. The long wet-and-dry fight began with the Beale local option law and the Anti-Saloon League. State Representative James H. Beale, born at Blake's Mills, wrote the Beale law in 1902, but it went down to defeat in Tuscarawas County. In 1907, the Aiken Law went into effect, raising saloon licenses to $1,000 a year, limiting saloons in New Philadelphia to 17. In 1908, Tuscarawas County was voted dry under the newly enacted Rose Law, but without the saloon tax income, law enforcement could not keep enough forces to keep order. Soon, liquor cases, the result of police raids on "speakeasies," cluttered the courts. In 1910, Woman Suffrage agitation was in full swing, and efforts to enforce prohibition brought on a demand that all laws be enforced, including the so-called Sunday "blue laws." Efforts were made to prevent Sunday newspapers, movies, slot machines, punchboards, and other operations. In December 1911, as soon as the law's three-year term passed, a new petition was circulated. New Philadelphia again turned into a "wet" city.

The State of Ohio voted dry in November 1918, and saloons went out of business on May 24, 1919. National prohibition began on January 20, 1920. The voters of Ohio, who in 1919 had rejected the proposed Crabbe Act for enforcement of state prohibition, ratified a second Crabbe Act, which passed in the 1920 election. Fines up to $2,000 were imposed and collected, but bootlegging of liquor continued. Police Chief A.L. Espich was caught in one crack down and forced to resign. The climax of the law enforcement fight in 1921 came on the morning of June 10 when County Prosecutor Bowers' home at 627 Tuscarawas Avenue was bombed. The two men responsible, both from Dover, were caught. One served a term in the Ohio Penitentiary, and the other committed suicide.

With the election of President Roosevelt, legal beer came back on April 7, 1933, after nearly 14 years, and the prohibition amendment was repealed.

OFFICE FAIRMOUNT NURSERIES;

TROY, OHIO.

FAIRMOUNT NURSERIES, TROY, OHIO. GEO. PETERS & SON. Proprietors. & SON ESTABLISHED 1838 IN PENNA.

DEAR SIR:

THE trees etc.you bo't of our agent will be delivered at Exchange Hotel, in ***NEW PHILADELPHIA, FRIDAY. NOV. 2, 1883,*** (Unavoidable delays excepted,) as per contract. As we have similar engagements to meet at other places, you will please be there promptly on that day to receive your trees and cancel your obligation.

GEO. PETERS & SON.

N.B.--As some fail to get this notice, please tell your neighbors.

Dr. Johnson had built the Exchange Hotel, one of the oldest brick structures in town. The Exchange was later converted into other uses, and a new Exchange Hotel (Delphian Hotel) was built on the south side of West High Street. In 1861, on East Front Avenue, William And Davis Hemenger established a wagon maker's shop.

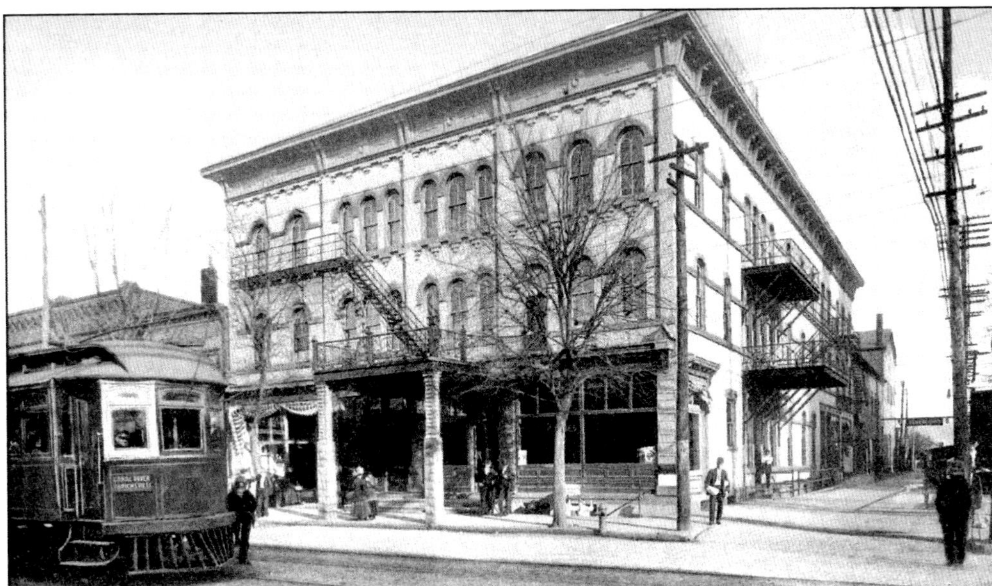

In 1881, Ernest Schmidt erected the Schmidt (Sherman) House on North Broadway just north of the courthouse. Before this, the old Grimm House on Front Avenue was a well-known and popular resort for travelers during the Civil War. In 1883, the Grimm House was demolished, and Harrison Kail erected a large three-story brick hotel on the northeast corner of Broadway and Front (later known as the Empire Hotel).

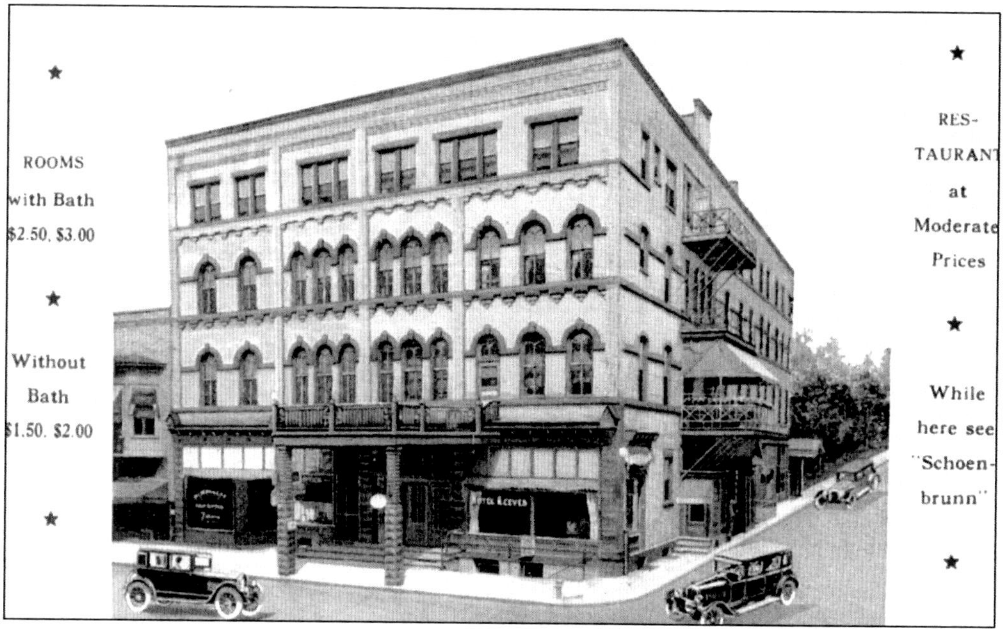

In 1905, the Schmidt House became the Reeves Hotel. It was torn down in 1968. Another hotel, the Lion House, served as a hotel longer than any other.

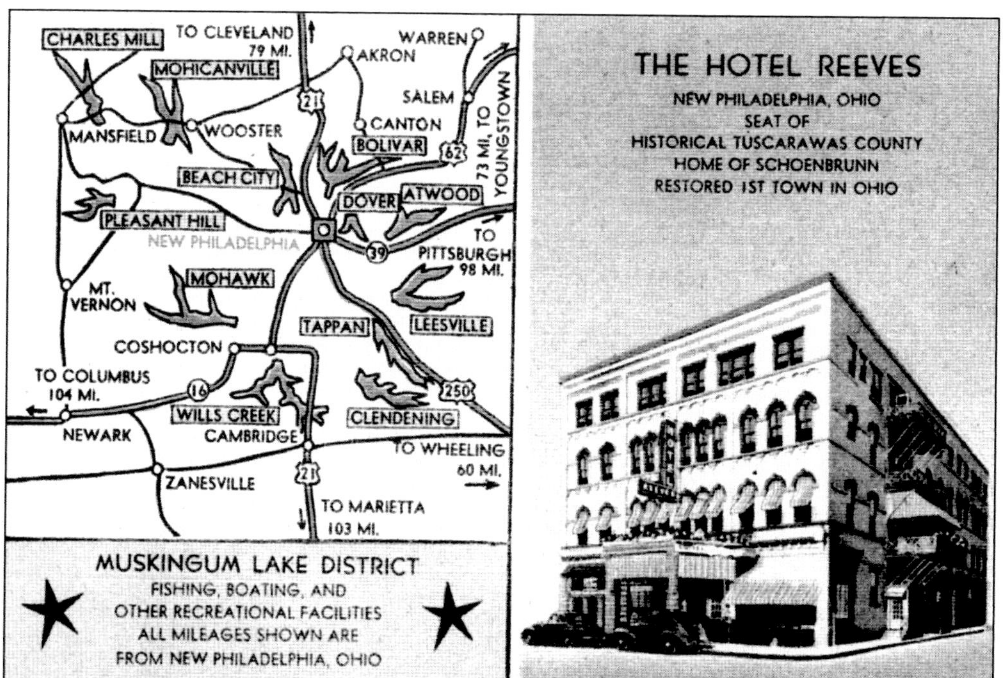

Built *circa* 1820, Baker Grist Mill specialized in custom work, but survived only a few years. Tobacco became the county's first leading crop 1825–1840, but due to successive tobacco planting and erosion, the soil was depleted. Out of necessity, the agricultural community began producing wheat, corn, and other grains, making them the leading industry. By the time of the Civil War, Tuscarawas County was predominantly agricultural. Grain acreages were large enough to support the New Philadelphia Agricultural Works, a company that manufactured the Pitt's Separator, the thresher, sulky corn plows, and hay rakes.

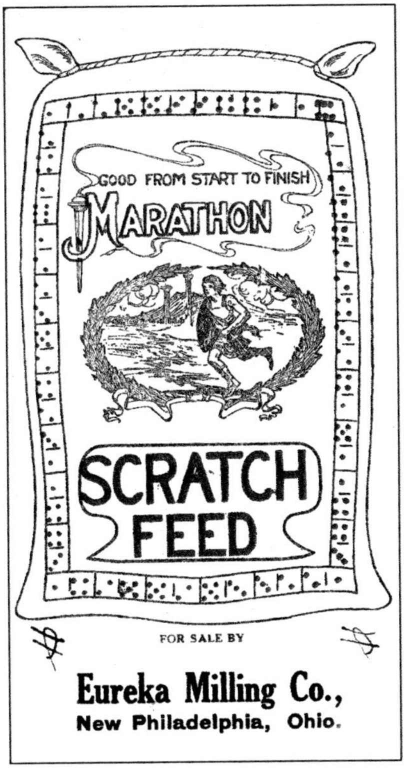

In 1854, Walter M. Blake built a gristmill at 715 Goshen Avenue. It contained three runs. The property was sold to Richard Johnson and then to J.W. Patterson, who added a fourth run. In the summer of 1883, he adopted the roller process and refitted the mill with new machinery. The water-powered mill produced custom work and flour. Today the gristmill is remembered as Blake's Mill. It was torn down in the 1970s. Williamson and Black erected a frame, steam gristmill in 1865 on lot 350 Kay Street. It burned to the ground in 1871. Another structure was built, but it was also destroyed by fire.

The Patrons of Husbandry, the official name of the Grange, was incorporated in January 1873, and the New Philadelphia Grange was established on April 14, 1874, the first in Tuscarawas County. In 1918, the Farm Bureau organized, and an agriculture agent showed farmers how to increase production. A female home demonstrator taught housewives to can and preserve foods from their gardens, and farm boys and girls organized pig clubs. This movement was the beginning of the 4-H clubs of today.

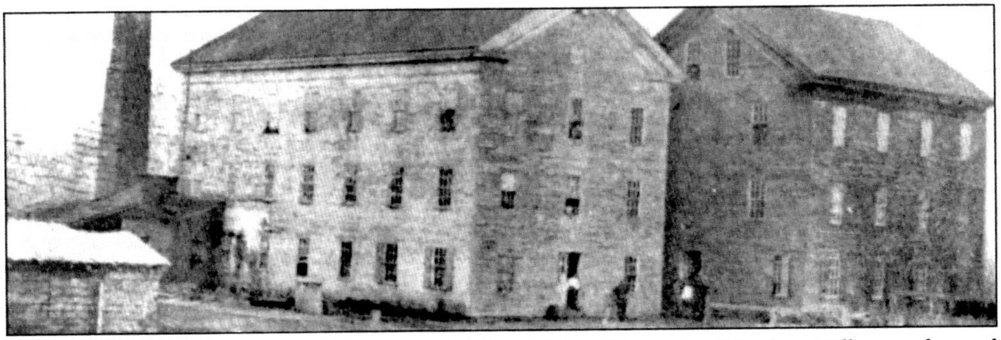

The oldest manufacturing establishment of New Philadelphia, the Woolen Mills, was located east of Broadway and south of the Cleveland, Lorain, and Wheeling Railroad. They produced flannels, blankets, cassimere, satinets, jeans, yarns, and hose. The Mills used Eli Whitney's principle of the interchangeability of parts and segregation of factory processes. Fire destroyed the buildings September 17, 1885.

The Smith Foundry Company organized in 1882 when the citizens donated a subscription of $10,000, and a large building measuring 246 by 100 feet was erected east of the rolling mills. Another building was added later. Besides general foundry work, it manufactured gas and water pipes and employed 20 men.

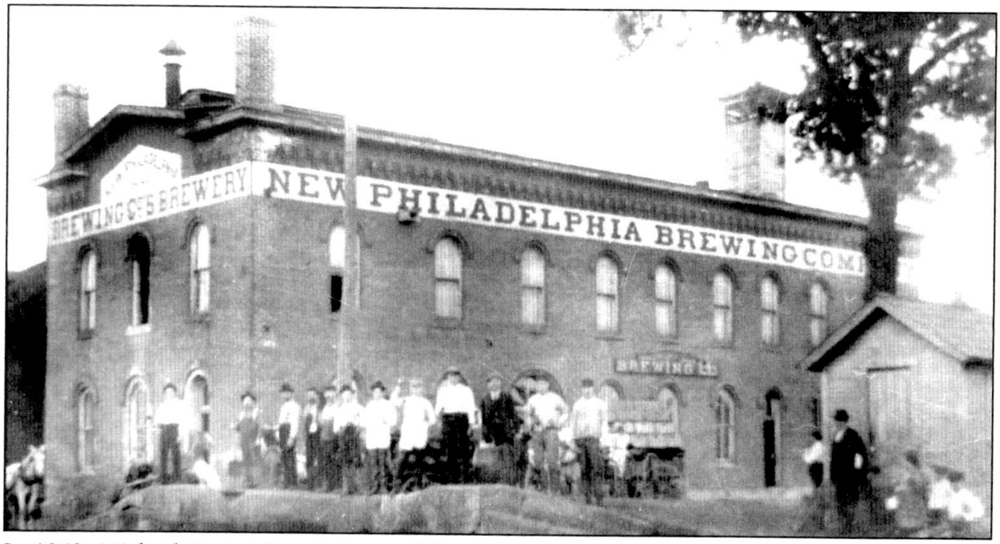

In 1863, Michael Berger founded a small brewery along the banks of the Ohio Canal on South Broadway. Upon his death, the plant transferred to Rudolph Kapizky and was later purchased by Michael Seibold and Adolph Hafenbrak. Seibold renamed the company the New Philadelphia Brewing Co. On March 21, 1905, the brewery joined a partnership with the Schuster Brewing Co. of Massillon, the Canton and Stark Brewing Companies of Canton, and the Christian Bernhardt Brewery of Dover. The new company was called the Stark-Tuscarawas Brewing Company. During prohibition, the company produced soft drinks and near beer. The company was sold in 1933, and the company changed hands again and became the New Philadelphia Brewery, Inc. The brewery shut down in 1949. The plant remained vacant until it was razed around 1963. Currently, the State Route 250 bypass runs directly through the site.

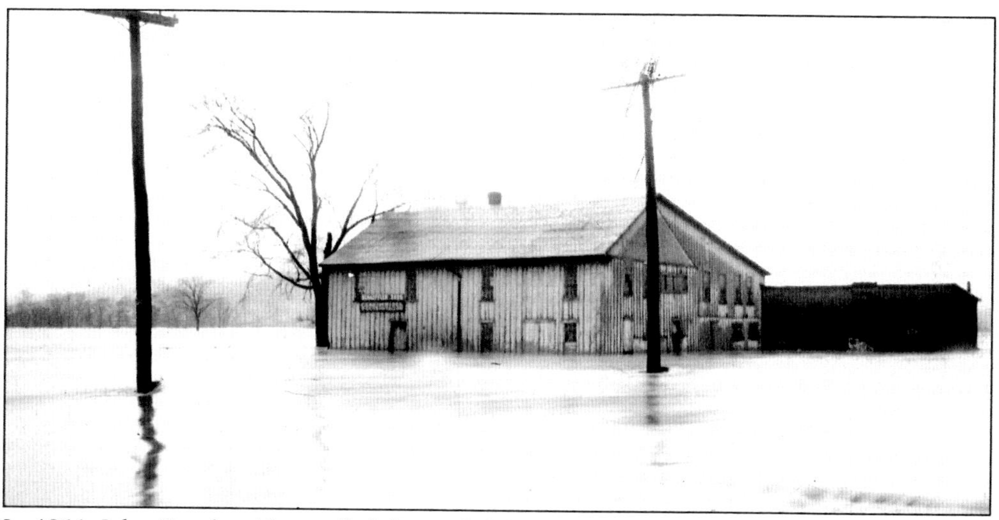

In 1866, John Kunsley (also spelled "Kuensli," but pronounced "Knisely") and Co. built the Tannery south of the railroad off of South Broadway, along the south bank of the Tuscarawas River adjoining the village of Blake's Mills. In 1872, Bigler and Leus purchased and enlarged the property, and four years later, the Bigler Brothers obtained possession. In 1882, they enlarged the facility, added new machinery, and adopted the steam process of tanning.

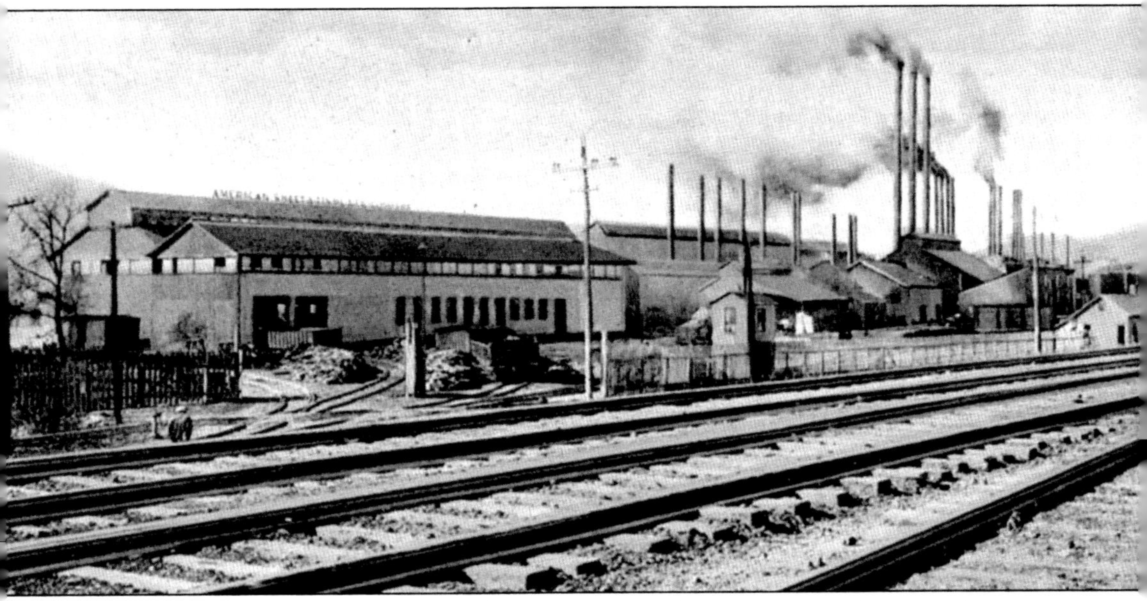

The leading industrial works of New Philadelphia was the Ward Rolling Mills. The Ward Iron Company of Niles agreed to build a new rolling mill at New Philadelphia to employ 250 men if the town donated $40,000 and 20 acres of land. Construction began in March 1882 southwest of town, near Beyer's Mills. Ward Rolling Mills opened March 15, 1883. Managed by Mr. W.E. Ward, about 50 tons of muck iron and 20 tons of sheet iron were produced daily. Work was suspended in July 1883.

In 1899–1900, a wave of iron and steel mergers swept the country. American Sheet Steel and Tin Plate Company, a subsidiary of the United States Steel Corporation, purchased a tin mill, along with the Dover and New Philadelphia rolling mills (both mills were abandoned in 1931).

The American Sheet Steel and Tin Plate Company later became the Warner and Swasey Company before becoming Gradall JLG. The telescoping boom was introduced in 1946, leading to Gradall's move to New Philadelphia in 1950. In 1980, the Bendix Corp. acquired Warner and Swasey Gradall. By 1982, Warner and Swasey's Gradall Division produced four sizes of wheeled and crawler-mounted hydraulic excavators with telescoping booms in a 500,000-square-foot facility. In 1983, Gradall was bought for $18 million by a group of Gradall executives, headed by Bill Gray. In 1985, International Consulting Management Group of Chicago acquired Gradall, and the company experienced a one-week strike in 1994. But by 1995, the company received the Equipment World's Reader's Choice Award. In October 1995, the company was purchased by Morgan, Lewis, Githens, and Ahn (MLGA), an investment banking company of New York.

In October 1998, the material handler line was shifted to Orrville. Gradall spent $50 million in capital improvements between the New Philadelphia and Orrville plants. In 1998, President and CEO of Gradall, Barry Phillips, was awarded the Northeast Ohio Entrepreneur of the Year award, and the same year, Ernst and Young awarded Gradall with the Entrepreneur of the Year Company award. Again, the company was purchased in 1999 by JLG Industries, Inc. of McConnellsburg, Pennsylvania. By 2000, Gradall posted $250 million in sales and employed more than 900 people. Shortly after, the Orrville plant was closed. Gradall JLG continues at New Philadelphia as one of the county's largest industrial employers. Gradall equipment is sold worldwide.

Betz Laboratories, Inc. produces metal chemicals used to prevent corrosion, scaling, and microbiological fouling problems in industrial water-related equipment. In 1990, Betz Laboratories, Inc. was named a Fortune 500 company, doing $600 million in sales.

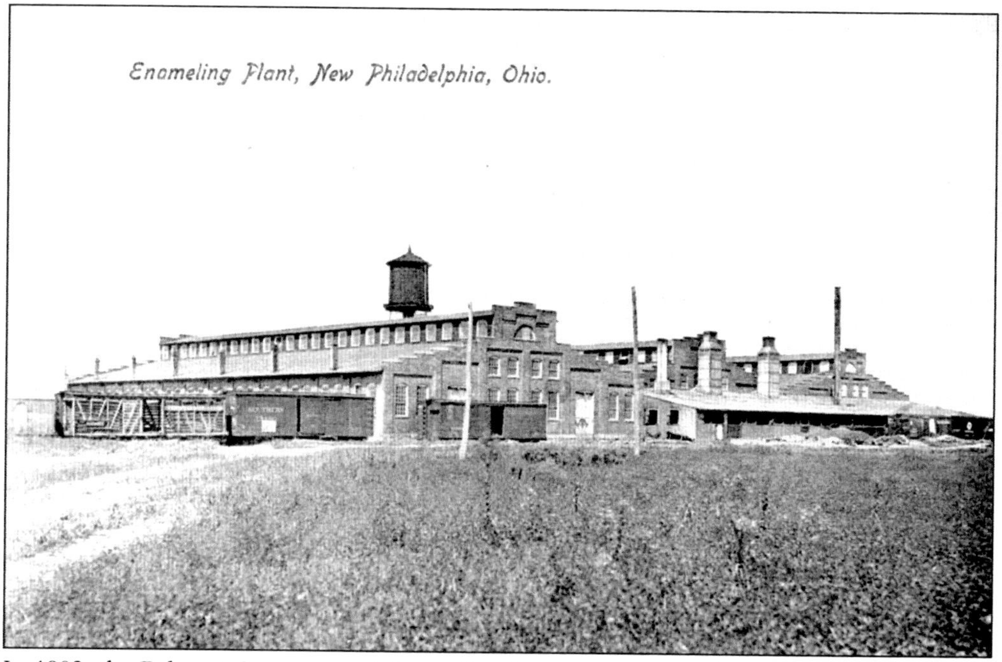

In 1902, the Belmont Stamping and Enameling Company organized and built a plant in New Philadelphia that would later become a flourishing manufacturing plant that continued for almost half a century.

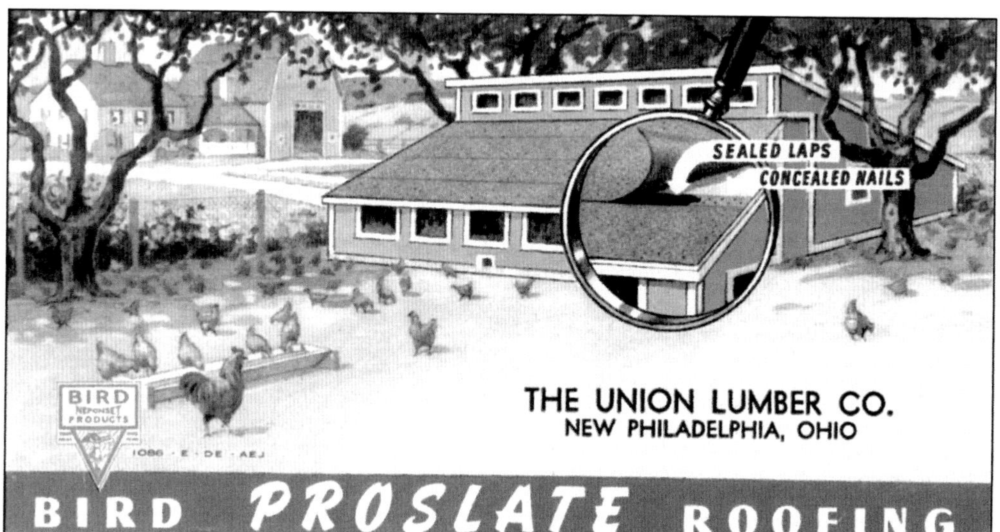

In 1903, a number of leading businessmen of New Philadelphia and Dover incorporated the Union Lumber Company, a building contractor business taking orders for wood, brick, or cement block.

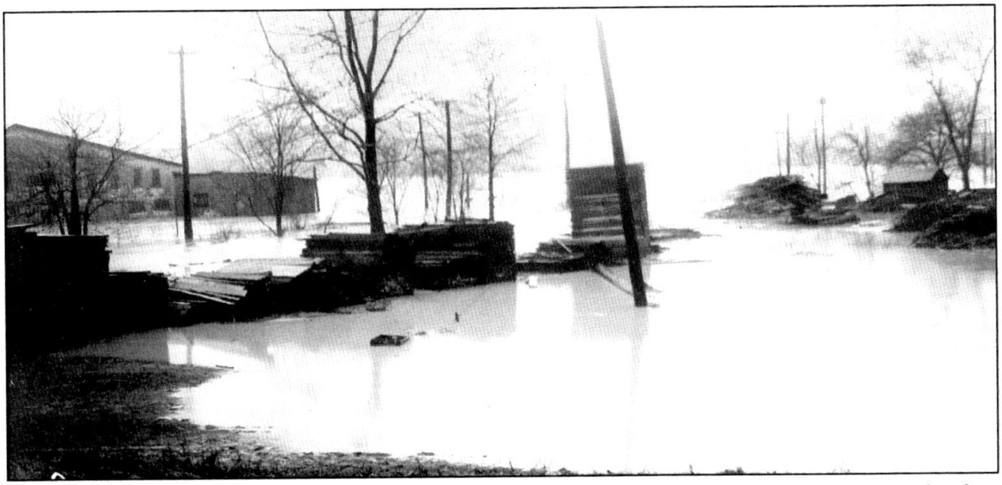

On Wednesday, May 10, 1916, the Spicer Manufacturing Co. (Spicer Works) was swept by fire. The LaDel Conveyor and Manufacturing Co., originated in the mid-1800s as a foundry, was established on the site. The business was later acquired in 1921 by a group of local businessmen under the name of the LaDel Conveyor and Manufacturing Co. (as in New Phi-ladel-phia).

The Joy Manufacturing Company purchased the LaDel Manufacturing Company in 1946. In 1986, Joy Technologies, Inc. merged with Ecolaire Corp., and Ecolaire's Green Fan division was transferred to New Philadelphia in 1989. It is the leading producer of highly engineered axial fans for commercial heating, ventilating, air conditioning systems, industrial applications, nuclear power plants, navy and maritime shipboard ventilation, mining, tunneling, public transit systems, and custom applications. In 1994, Harnischfeger Industries Inc. of Milwaukee, Wisconsin, acquired Joy/Green Fan Division, and in January 1997, the name changed to New Philadelphia Fan Company. Today, Howden Buffalo Co. owns the company, a 240,000-square-foot facility still located on South Broadway.

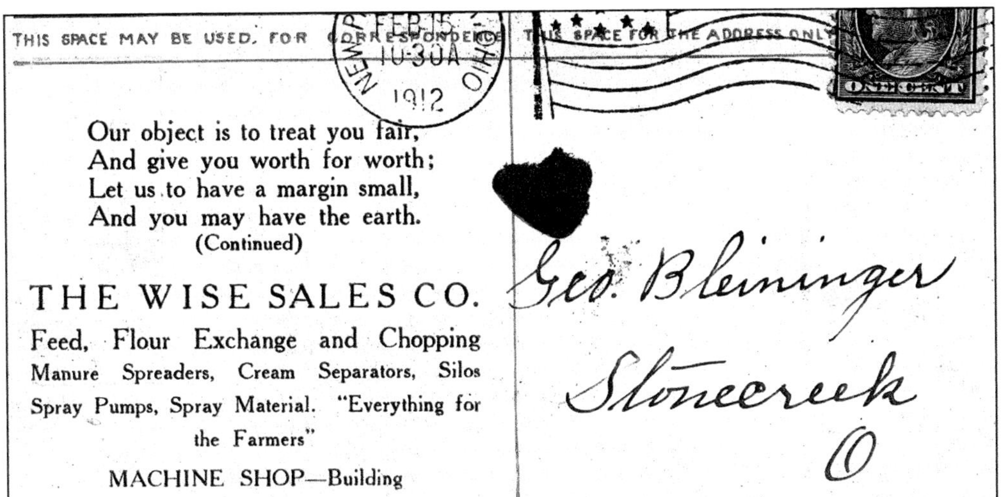

In 1917, the Wise-McClung Manufacturing Co. was organized in New Philadelphia to manufacture electric vacuum cleaners and other appliances. In the 1950s, the Timken Roller Bearing Plant acquired the Cardinal Products plastic building at Schoenbrunn. They produce precision tapered roller bearings for a global market in the machining, aerospace, and printing industries.

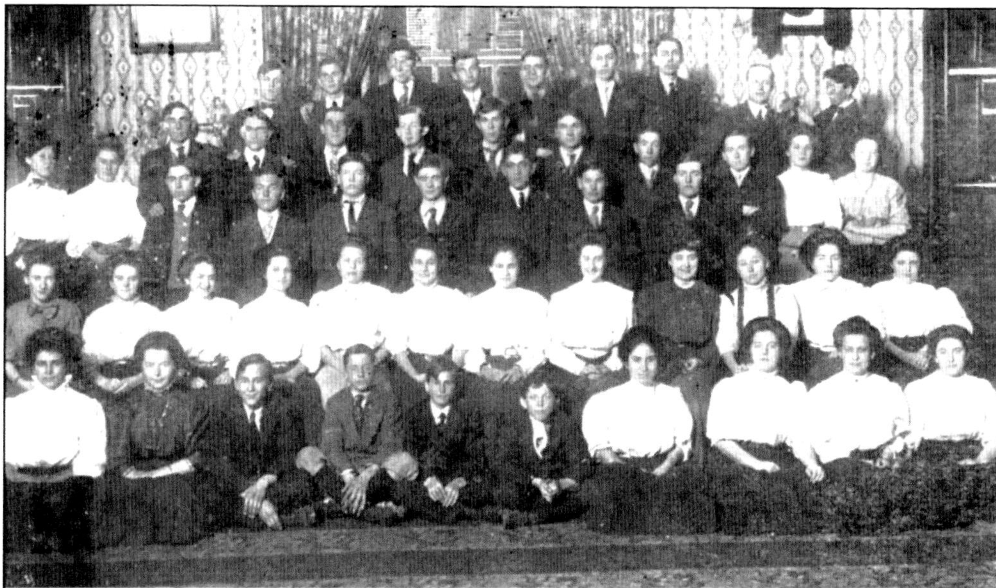

Student Group, Yocum's New Philadelphia & Dover Business College, '08.

John and Alexander McConnel opened a clothing store on the southeast corner of the square. The Boston Clothing Store then operated from the location from 1880s–1960s, with the Yokum's Practical Business College of Dover and New Philadelphia and New Philadelphia's BPOE No. 510 Lodge on the third floor around 1908. The second floor was leased to lawyers and dentists. The BPOE later constructed their own building a few doors down in 1928 (Knisely Centre). The House of Stones, a jewelry store, operates from the building.

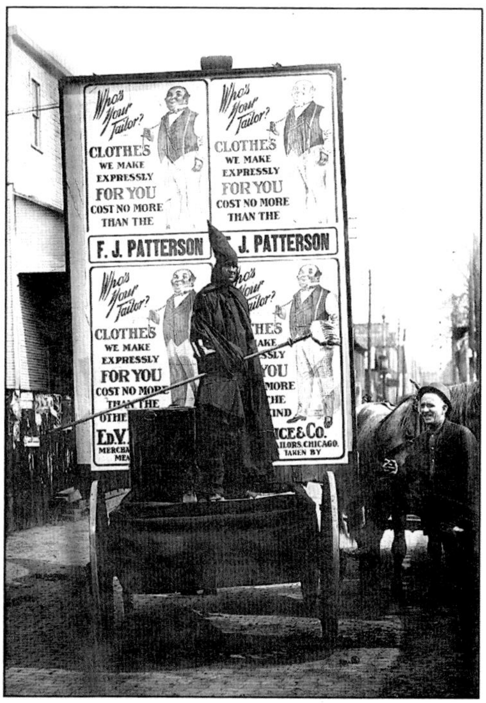

Many retailers used advertisements to lure customers into their shops. 1821 advertisements for New Philadelphia businessmen include: Dr. Orange Ranney, William Albert's tavern, and druggist Tie. Patent medicines could be bought at Tie's, including Bateman's Drops, Godfrey's Cordial, Anderson's Pills, Itch Ointment, Golden Tincture, British Oil, Balsam de Malta, Harlem Oil, and Lee's Antibilious Pills. Other business men included general merchants J. Johnson and B.H. Warfield; gun-maker John White; chair-maker H. Williams; book-binder Samuel J. Bowlby; tailors Michael Ream, Samuel Lane, Robert Sergeant, John Hall, and William Neeriemer; furriers Benjamin and Jacob Ream; shoe-maker Mathias Springer; earthenware dealer Peter Cribbs; ginseng cultivator, tin and stoneware salesman, and merchant Charles F. Espich; attorney Wright Warner; and tanners Joseph Landers and Thomas Sergeant.

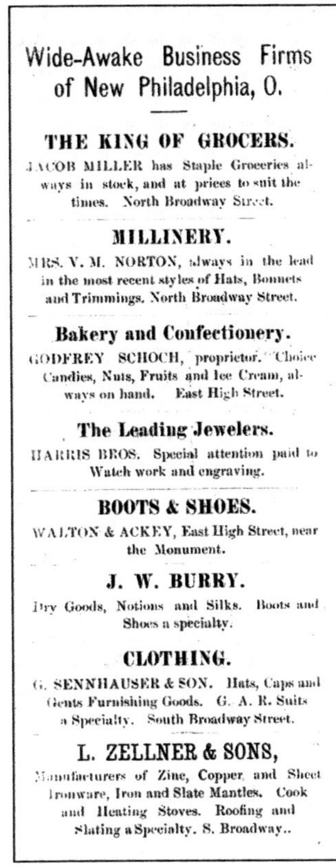
Wide-Awake Business Firms of New Philadelphia, O.

THE KING OF GROCERS.

JACOB MILLER has Staple Groceries always in stock, and at prices to suit the times. North Broadway Street.

MILLINERY.

MRS. V. M. NORTON, always in the lead in the most recent styles of Hats, Bonnets and Trimmings. North Broadway Street.

Bakery and Confectionery.

GODFREY SCHOCH, proprietor. Choice Candies, Nuts, Fruits and Ice Cream, always on hand. East High Street.

The Leading Jewelers.

HARRIS BROS. Special attention paid to Watch work and engraving.

BOOTS & SHOES.

WALTON & ACKEY, East High Street, near the Monument.

J. W. BURRY.

Dry Goods, Notions and Silks. Boots and Shoes a specialty.

CLOTHING.

G. SENNHAUSER & SON. Hats, Caps and Gents Furnishing Goods. G. A. R. Suits a Specialty. South Broadway Street.

L. ZELLNER & SONS,

Manufacturers of Zinc, Copper, and Sheet Ironware, Iron and Slate Mantles. Cook and Heating Stoves. Roofing and Slating a Specialty. S. Broadway..

Gustave Senhauser founded Senhauser Clothing in July of 1854. Gustave's sons, Norman, Albert, and Gustave, joined him in the business, causing the name to change to G. Senhauser and Sons. The store was moved from East High Avenue to 110–112 South Broadway.

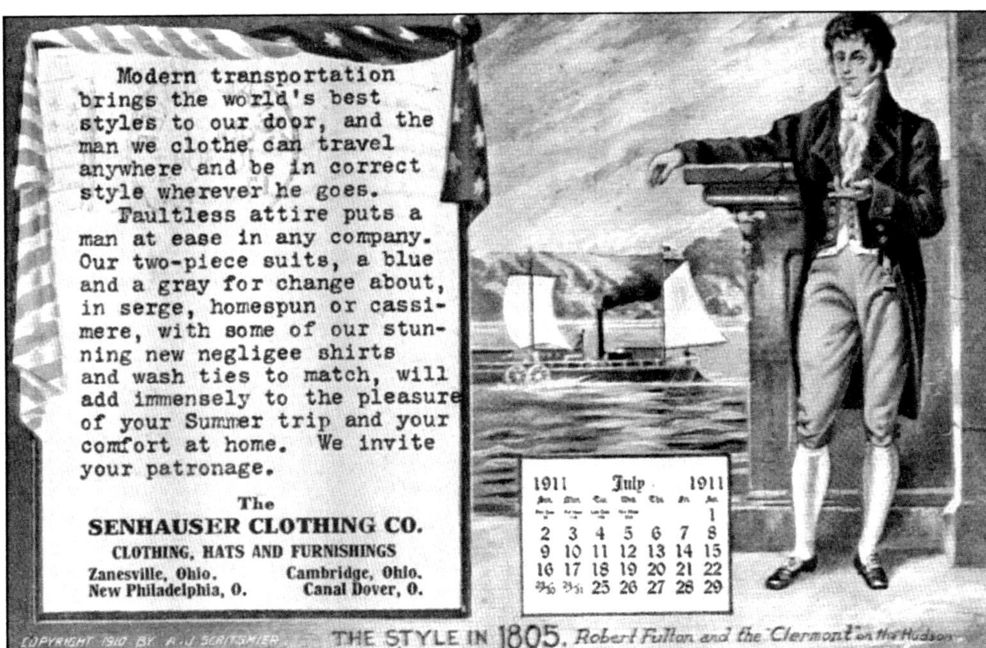

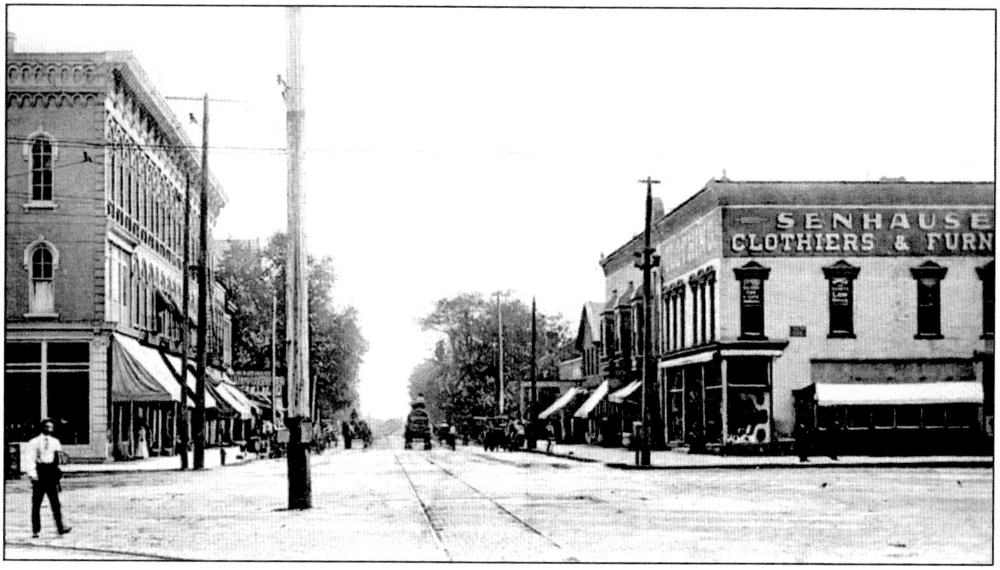

Later, G. Senhauser and Sons was incorporated as the Senhauser Clothing Store. Today, the building houses Fly Boy's Restaurant.

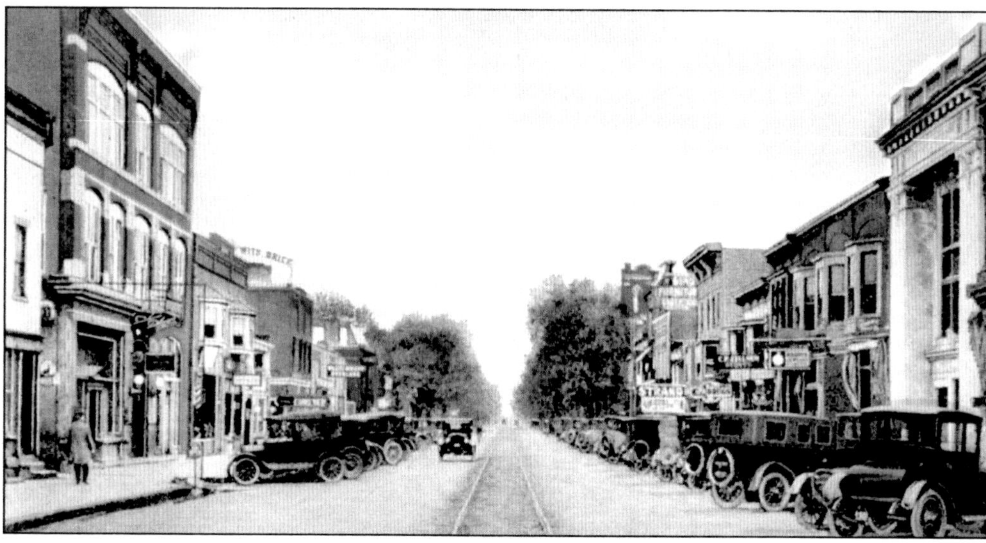

In 1865, John Christian Joss purchased William Nichols' interest in a long established business on West High Street that manufactured eyeglasses and jewelry. Joss used the West High structure as both a home and business. His two sons joined him in the business, and the business thrived. They added pianos, organs, a variety of musical instruments, and sewing machines. John E. Joss, son of John C. Joss, left his father's business in 1907, to start his own jewelry shop, the Watch Shop. This popular shop on North Broadway also existed for many years. It later became the Diamond Shop, which recently closed its doors after many years of operation by owner Jerry Lukens. John C. Joss' other son, George Joss, a banker, had inherited his father's musical talent, and he helped establish the Little Theater.

In 1922, Forrest Tucker established a printing business in a storefront on West High. Tucker's sons, Robert and Richard, succeeded him and sold the storefront to Harold Tedrow, whose sons Jeffrey and Tracy operate the Family Office Equipment Inc. today at the same location.

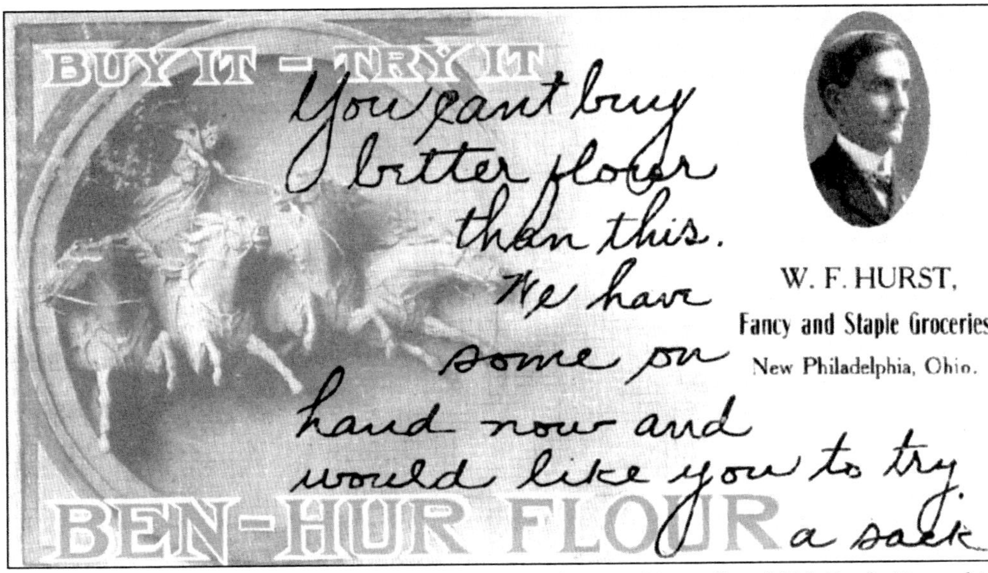

C.L. Hurst owned Hurst Grocery in 1893 when David Henry Troendly sold his Bucks Township farm, moved his family to New Philadelphia, and purchased a lot on the southeast corner of Fair Street and Tuscarawas Avenue to open another grocery store. Troendly eventually built a two-story, multi-shop building, a harbinger of today's shopping centers, which over the years housed the grocery, meat market, Dr. Battershell's dentist parlor, Mr. Hiller (and later Thomas McCue's) Candy Shop, Tommy Garabrandt's barber-shop, and Joe Rieker's shoe repair shop.

David and Elizabeth Troendly 's daughter Adelia married John C. Miller, but he left the family, and Adelia and her sons Edgar Hugh and John Henry (J. Harry) moved back in with the Troendly's. Adelia died young, and the two boys opened a bicycle repair shop around 1908. J. Harry married Clela McDermott in 1911, and they moved into the Troendly family's apartment at 724 West Fair Avenue. In 1923, they moved to 224 Seventh Street and had three children. Edgar married Cecelia Mathieu in 1913, and Troendly built the couple a home next door to the apartment and business where they had four children. This home still houses the art department of Miller Studio.

Miller Studio began in 1908 on Clela Miller's kitchen table. Max Troendly Miller's book, *Straight from the Kitchen Table*, states that his mother would paint china on the kitchen table to put food on the table. Clela taught other women to paint their own china. In the 1930s, Clela's small gift shop was moved from her home to the former West End Garage showroom, which they still owned. Due to the closure of West End Garage, J. Harry went to work for the Seibold Brothers, owners of the Lockport Brewery, to operate their Bel-Mar Pottery in East Liverpool. When the Pottery was closed, J. Harry returned with three truckloads of leftover pottery as a bonus. Miller Studio began with J. Harry Miller and his wife Clela and their sons Max and Richard. There other son, Robert, later joined the group. They began making wall plaques around 1934 and still make them today. For many years, beginning in the 1950s, Richard Miller decorated the front point of the triangular building with a face of a woman made from pieces of plywood or with a Santa Clause face for Christmas season. Richard left the business in 1961 and became a well-known sculptor in New York City. Max took over in 1961. They produce more than 150 items, including three-dimensional wall plaques, wall clocks, and Magic-Mount wall hangers. Miller Products Inc. has grown into a business with sales approaching $100,000,000 annually, occupying more than 350,000-square-feet of manufacturing space with nearly 600 employees. The facility is still located at the corner of Fair Avenue and Tuscarawas Avenue NW. It is one of the oldest continuously operating companies in the county.

Max and his late wife Erma donated funds for many area projects, many anonymously. Among some of the known projects are Park Place youth center at New Philadelphia's Tuscora Park and the city's skate park.

Several famous artists have lived in New Philadelphia: William T. Mathews, presidential portrait painter; Vic Donahey's brothers James Harrison (Hal) Donahey, one of the country's top cartoonists whose drawings were a daily feature in the *Cleveland Plain Dealer*, and William Donahey, illustrator for Teenie Weenie books; and Norman Bel Geddes, a widely-known state and industrial designer.

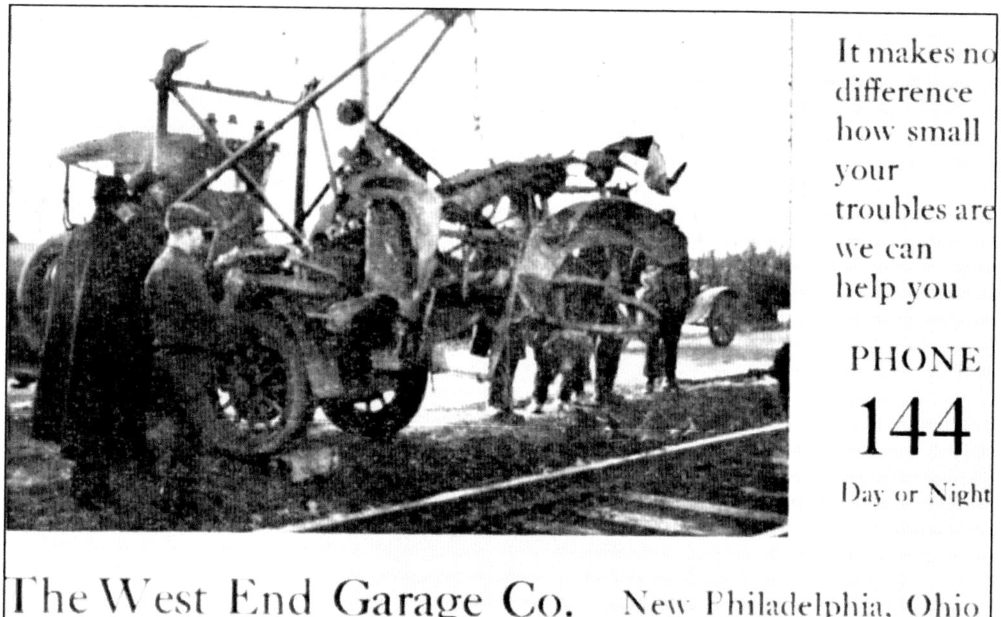

David Troendly sold nursery stock purchased from Hooker Nursery Company of Rochester, New York. Later, the business became an automobile repair shop and then one of the first full-service auto dealerships in Eastern Ohio, West End Garage. Full-service then included a full line machine shop including lathes to turn out needed parts, a carpenter wood working shop to rebuild damaged car roofs, industrial sewing machines to repair or replace upholstery and roof tops, and a full line paint shop to refinish any requirement. They sold Cadillacs, Hupmobiles, and LaSalles. Baseball-pitching great Cy Young bought his LaSalle automobiles here.

In the early 1920s, West End Garage had an orchestra, the Saxophone Serenaders, which played at Cleveland and broadcast performances from the garage. It was one of the first wireless broadcasts in Tuscarawas County. They would provide food and treats, as well as a clean showroom for dancing. The West End Garage was one of the largest in the state. The 20,000-square-foot facility had entrances on three different streets: Fair Street (now Fair Avenue), Tenth Street (now Seventh Street), and Tuscarawas Avenue. The garage declared bankruptcy in 1932 during the depression when debtors could not pay their bills. The bank repossessed the garage portion of the business.

Many businesses have since gone in, including the Cummins Diesel Sales and Service; Ed Miller (a relative of the Millers) opened Adelphia Studios where he built authentic, true-scale model trains and elaborate track layouts; and Allied Machine and Engineering Corporation, owned by William Stokey.

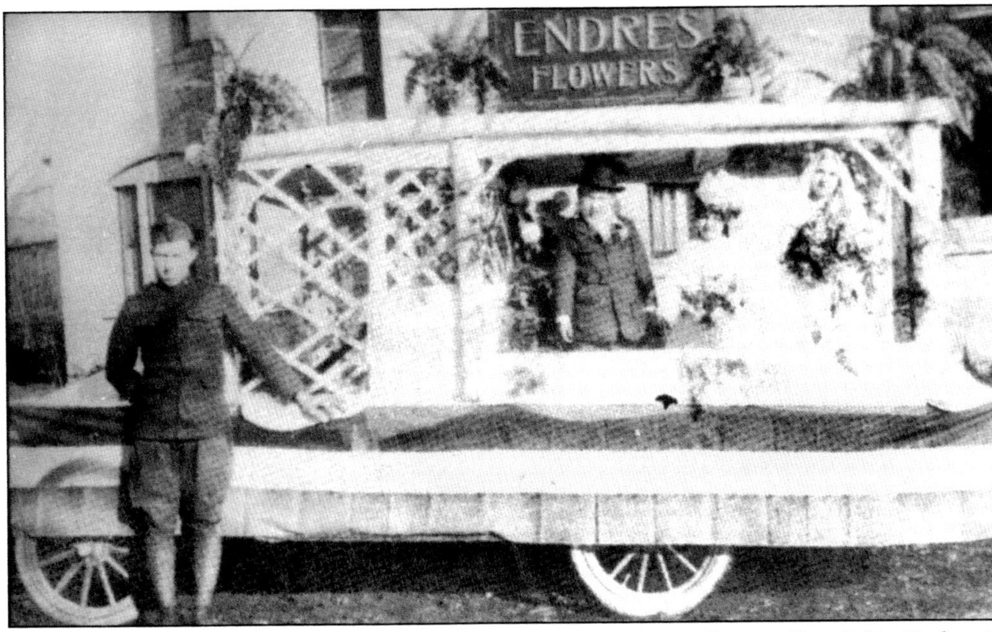

Louis Endres Sr. founded Endres Floral Company in 1913 on County Road 21. Endres is Tuscarawas County's oldest floral retailer and Ohio's largest rose grower. Sons Gene, Louis Jr., and Bill joined the business over the years. In 1984, Endres operated a wholesale greenhouse, a retail shop in New Philadelphia (now the site of the Dover-Phila Federal Credit Union in New Philadelphia), and a business cart at Monroe Mall. Gene Endres became better known as "Mr. Rose," serving as president of the Ohio Florist Association; as president of Roses Inc., an international organization boasting a membership of 3,000; as president of the Ohio Agriculture Council; and as ambassador for "Beautiful Tuscarawas County." Producing over 24 varieties of roses, Endres is Tuscarawas County's largest agricultural entity. In the late 1980s, Endres expanded their business to include geraniums, perennials, gift baskets, and balloons. The business cart at Monroe Mall faded away when the mall shifted from retail to service-oriented businesses after New Towne Mall was constructed on Mill Avenue behind Buehler's. Endres' retail shop at 635 West High Avenue closed its doors on August 15, 1995.

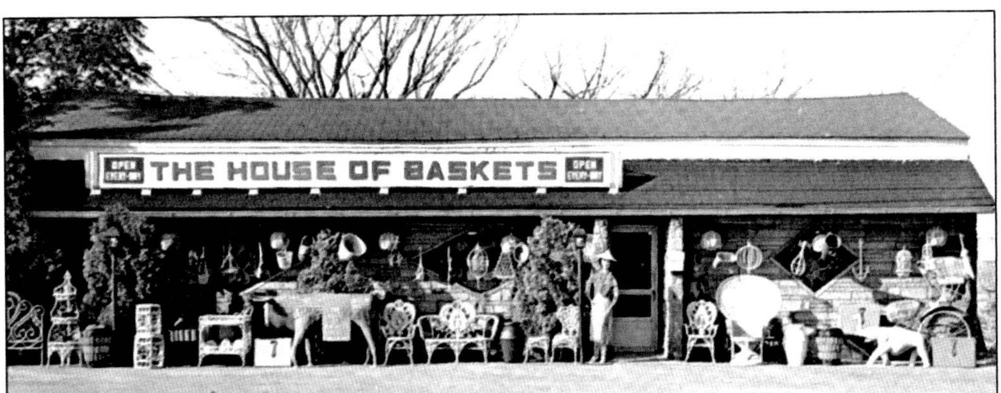

The House of Baskets began business around 1950 owned by Bud Stratton. At one time it was a major stop for tourist buses. Bud's daughter, Susan Smith, took over operations until they closed their doors in 2002.

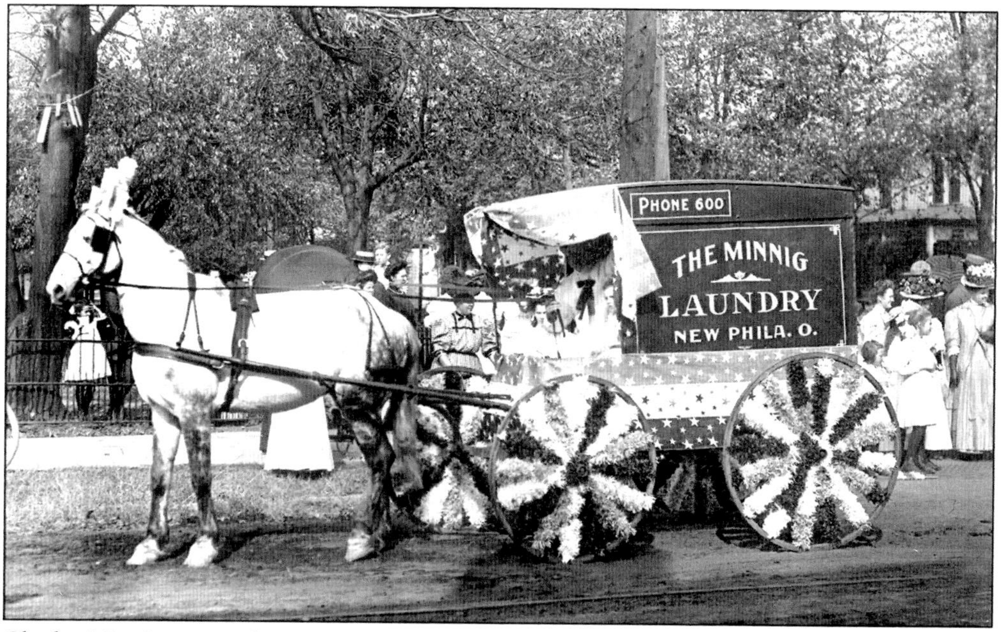

Charles Minning owned Minning Laundry, which was located on Second Street NW by the former Goshen Dairy.

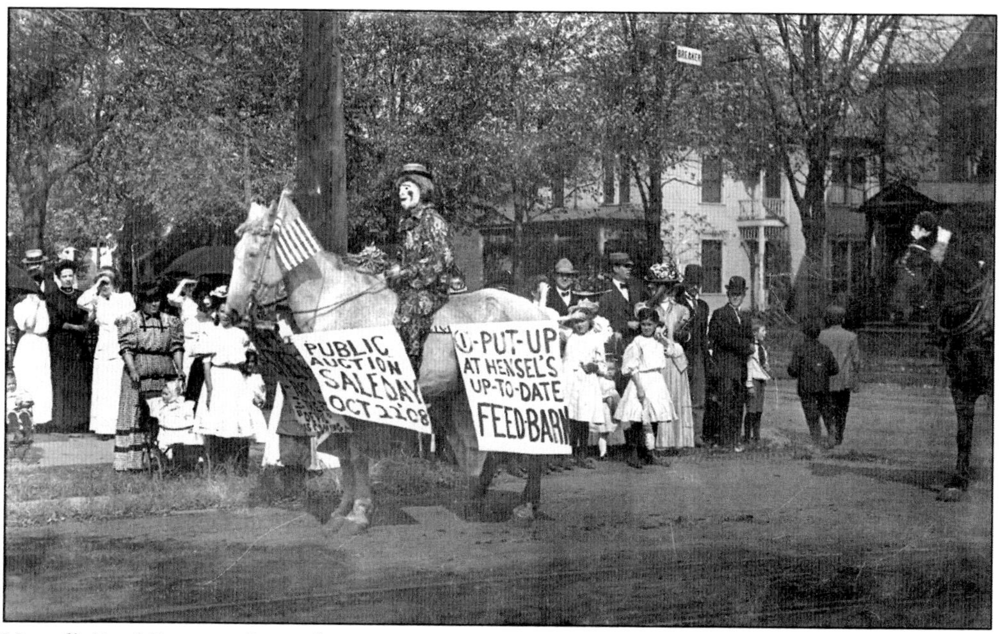

Hensel's Feed Barn was located on Front Street and St. Clair Avenue NW. Hensel's also owned a rolling mill.

Today on Front Avenue at 1203 in the former Rink's department store is Riverfront Antique Mall, opened July 1, 1992 and owned by Al and Teresa Bringardner. It is touted as the largest antique mall in Ohio and perhaps the Midwest.

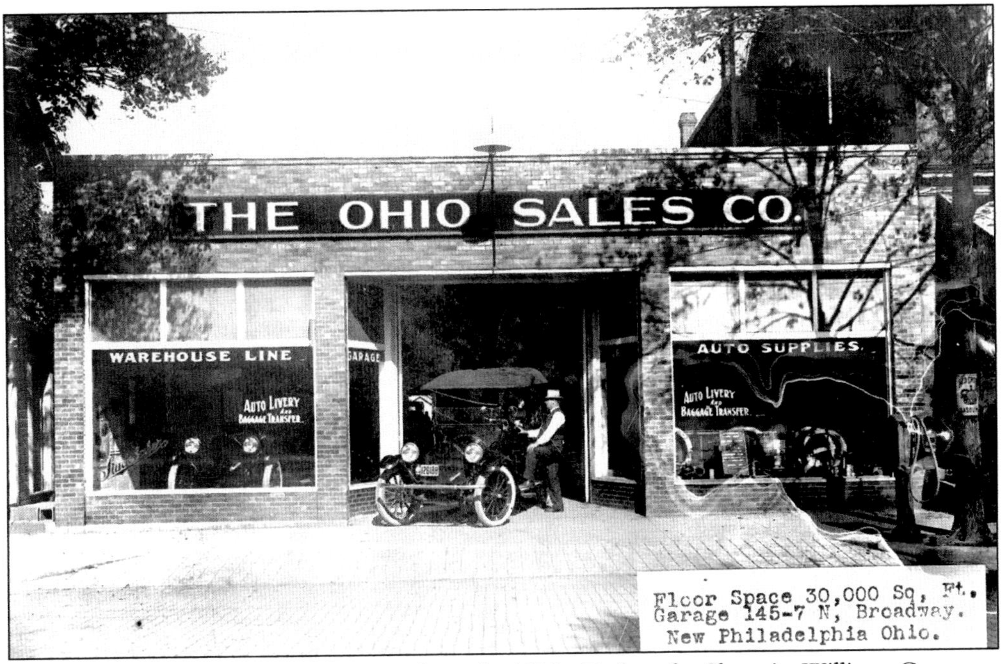

The Ohio Sales Company operated in the early 1900s. Today, the Sherwin-Williams Company is located at the same site, at 157 North Broadway.

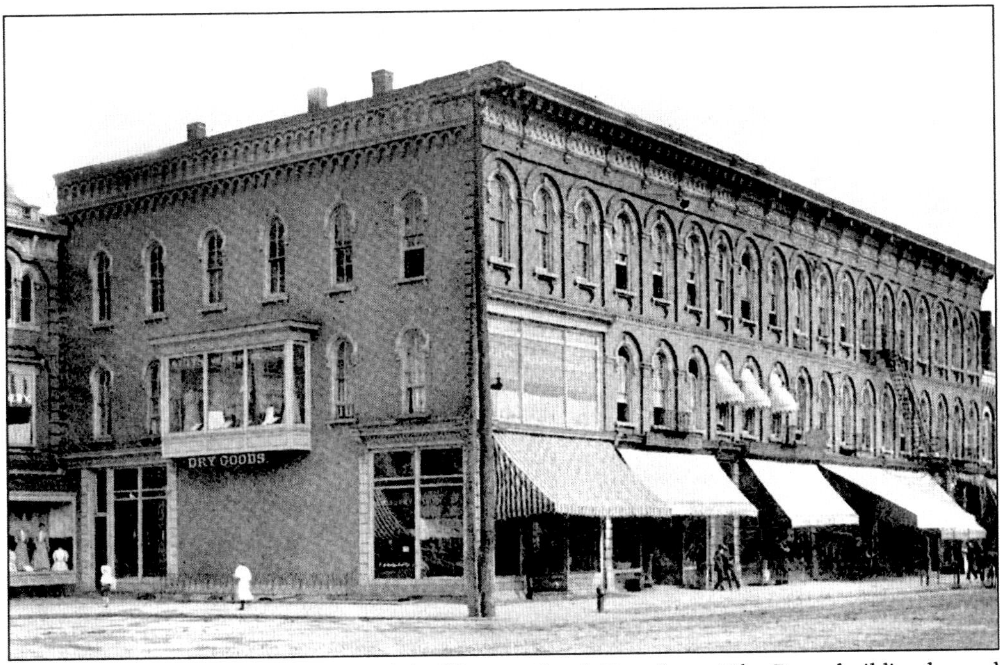

In 1869, John Burry built a large brick building on South Broadway. The Burry building housed the Albert Reiser Grocery and the Albert Reiser Saloon. Today the building is owned by Attorney Michael Johnson and houses numerous businesses including the law practice of Johnson, Urban, and Range.

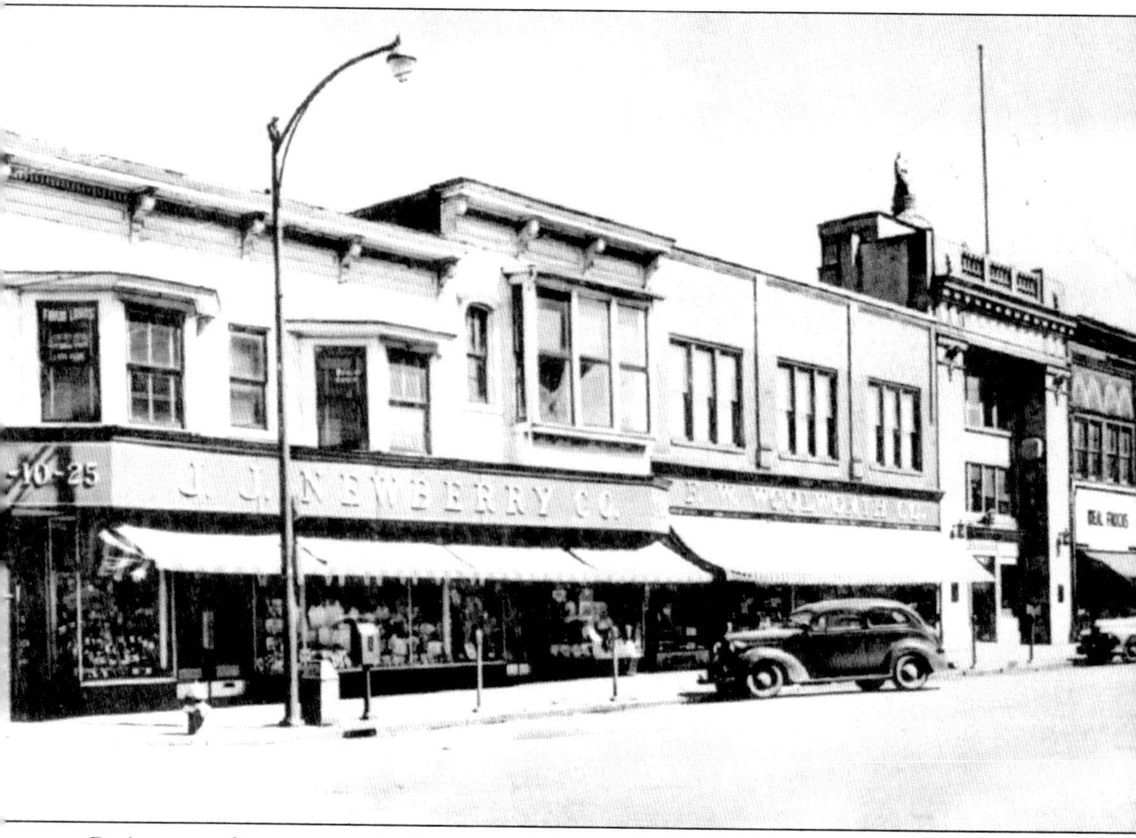

Business people were attracting buyers to their stores in a creative manner. The business people came together with a one-day shopping idea they called "Your Lucky Day—Friday 13th." Many special bargains with a "13" in their price were advertised for Friday, April 13, 1951. People lined up by the hundreds at their favorite stores to be the first to get a good bargain. Stores involved in the promotion included the Better Dress Shop, Reeves Hotel, the Weaver Car Lot, LaFountain Store, J.J. Newberry, and W.T. Grants.

On June 17, 1955, shoppers were once more enticed to stores by the Retail Merchants Council of New Philadelphia. A give-away of $100 cash was being featured in area newspapers. The "Barrel of Luck" contained the names of everyone over the age of 18 listed inside the city directories of New Philadelphia, Dover, Strasburg, Uhrichsville, Dennison, Newcomerstown, and their rural areas. Each Thursday, a drawing would be held at a featured store. To win the $100, any participant wishing to win had to register in the store, thus getting shoppers into the featured store. Twenty-nine merchants participated. The rules of the contest included having the winner's signature on the registry authenticated by three bankers. The rules were referred to as the rules for the "Lucky Barrel," which is a name that has lasted over the years. This particular fun will be revived for the Bicentennial Celebration when the city merchants once again take part in the "Lucky Barrel" contest.

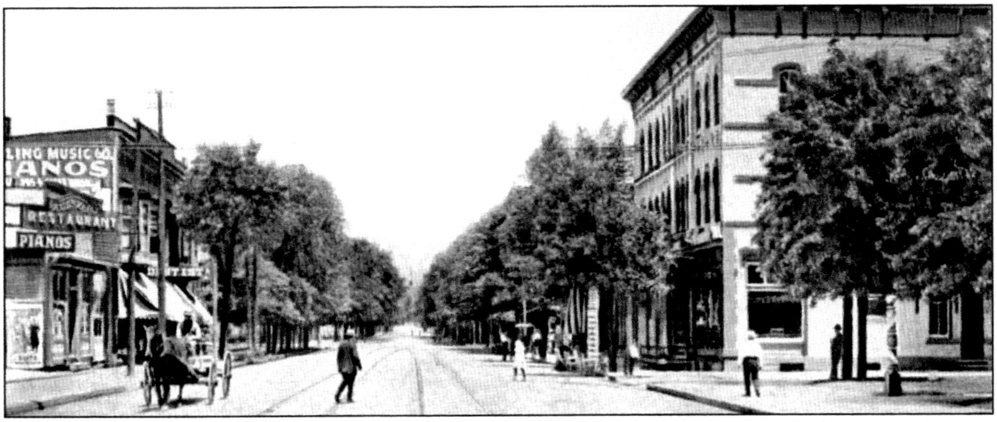

This view of North Broadway shows the Kuenzli Restaurant on the left, right between the two Piano signs. A notable food business today is Litty's Cakes and Cookies. Steve Litty's popular pieces of cake for sale at the Tuscarawas County Fair for 5¢, led to the opening of Litty's Cakes and Cookies at 185 Fifth Street NW on October 4, 1993. Today, it produces 30,000–35,000 cakes annually, plus a similar volume of cookies.

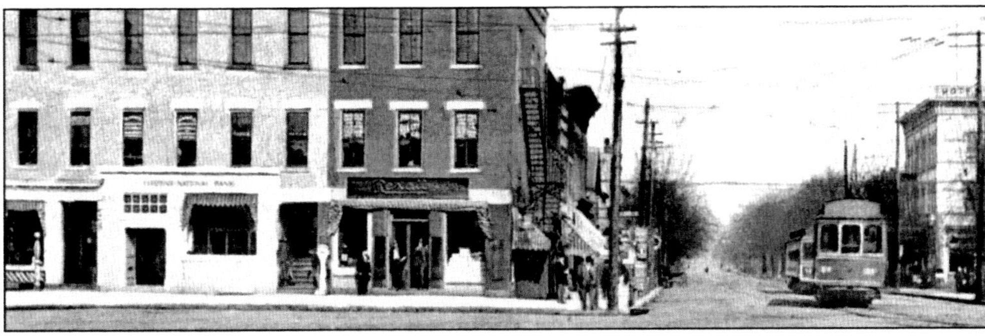

Blickensderfer's Bank, on lot 150, High Street, the first and only bank for many years, was established in New Philadelphia in 1817. In that day, money was scarce, and banks actually issued their own paper money ranging from sixpence upward. Mr. C.H. Mitchener remembered, "Like all other banks of that day in Ohio, it was honestly run on paper money only, although the bills promised to pay in gold or silver on sight. The bank was started to build up the town but failed when a stranger stopped in with $10,000 of the bills and demanded gold and silver. The officers told him to call in again and then disappeared. About 1852 or 1854, Peter Hines found the bank safe in a garret. The safe was an old-fashioned trunk lined with newspapers, behind which he found two Spanish quarters dated 1796 and 1800, which he purchased for $1 so that he could boast of having all the money of the first bank of New Philadelphia!

In 1866, Andrew Patrick and Henry Kaldenbaugh opened the Citizens Bank with a stock of $75,000. In 1872, it was merged into Citizen's National Bank, and in 1910, it took over the Kaldenbaugh Bank. The City Bank, an unincorporated institution, opened in the spring of 1876. The Merchants State Bank was also organized at New Philadelphia.

Employees of Gradall began a credit union for their employees on August 5, 1953, known as the Warner and Swasey Employees Federal Credit Union, at 113 Fourth Street NW. The successful Credit Union expanded its services to others in the community, changing its name to the Dover-Phila Federal Credit Union on December 23, 1983. The Credit Union has expanded to Filmore Avenue in Dover, West High Avenue in New Philadelphia, Wooster Avenue in Dover, and East State Road in Newcomerstown. Assets now total $185,738,632 with over 28,000 members.

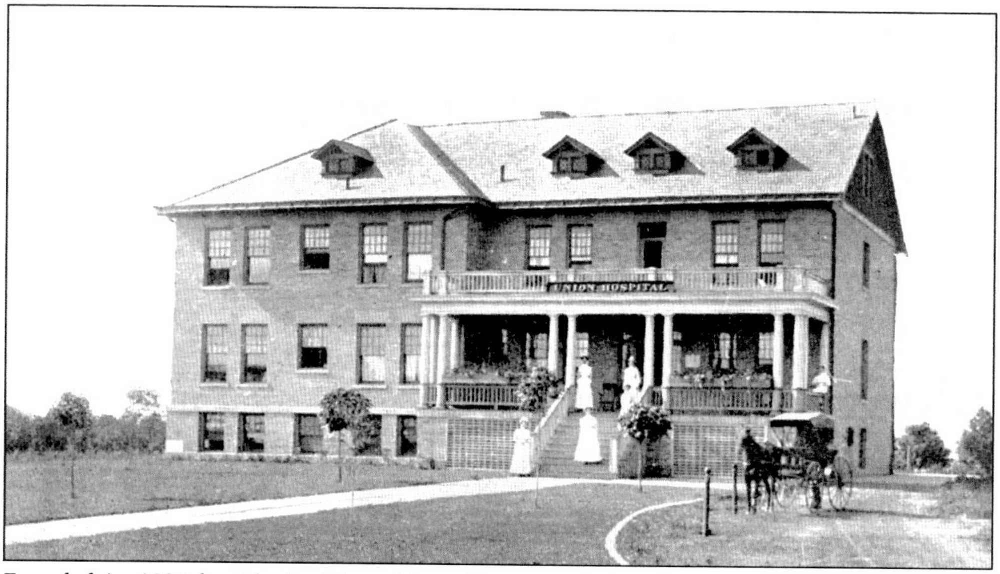

Founded in 1924 by Charles Marr, Marr, Knapp, and Crawfis Associates Inc. (MKC) have stamped its imprint on the Tuscarawas Valley. The firm provides a full scope of architectural, engineering, planning, and interior design services. Among signature buildings designed by the company are the Tuscarawas County Public Library, most area schools, the Municipal Building, the Elks building (now the Knisely Centre), the Tuscarawas County Home (Colonial Manor), Muskingum Watershed Conservancy District building, Kent State University Tuscarawas, Tuscarawas County Office Building, Tuscarawas County Jail, Empire Affiliates Credit Union, Boulevard Honda, the Geib Family Center, Emmanuel Lutheran Church, Tuscarawas County YMCA, Union Country Club, and Atwood Lodge.

Other MKC projects include Union Hospital, New Dawn Health Care and Retirement Center, and Hennis Care nursing centers. For 47 years, the firm was located in part of Marr's residence on Ray Avenue NW. Because it had outgrown the quarters by 1983, MKC was moved to the Sharp Building at the corner of Fair Avenue NE and North Broadway—a building designed by Charles Marr in 1927.

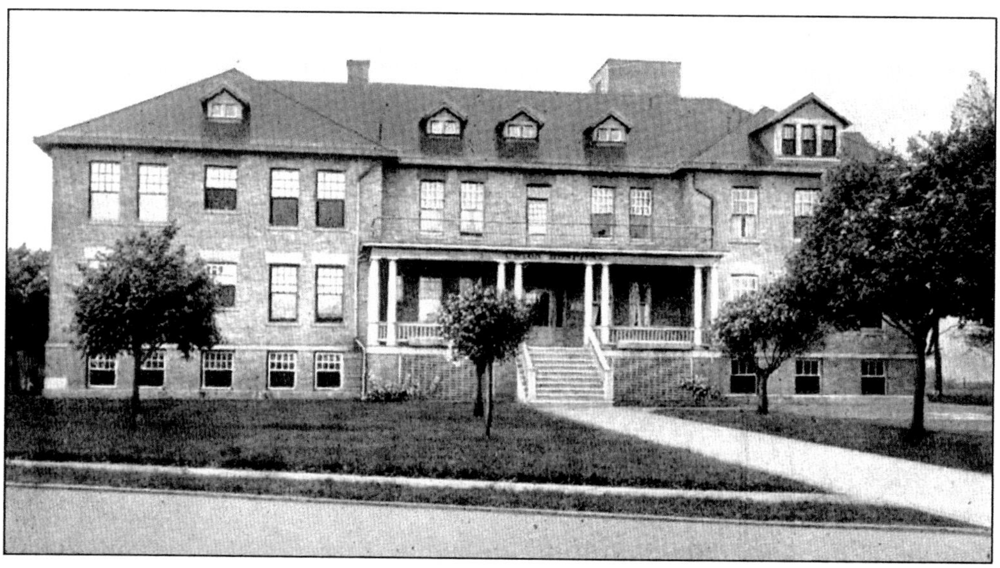

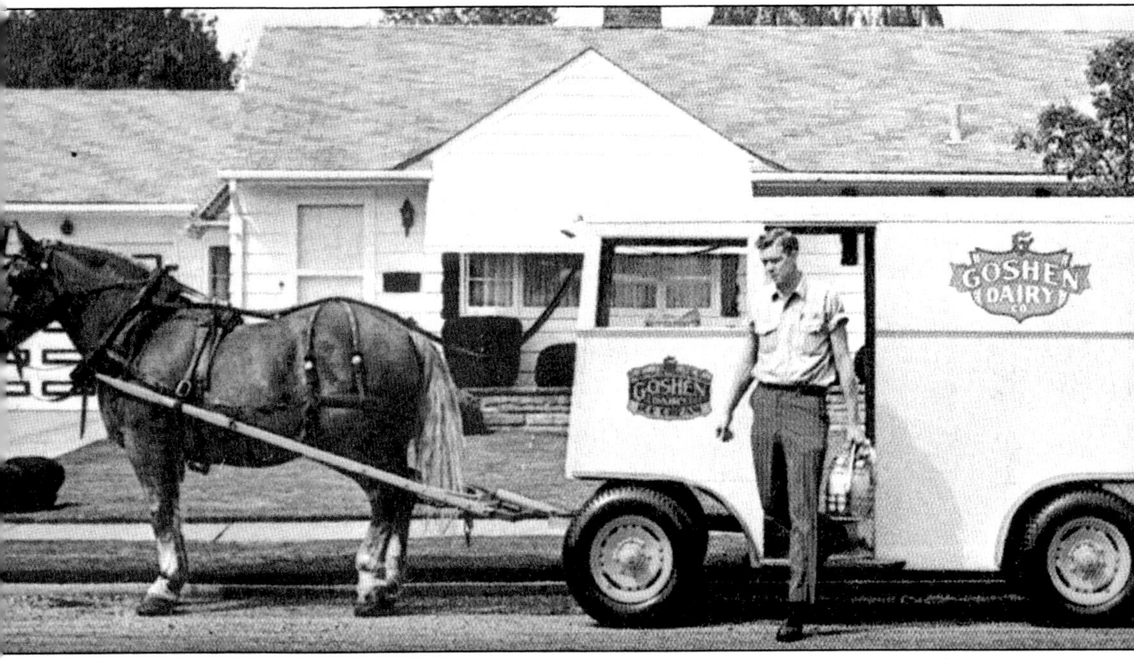

This 1963 postcard, printed by Schlabach Printers Ltd. in Sugarcreek, shows a Goshen Dairy horse-drawn cart being pulled by Dewey with driver Dan Buss. The picture was taken in front of Jim Wallick's home at 816 Oak Street NW.

With the great expansion of the railroads, it was time for drastic agricultural change in the county. Tuscarawas County farmers, who were predominantly German and Swiss, possessed the knowledge necessary for dairying. Cooperatives were established to purchase the expensive equipment needed to manufacture the county's specialty—Swiss cheese.

William Bichsel Sr. founded the Goshen Dairy Company in 1920. It began in a one-room building at 139 Second Street NW. Milk and dairy products were delivered door-to-door by three horse-drawn wagons. In 1930, Goshen Dairy purchased the Espenshied Dairy Company of Dover and opened a retail store there on Second Street. A retail store in front of the 139 Second Street NW property in New Philadelphia followed in 1932, selling products such as Cream Top Bottle, Skyrocket Ice Cream Cone, and the Goshen Dairy Happy Bar. The business continued to expand, adding another retail store in 1971. On March 13, 1972, the era of dairy delivery by horse-drawn carriage ended when the barn was struck by lightning and destroyed.

Goshen Dairy opened other retail shops in Sugarcreek, Uhrichsville, Carrollton, Beach City, Bolivar, Malvern, North Canton, Canton, Coshocton, Bolivar, and on New Philadelphia's south side. In 1987, the business offices were moved to Cookson Avenue. By the 1990s, Goshen Dairy was producing 35–45 different flavors of ice cream and eight yogurt flavors. Their products were distributed to retail and wholesale outlets, schools, restaurants, hospitals, nursing homes, and convenience stores. Satellite distributors were located in Salineville and Zanesville. In November 2000, Goshen Dairy purchased the D and G Dairy of Mount Vernon, expanding their distribution to Knox, Coshocton, Delaware, Licking, and Ashland Counties.

Smith Dairy Products of Orrville bought Goshen Dairy Company on February 1, 2002. Goshen convenience stores, known as Goshen-On-The-Go, are separate entities from the Goshen Dairy Company, so Goshen-On-The-Go still operates convenience stores on New Philadelphia's south side, at Malvern, Uhrichsville, Gnadenhutten, Sugarcreek, and Dover. On August 12, 2003, all remaining Goshen Dairy Company items were auctioned off, including four horse-drawn wagons bringing $8,250 to $11,000 each and three bicycle ice cream carts at $9,000 each.

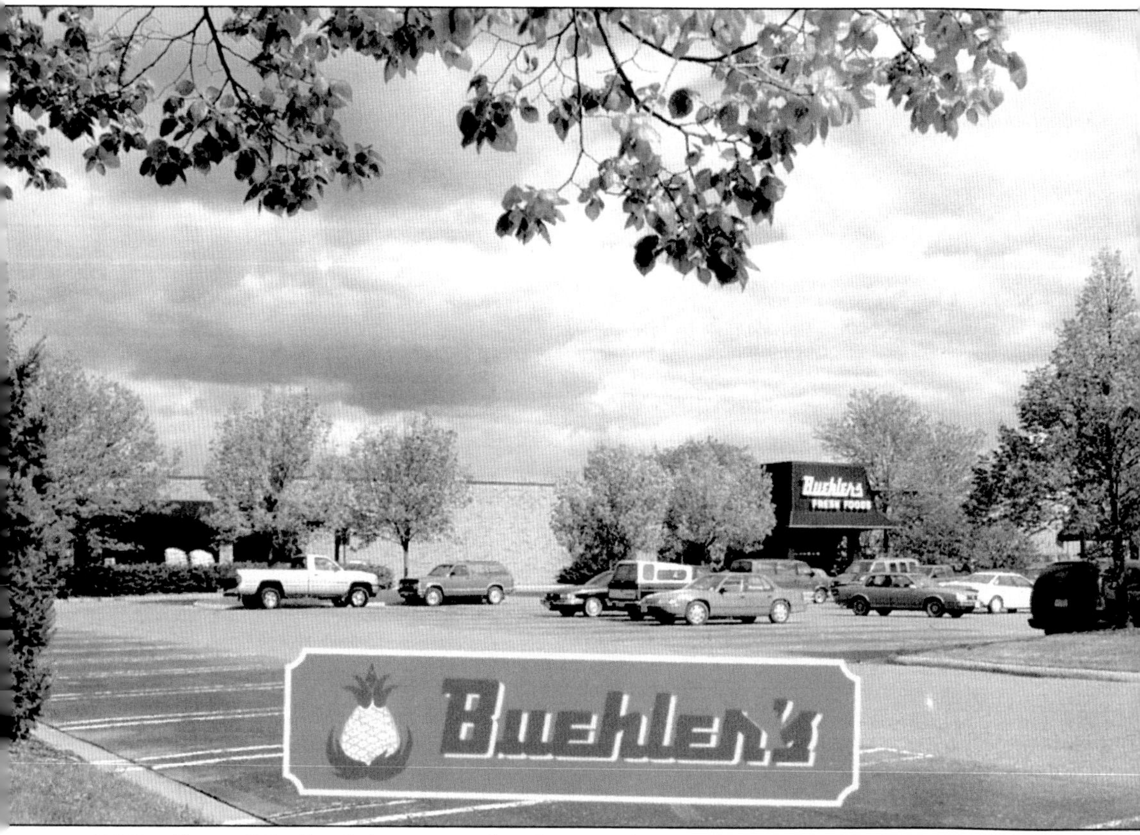

Ed Buehler and Dudley Sulzner owned and operated Fairview Dairy on County Road 21 in the Stone Creek Valley, delivering milk door-to-door. Edward and Helen Buehler opened the first Buehler's grocery store in New Philadelphia in 1929. The store located on West High Avenue at the site of the current Gospel Book Store was a 26-foot by 70-foot space. The second store opened in 1911 at 223 West Third Street in Dover, Ohio. In 1957, the Dover store moved to 420 West Third Street. The second New Philadelphia store opened on Second Street NW in 1964. This store has since become Drug Mart. The third New Philadelphia Buehler's, the one we are familiar with at the corner of Mill Avenue and South Broadway in front of New Towne Mall, opened in 1984. The store was built on an old landfill.

The Buehler's and their children expanded the business over the years to include other cities. The Orrville store was opened in 1959, Medina in 1964, Coshocton in 1968, Delaware in 1969, Wooster in 1981, Wadsworth in 1976, and Ashland in 2000. Most Buehler's stores include a pharmacy, a bakery, a restaurant, an FTD floral shop, a photo express, video rentals, a deli, a card and gift shop, and gasoline.

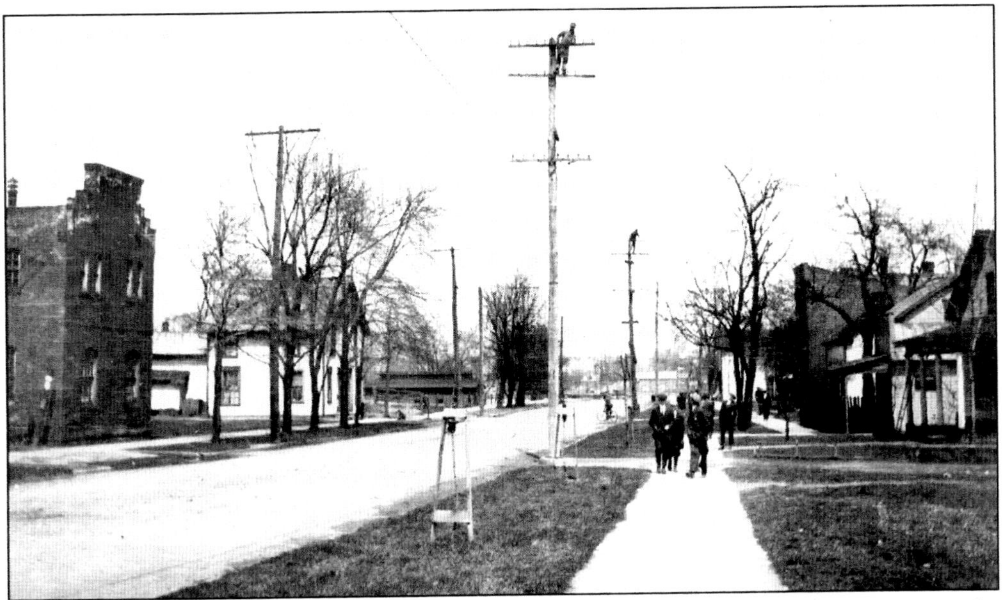

In 1898, the East Ohio Gas Company (Dominion) came to New Philadelphia. In 1908, the old oil and gas lamps were replaced, and the town was lighted by 35 arc lights. By 1910, New Philadelphia claimed that it was "the best lighted city of its size in the state." In 1911, the American Gas and Electric Company acquired the Twin City United Electric Power Company, which was later known as the Ohio Service Company. The company had already acquired the Augustus Beyer Power Plant of New Philadelphia and the United Service Company. This was the formation of the Ohio Power Company (AEP).

DUE DEC. 1, 1910

To The New Philadelphia Heating Co. Dr.

PAYMENT NO. 2

No. ....

Collections made in six equal amounts.

THIS BILL IS NET.

If not paid before the 10th of each month, service will be discontinued and $1.00 will be charged for reconnecting.

Amount - - - 8 34

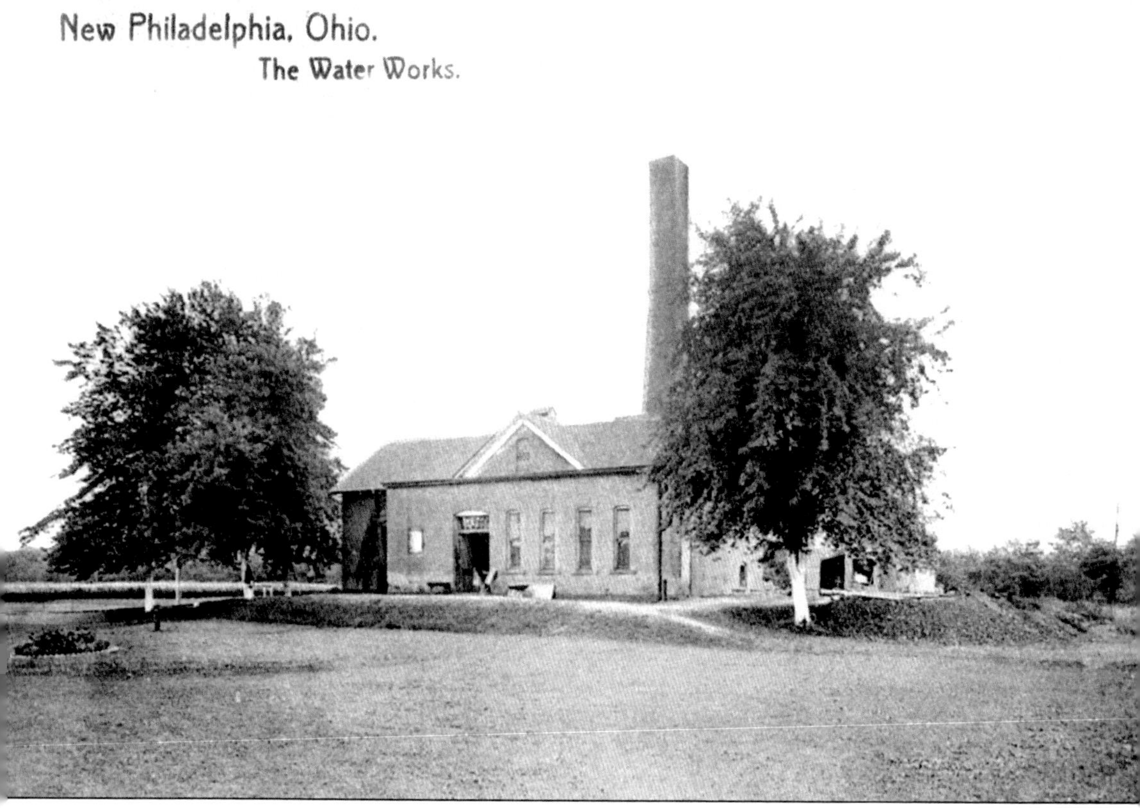

In 1910, new sewer plans were approved by the city council, and a water filtration plant was purchased at a cost of $130,000.

Seven

Transportation

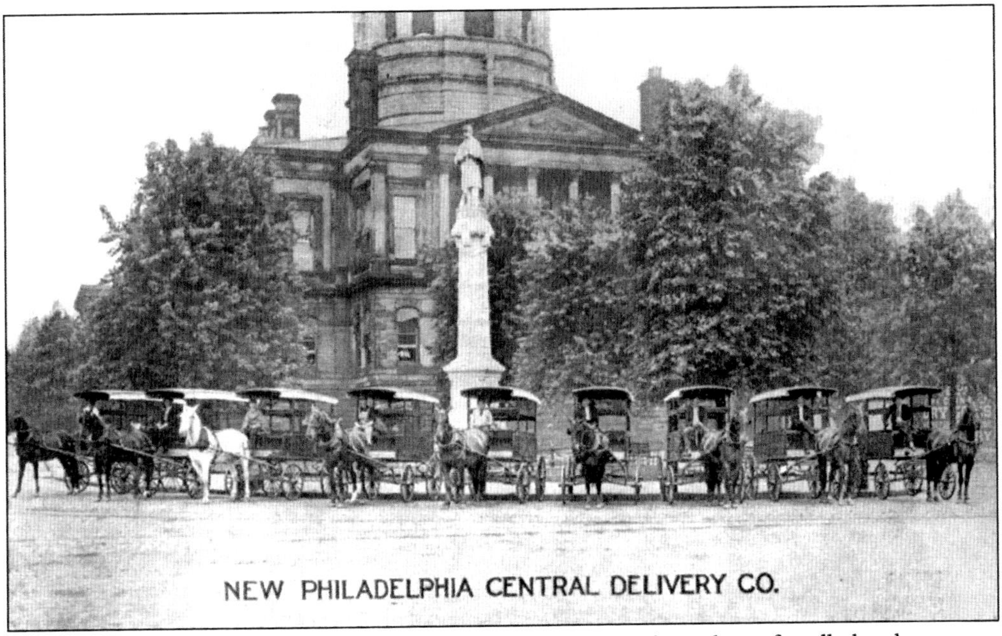

The New Philadelphia Central Delivery Company delivered products for all the downtown businesses directly to customers' homes. The company later used some trucks.

By the 1820s, widened and graveled or mud roads led to towns and settlements within the county and to the cities beyond. In February 1827, the following announcement appeared in an issue of the *Tuscarawas Chronicle*: "The subscriber informs the public that he has fitted up a New and Handsome Stage which regularly runs once a week (from New Philadelphia) . . . The new Stage will afford an easy and comfortable conveyance . . . It will pass on its route through Dover, Leesburg, New Hagerstown, New Robley, Jefferson and Annapolis."

J.P. and D.T. Bartles on West Front Avenue erected the first carriage works in the county, Bartles and Son, in June 1846. In 1871, J.P. became sole proprietor and took his son into partnership. They manufactured 60–80 vehicles annually, employing eight to ten men. Charles Houpt owned the only other buggy and carriage manufactory in the New Philadelphia. His shops were located on South Fifth Street and were erected in 1868. He manufactured 35–40 buggies each year.

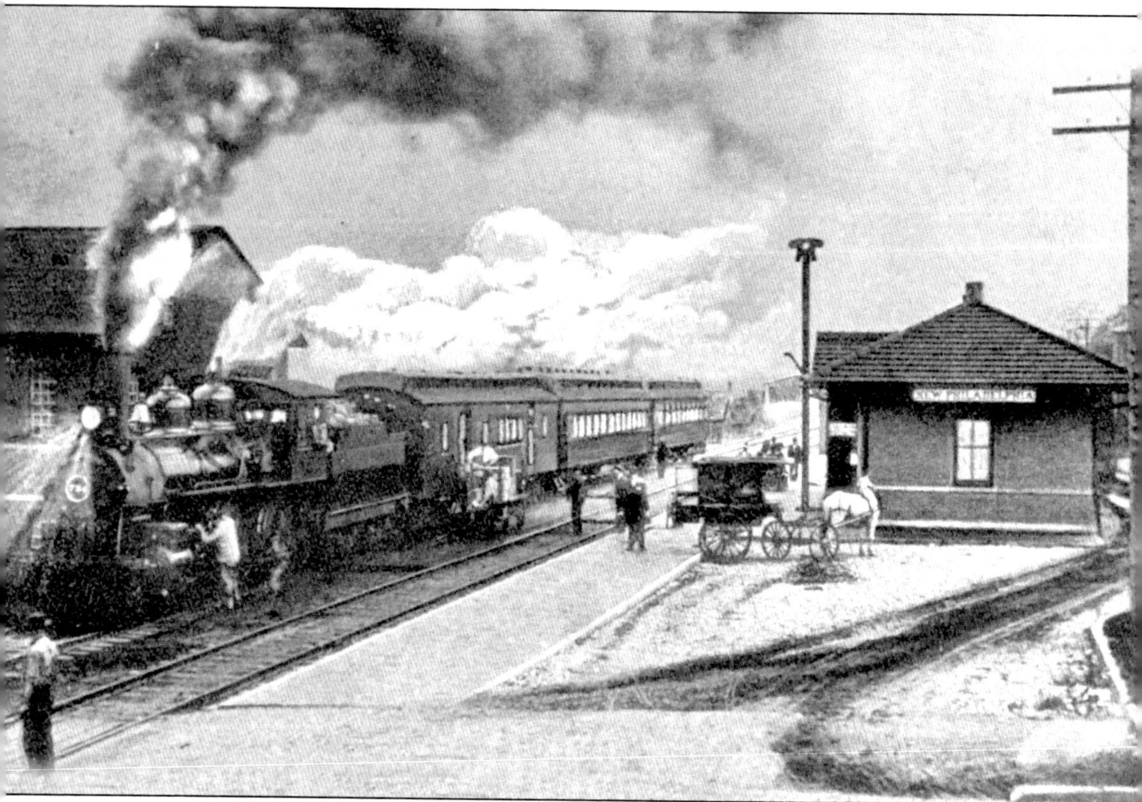

In 1854, the Cleveland and Pittsburgh Railroad began construction of a branch line from Bayard in Columbiana County to New Philadelphia. Its freight depot was located on North Broadway. A network of rails gradually supplanted the canal system, unable to accommodate the vastly increased traffic burden or meet the demand for greater speed. In the pre-auto days, there were also a number of local passenger trains. Among them was the coal miners' train from New Philadelphia to the Roswell mines.

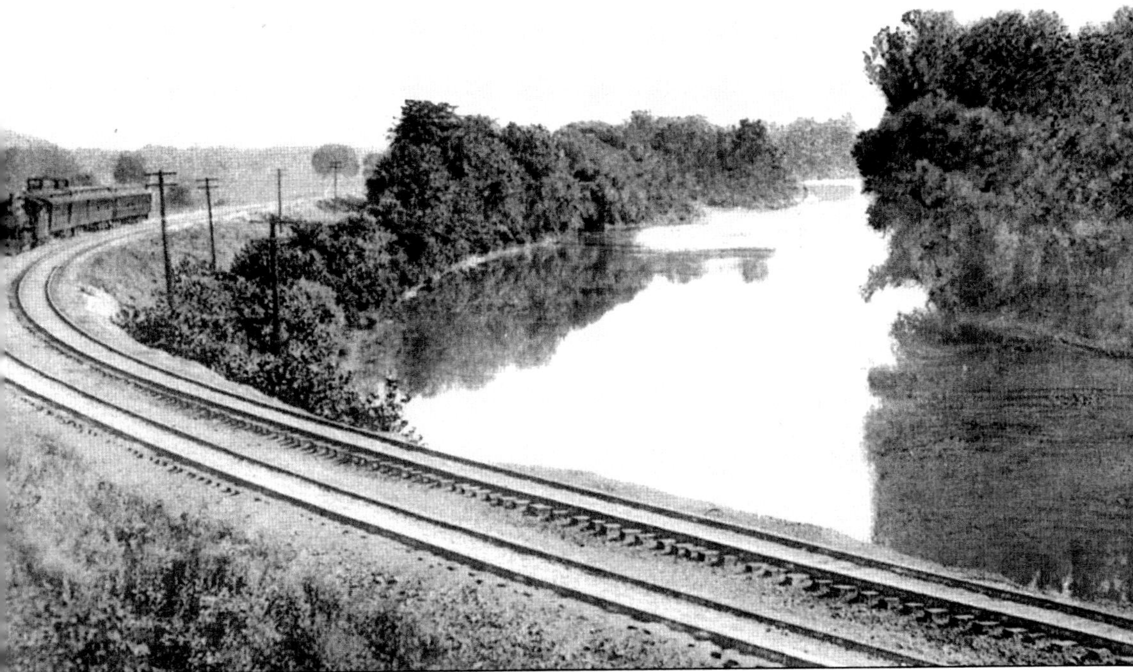

Businesses and industry continued to flourish during the late 1800s, and in the early 1900s, the population had swelled to over 5,000. The year 1901 saw the merger of the Tuscarawas Railroad Company, operating a trolley line from New Philadelphia to Uhrichsville with the Tuscarawas Electric Company operating in Dover and New Philadelphia. Work was also started on the Northern Ohio Traction electric line from Cleveland to Dover and New Philadelphia, which later absorbed the Tuscarawas Traction Company. They failed because there was no large city in or near Tuscarawas County and because the countryside was sparsely settled. The coming of the automobile hastened their collapse in 1929.

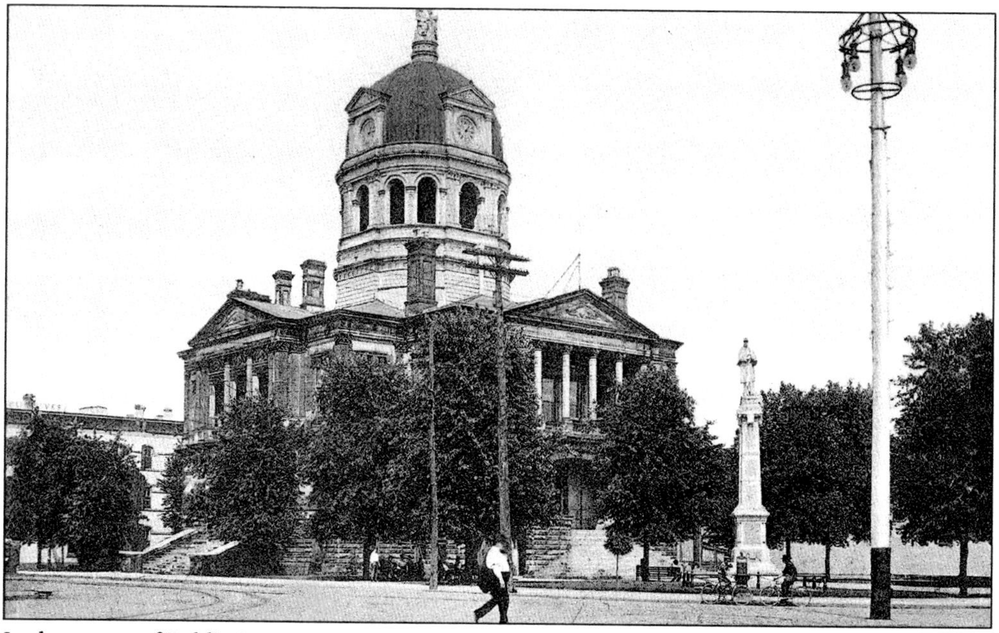

In the center of Public Square sat an electric streetlight where wires were hung for the Interurban transit. In 1904, the city fathers discussed the future of the square, deciding the center light pole was in the way. The *Tuscarawas Advocate* wrote, "If left to a vote, a very large majority of the people of New Philadelphia would say 'Let the electric light mast remain on the public square'." Better lighting, a place for the posting of the colors on special occasions, and the hanging of strands of lights from the mast to various corners of the buildings during special seasons were just a few of the reasons. On Friday, October 21, 1904, the center mast was moved by a group of electric railway men. A new pole was placed 14 feet towards the Courthouse to allow the Interurban straight passage from North to South Broadway. The new pole was removed sometime after the closing of the Interurban in 1929. Traffic light islands were eventually erected at each of the four corners of the square. In the 1960s, these islands were also removed and overhead traffic signals were strung.

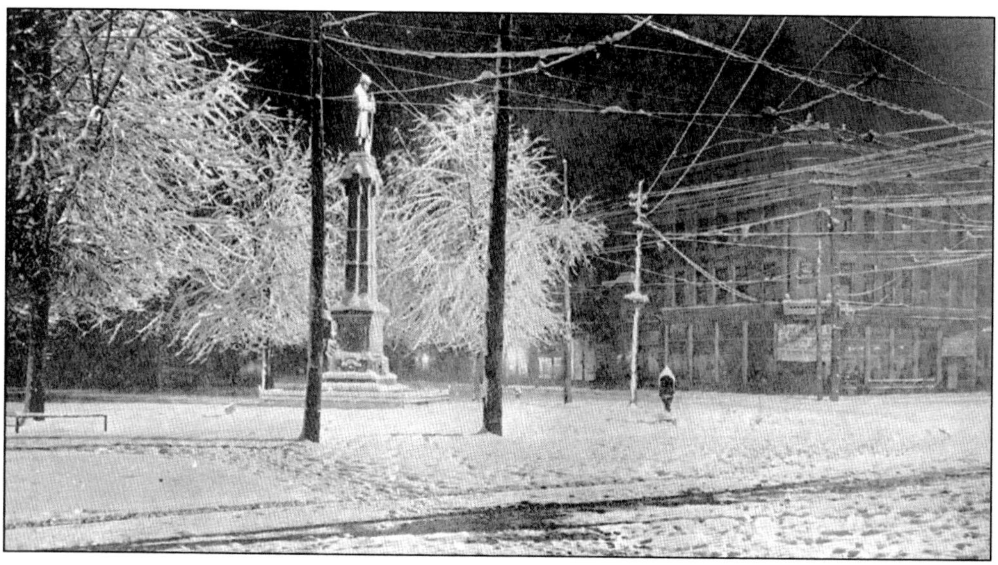

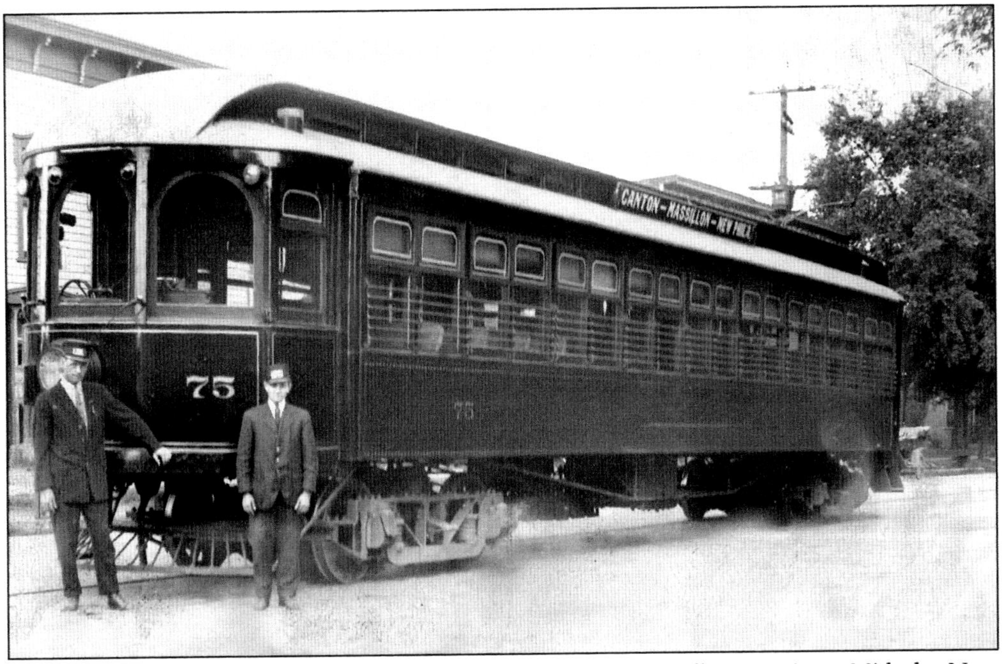

The Northern Ohio Power Co. Interurban connected Uhrichsville, Dennison, Midvale, New Philadelphia, Dover, Parral, Louden, and Strasburg with all points north to Cleveland. The cars were operated with overhead electric wires. In Tuscarawas County, the Interurban ran from April 29, 1903, until 1929. On July 2, 1904, the *Tuscarawas Advocate* described one of the cars stopped in New Philadelphia for people to examine: "This car is one of the handsomest that is built for electric roads and compares favorably with many of the new Pullman steam railroad choices. It is 57 feet long and weighs in the neighborhood of 40 tons. The color is dark green; the interior is mahogany of fine quality and finish; the reversible seats are upholstered in dark green brocaded plush and the metal work is all polished brass. It is geared to run at 65 miles per hour." The interurban era ended on June 1, 1929, and was replaced by the Northern Ohio Power Co Bus Line. The old interurban lines were removed.

Union Terminal bus line was located a half block north of Public Square for the Gold Star, Penn-Ohio, Dover and New Philadelphia, and Red Eagle lines.

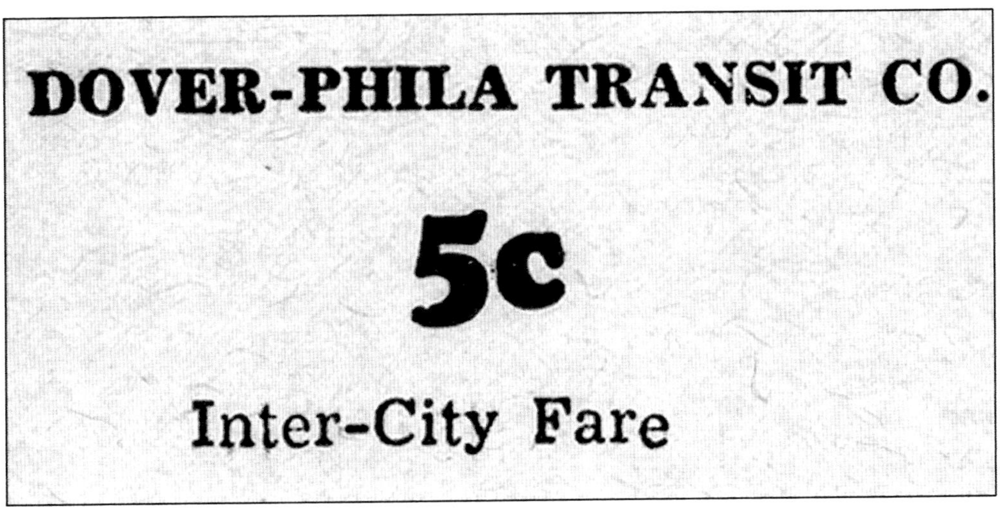

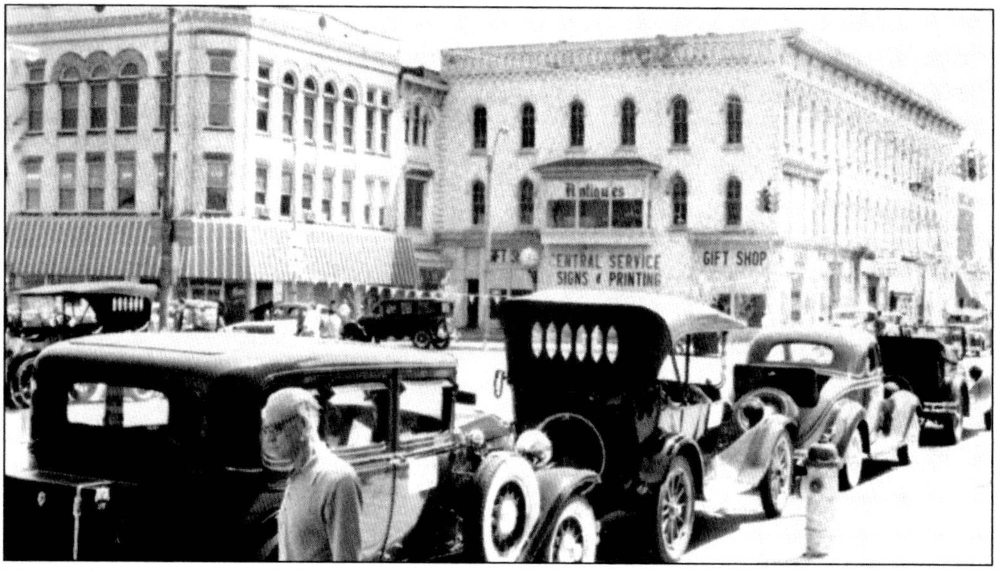

The settlers first petitioned the Tuscarawas County Commissioners for better roads as early as April 1808. By 1906, there were enough automobiles in use to give demand for better highways. The National Good Roads Association convention was held at the Union Opera House on January 19. A program was outlined that launched the highway building system. In 1912, the first Tuscarawas County Automobile Club was organized.

In 1927, a man named Ab Jenkins, a Salt Lake City contractor, decided to see if man and machine could set a new road record for ocean-to-ocean travel. There were speed records for the train, airplane, why not the "machine" as many people referred to the automobile. Ab, driving a Studebaker Commander sedan, set out from New York City at 8 p.m. on August 30th and made his first stop for fuel at 10:05 a.m. on August 31st at the Cope-Shank garage, the local Studebaker dealers located at 160 South Broadway. Ab pulled into San Francisco, California, on September 3rd at 2 a.m., establishing a record of 77 hours 40 minutes.

The 1926 Ohio Department of Transportation on West High Street was expanded four times; plus, modular units were added. A new headquarters for the Ohio Department of Transportation District 11 was built in the Knisely Industrial Park at 2201 Reiser Avenue SE in 1996.

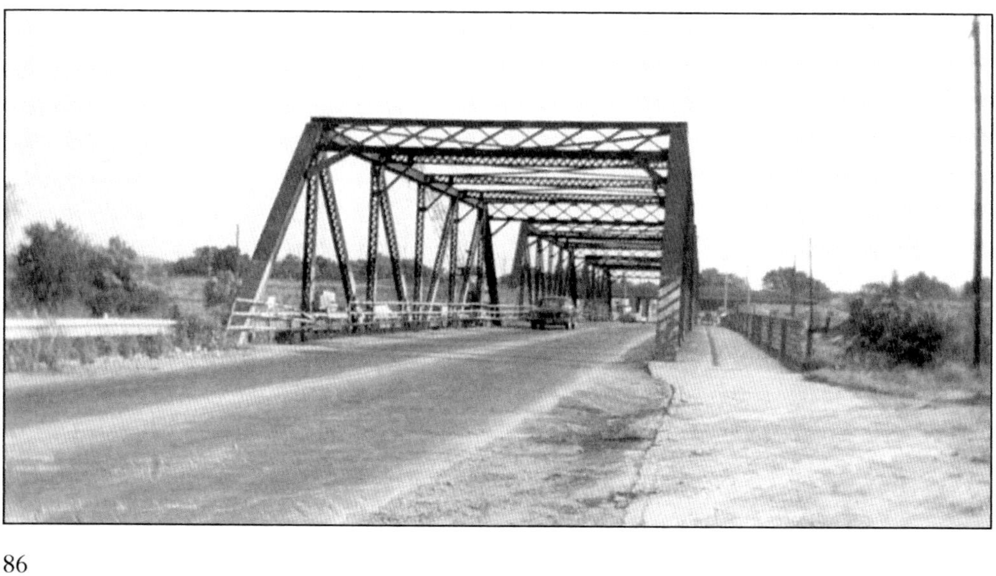

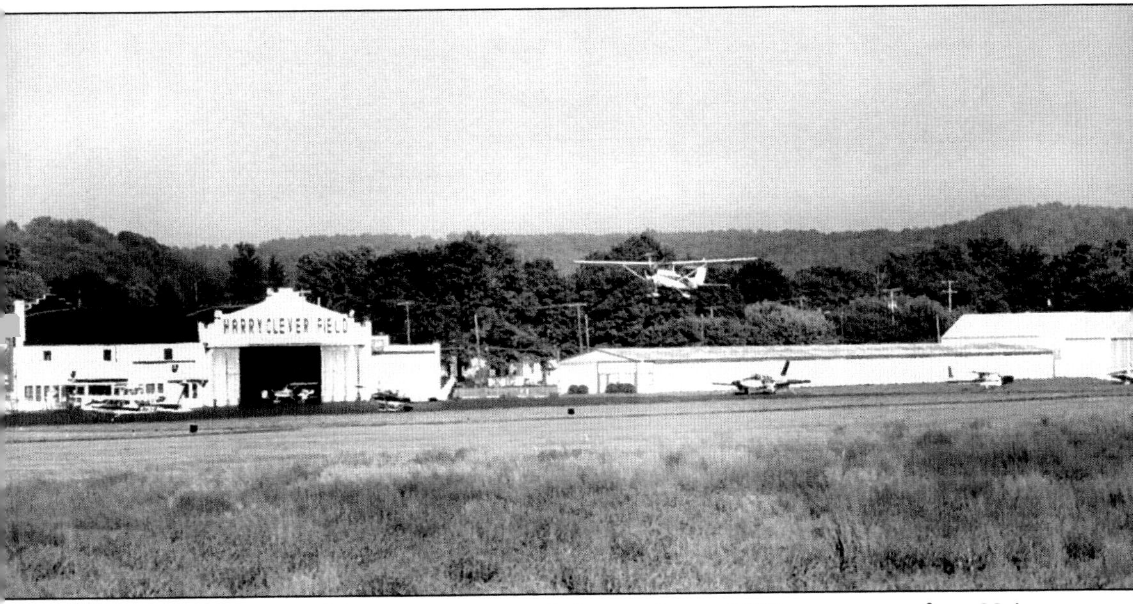

In 1927, the Chamber of Commerce proposed the purchase of 125 acres across from Union Hospital to build an airport, but was turned down by the voters. Meanwhile Harry Clever, having returned home from the Army Air Service where he learned to fly, had purchased a plane and started to fly at Schoenbrunn. He and a group of others incorporated Tuscarawas County Aviation, Inc. in 1928, with Harry as the local manager. The land was leased from the Della Brown farm, a relative of Harry Clever. They constructed two tin hangers and converted an old barn into a hanger.

In 1934, the city assumed control of the field in order to qualify for Federal funds and changed the name to Municipal Airport. In 1935, the city purchased one acre from the Della Brown farm and constructed the current brick hangar. A year later they built a hangar measuring 100 foot by 80 foot, along with a small structure beside it that was opened as a restaurant. In 1939, the city leased all of the Brown Farm for five years with an option to purchase. One year later, the U.S. Civil Aeronautics Authority gave the Schoenbrunn airport a $261,000 grant to develop the field further.

The city bought half an acre more from the Brown Farm to construct a repair shop adjacent to the brick hangar, and in 1945, the city purchased the 72 acres from the Brown Farm and also purchased an additional 17.23 acres from the Cemetery Department. In 1949, an additional 4.06 acres were leased for 20 years at $5 a year from the Ohio Historical Society, and in 1955, Tuscarawas County Aviation, Inc. built 14 metal T-hangars, which the city acquired.

On June 7, 1969 the airport name was officially changed to Harry Clever Field, but the Tuscarawas County Aviation Company dissolved shortly after. Today, the New Philadelphia Airport Commission controls the airport. They have plans for airport expansion, hoping to become a regional airport. Plans show a projected 4,400-foot runway, which will cross 21st Street SE and consume property and homes. The city is still seeking FAA approval.

Harry Clever Municipal Airport, located in New Philadelphia, was the site of Senator and Astronaut John Glenn's first solo airplane flight. In John Glenn's original flight book questionnaire, which all cadets fill out, Glenn answered the question on future plans to continue flying. Glenn handwrote, "probably but not certain." Glenn went on to set a coast-to-coast speed record of three hours in a jet plane. Later, he piloted his space capsule the same distance in a little over 10 minutes. Glenn's most notable accomplishment would be returning to space on the STS-95 Discovery for a nine-day space mission at the age of 77.

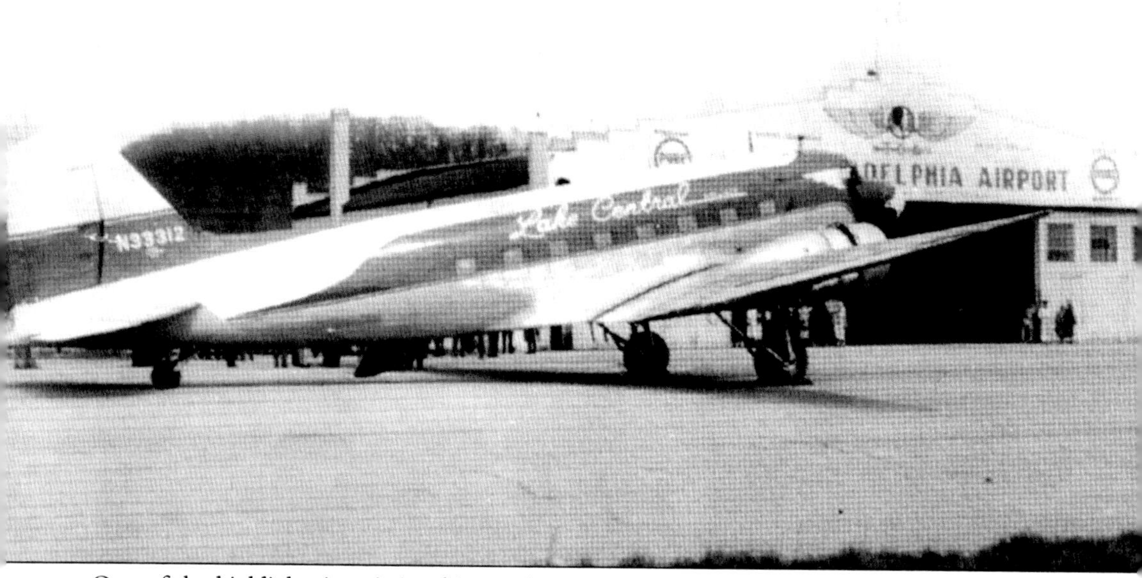

One of the highlights in aviation history for Tuscarawas County was the inauguration of Lake Central Airlines service. In April 1953, the first flight of Lake Central Airlines arrived in the county on Saturday the 13th. Passenger quotas were set in order to continue operation, but by the end of the 1950s, the quotas were not being met, and the airlines pulled out. People could hear the drone of the big plane miles away and would stop to watch as the plane made its final approach to the airport. If they were lucky enough to be near the airport, they would see what a feat had been accomplished by the skilled pilots in landing and returning to the air. The short runways taxed the skills of the pilots to the maximum. The airport was the scene of numerous air shows put on by civic organizations, and crowds would flock to the east end of the county seat to watch the stunt pilots.

Eight

Entertainment and Media

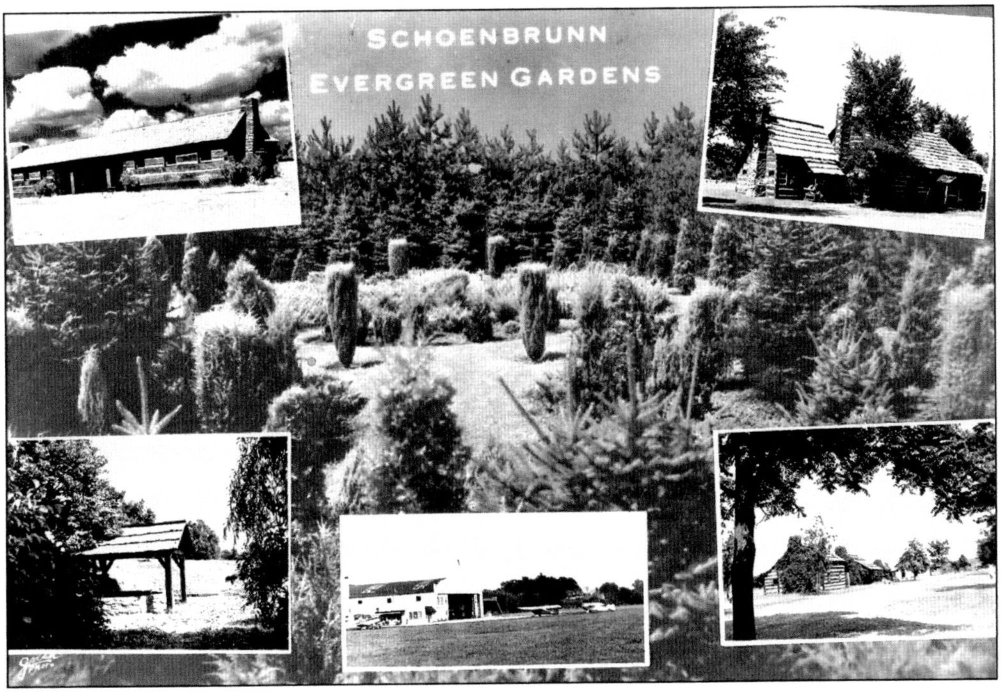

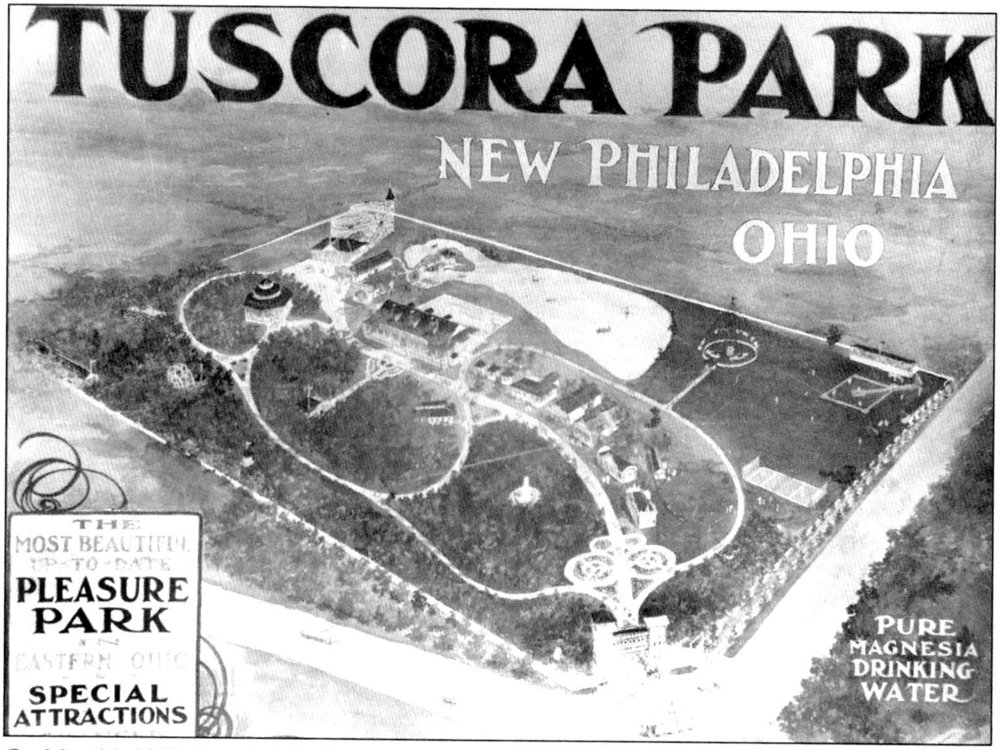

On May 16, 1900, Jeremiah E. Reeves, principal stockholder in the Dover rolling mill, purchased land for $20,000. The land encompassed several farms including the Gooding farm, the Legget farm, the Dr. Lewis farm, and land of Kirk Arnold and the Willis farm. A portion of this property purchased by Mr. Reeves would later be the location of Tuscora Park.

In 1907, the Tuscora Park Company, a corporate holding, was organized with a capital stock of $80,000. The stocks could be purchased by anyone from the adjacent towns to New Philadelphia, provided they had $50 per share to invest. The original area of the park was 10 acres.

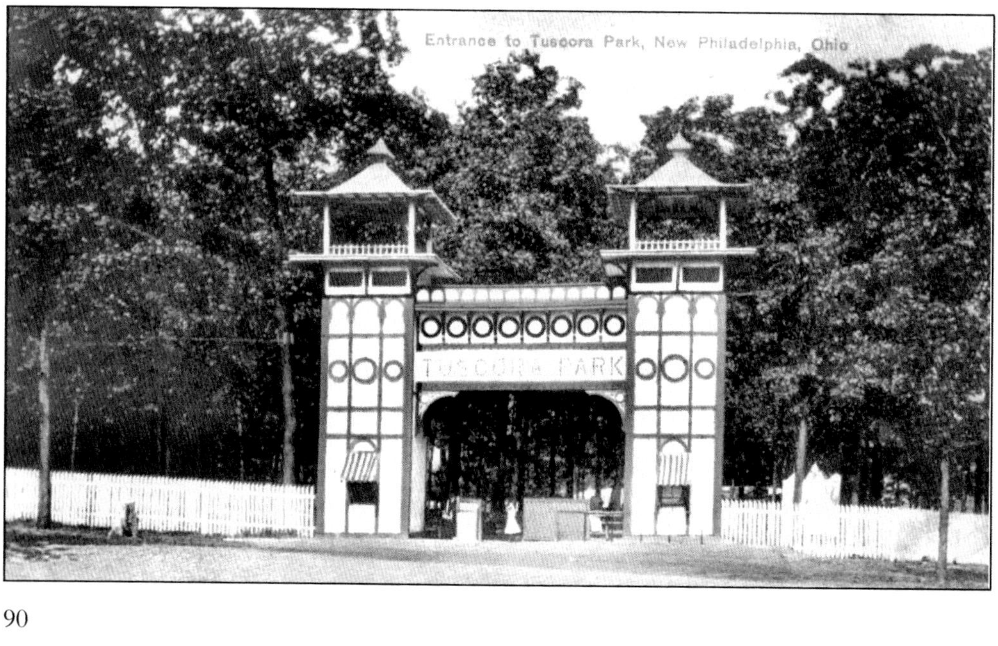

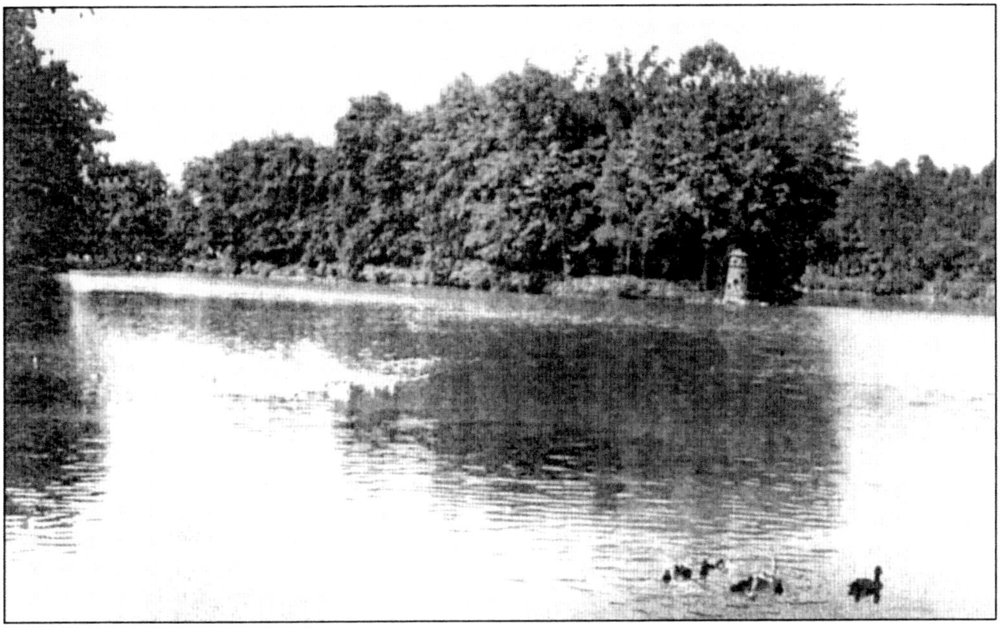

Opening day was Saturday, June 1, 1907. Over 1,000 people enjoyed a splendid concert. Attractions included the Dancing Pavilion, the swimming pool, the bowling alley, the Merry-Go-Round, the Country Store, the Miniature Railway, the Ice Cream Cone Stand, the Art Gallery, candy booths, tennis courts, knife racks, an artificial lake, the Electrical Theatre, the Figure Eight Roller Coaster, the Shooting Gallery, the Photo Gallery, the Sea Wave, a restaurant, cane racks, running tracks, baseball grounds, and more. On July 4th, over 14,000 people entered the gates. A switch point was acquired so the street rail could run into the park for those who did not own a car. Two more wells were also drilled so the swimming pool water could be changed twice weekly. A Columbus amusement company managed the park as a private venture. After just a few years, the private company dissolved, and the City of New Philadelphia bought Tuscora Park from Jeremiah Reeves on June 22, 1912 for $16,500. Additional acreage was purchased from the Davidson Land and Building Company as the venture prospered.

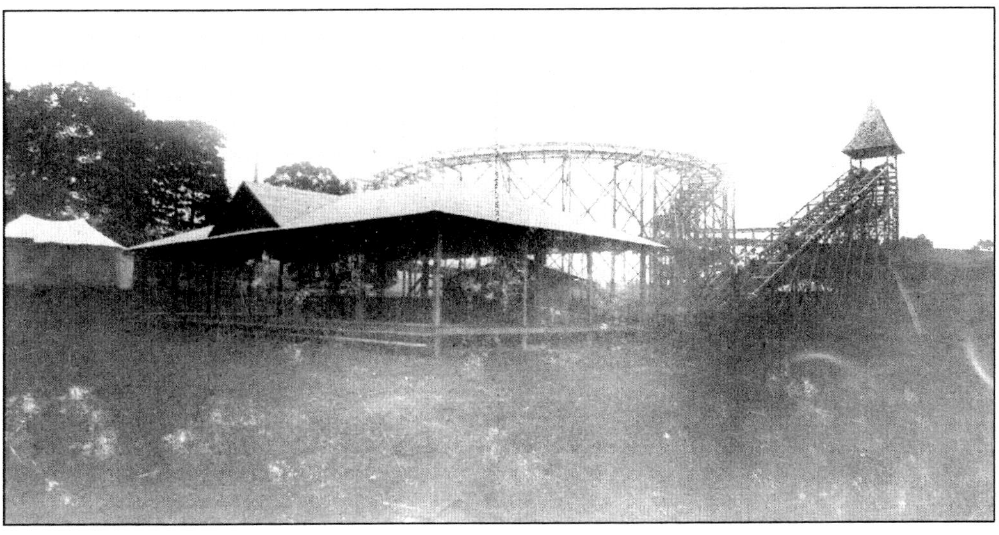

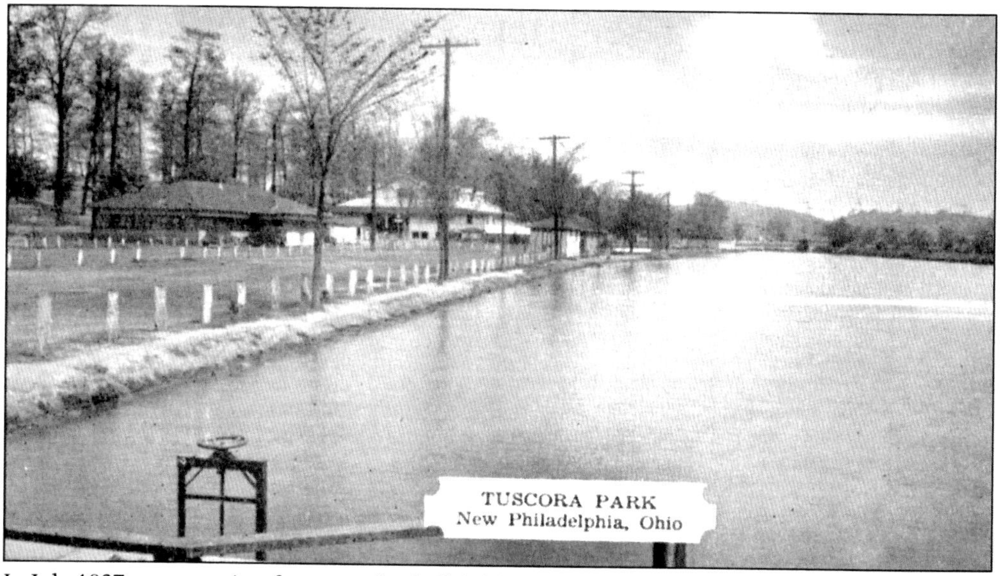

In July 1927, construction for a new football field and cinder track facility began. Quaker Stadium held its first game on September 29, 1928. In 1930, a miniature golf course was constructed. The first levy specifically for the park's operating costs passed in July of 1935. In 1942, playground equipment was purchased and the first lifeguard hired.

Many of the rides were purchased in the 1940s, including the Herschell-Stillman Merry-Go-Round, a 10-gondola Parker Wheel, a kiddy's airplane ride, and a kiddy's car ride. The Spillman Carousel was manufactured in 1928 and purchased second hand. It is one of the few all-wooden carousels in the country today. The 36 artistically carved wooden jumping horses and chariots have 350 individual lights. They travel around center panels adorned with 14 original oil paintings. A Wurlitzer-style 153-band organ provides music. The Carousel is 40 feet in diameter and weighs 10 tons. In 1988, Jerry A. and Donna L. Schwab provided the funds to construct the Douglas Lee Schwab Memorial Carousel Building.

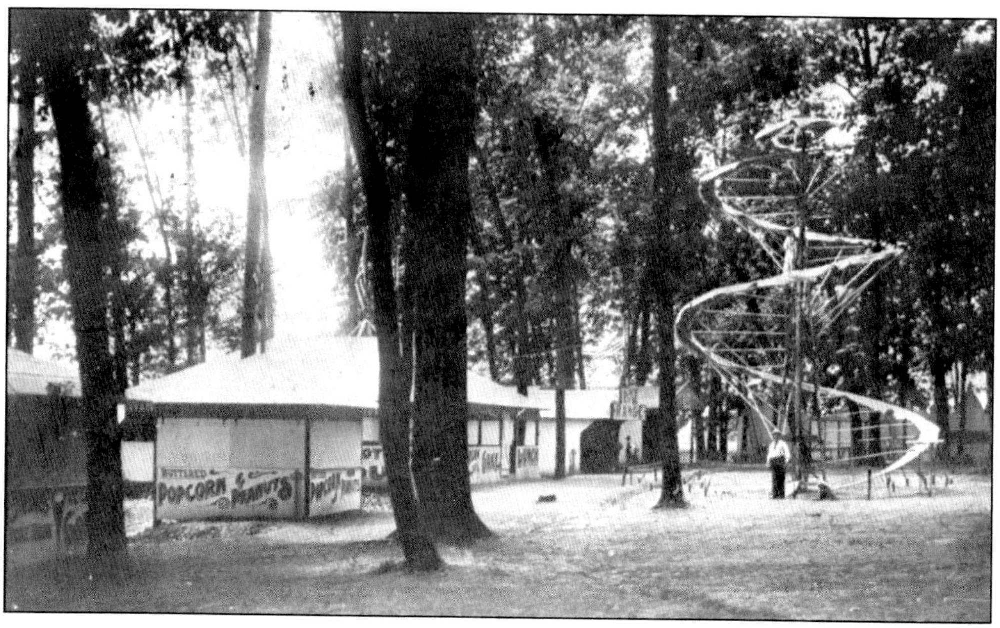

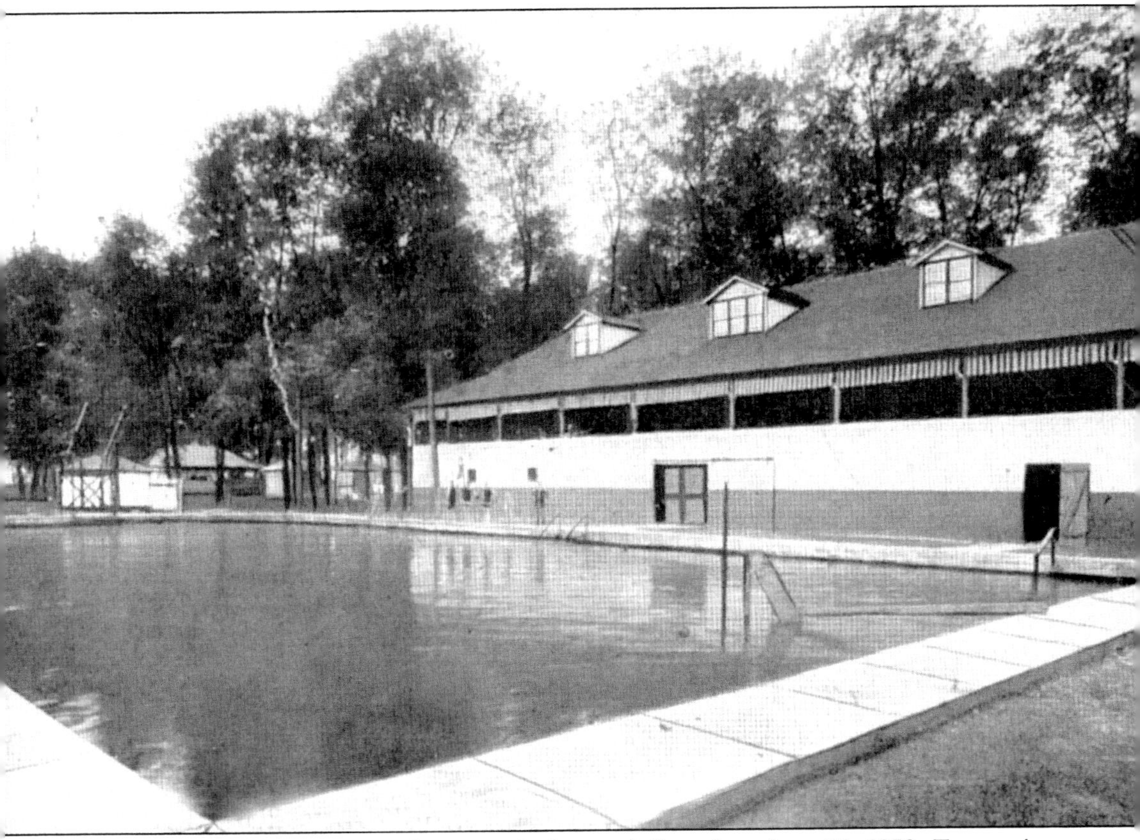

The new ball diamond on top of Tuscora Park was dedicated on June 15, 1953. Two major disasters followed in the next decade. On January 10, 1961, on a cold winter night, the pavilion that had provided sanctuary to many events burned down. The biggest tragedy was that the pavilion housed the animals of the zoo during the winter months. Then, on July 12, 1969, a tornado tore through Tuscora Park hitting Quaker stadium, destroying the press box, the fence, and the refreshment stand. Repairs costs totaled $10,165.

In the spring of 1985, a not-for-profit corporation formed by members of the New Philadelphia Rotary Club (RTY), funded the renovation of the existing rides and also purchased a miniature train and roller coaster. In 1986, this same group added a centripetal swing, improved the miniature golf course, and constructed batting cages. This same company later bought the rides from the city, making Tuscora Park once again a privately operated facility. Other improvements the park has seen are the enclosure of a large eating pavilion, construction of a new park office with pool bath house, a new swimming pool, the dredging of the lake, operation of the concessions, summer musical concerts (Summer Showcase) at the amphitheater, Park Place Teen Center, and the renaming of the football stadium to Woody Hayes Quaker Stadium in honor of the famous coach who began his successful coaching career right here in New Philadelphia at Tuscora Park. Each year, Tuscora Park is the site of New Philadelphia's "First Town Days" celebration during the week of July 4.

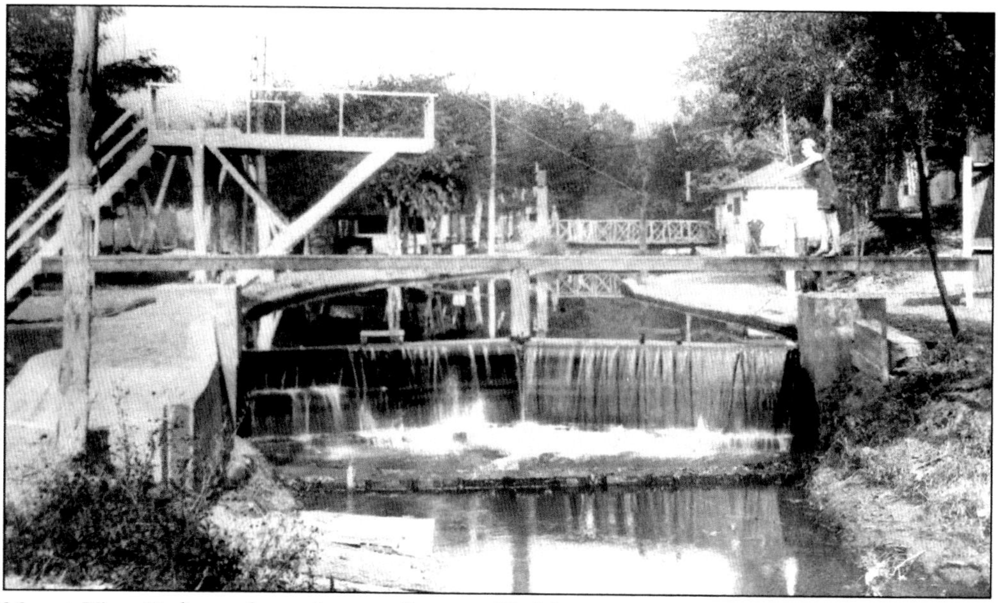

Mount View Park was located one mile east of Public Square during the 1930s and 1940s on what was then US 250 (East High Avenue and the north end of 12th Street). It was a seven-acre tract with a dance pavilion, baseball field, picnic facilities, tennis courts, and tourist cottages, as well as a swimming pool.

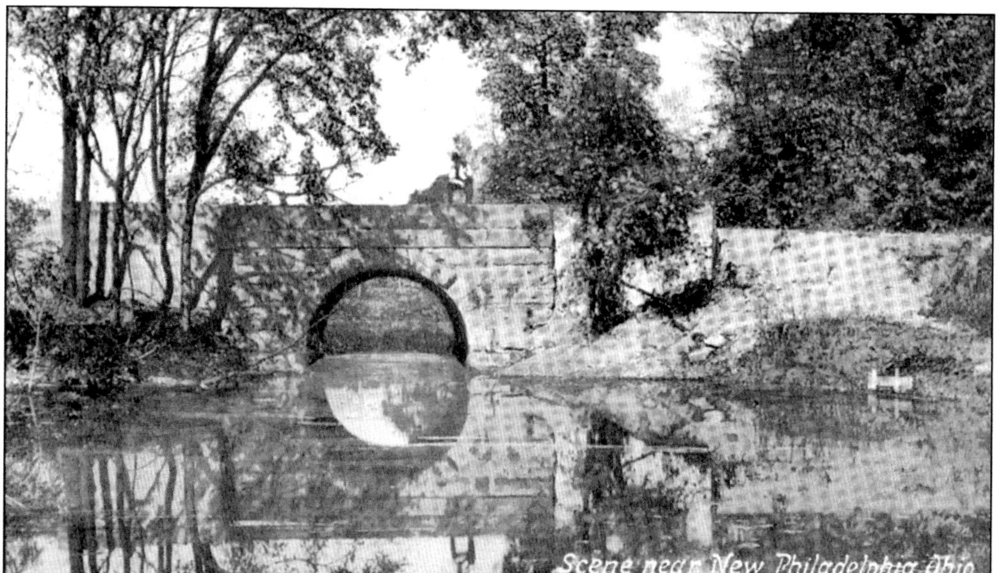

Springer's Park, developed by Leroy (Dee) Springer, was located west, one mile from the square of New Philadelphia. People came to this park to enjoy a summer picnic, skip stones in the river, fish, or take a much-deserved nap in the beautiful setting. The park had a hotel and a concession stand for guests. Unfortunately, the hotel burned to the ground. Leroy went on to develop the New Philadelphia Bottling of Carbonated Beverage Company and then Springer Contracting Business. The latter company paved many New Philadelphia streets during the early 1900s.

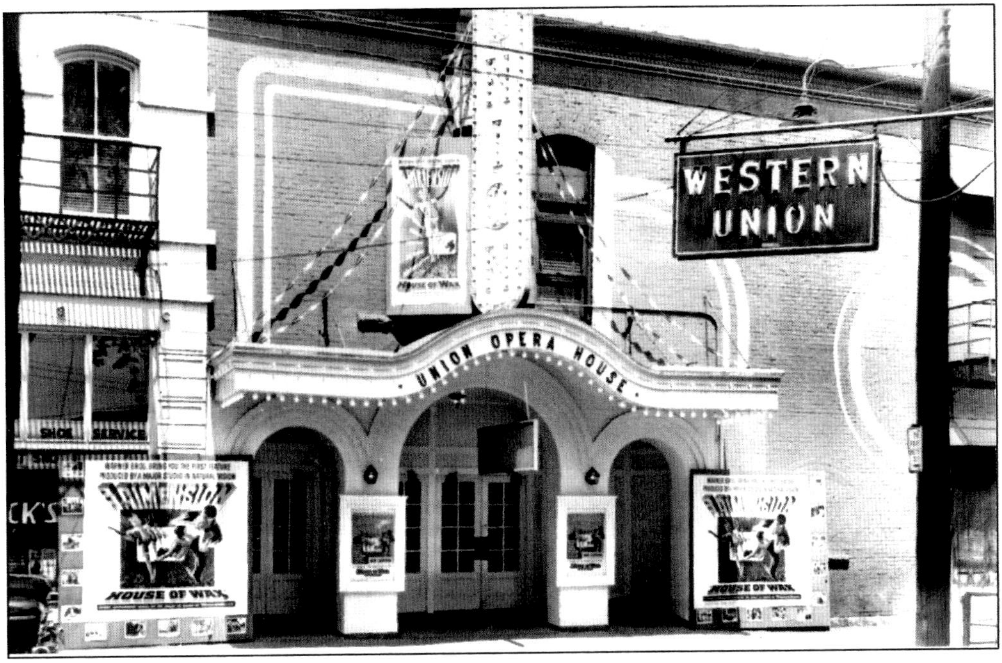

The Union Opera House, opened in 1897, hosted John Philip Sousa and his band on September 24, 1912. According to a newspaper ad, the price of the evening's entertainment was "20 Box Seats $1; 5 Rows Orchestra 75¢; Orchestra $1; Parquet $1; 2 Rows Balcony 75¢; Balance Balcony 50¢; Gallery 25¢." The New Philadelphia *Daily Times* review read: "There's no vaudeville about John Philip Sousa when conducting his great band; he is always the cultured American gentleman...and that's why he was actually loved by a good size crowd. The real treat of the evening was the young Hungarian violinist, Miss Nicoline Zedeler. She is a wonderful artiste, perhaps the most marvelous ever heard." Many political debates, conferences, and organization rallies were held at the Union Opera House. Below is a scene from *Mutt and Jeff*.

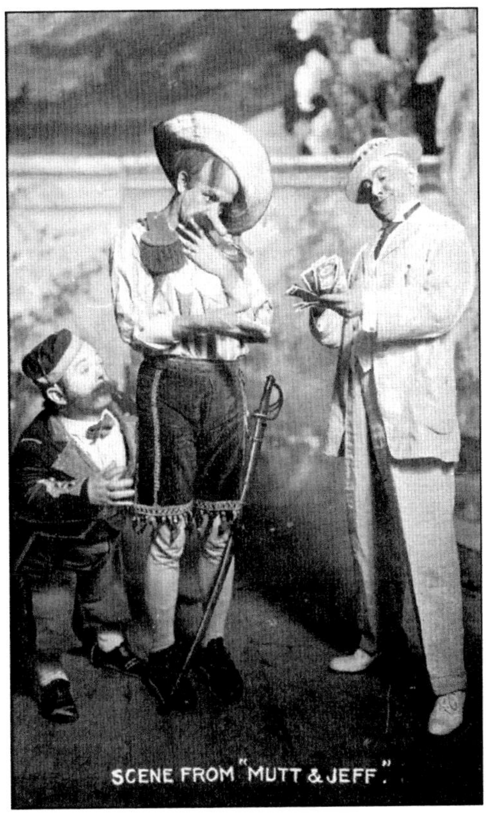

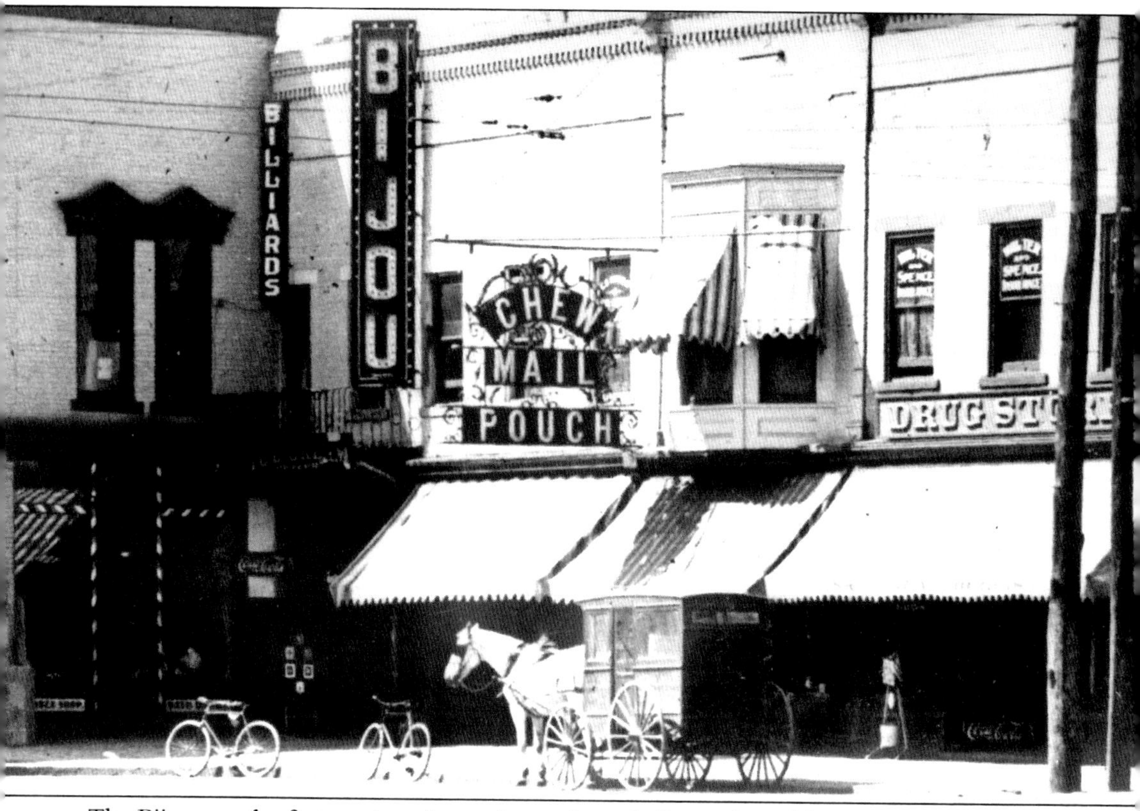

The Bijou was the first motion picture theater here. It featured an elaborately furnished interior and offered its guests 10¢ admission to experience the rapture of viewing the celluloid miracle. The 10¢ nickelodeons, the vaudeville of motion pictures, came along in 1902. *The Great Train Robbery* in 1903 was the first story movie and was silent. Far-sighted entrepreneurs in New Philadelphia shot one of the earliest pictures of the Bijou Theater. Dating back to 1904, it was shot on the Public Square where Beltone Hearing Aids and Fly Boys are now located. The 1907 *Daily Times* described the opening of the new Bijou "next to the old one"; movies were in the "B" ranking with some too "racy" for innocent eyes. Prices ranged from 10¢ to 35¢ for years, and in World War I, a "war tax" of 1¢ and 2¢ was added. The Bijou Palm Garden contained an amusement hall, moving picture show, and a penny arcade.

Leonard Marshall Beatty operated the Popcorn Wagon parked on the southwest corner of the Square in front of the Bijou Theater and the Earl E. Smith Store (Flyboys Restaurant is here now) for over 42 years (1920–1962). Beatty lost both of his legs in a terrible mine accident in Boswell, Pennsylvania, in 1911. Beatty came to New Philadelphia when he recuperated and supported his wife Lillian and sons Robert and Leonard by selling popcorn, peanuts, candy, and other items from the Popcorn Wagon. Beatty wore protective gloves and maneuvered on a board with wheels. He sold the wagon in 1962 due to failing health and died July 8, 1968, at the age of 81. The life of Leonard Marshall Beatty offers many lessons on living a full and useful life. He is buried in the East Avenue Cemetery.

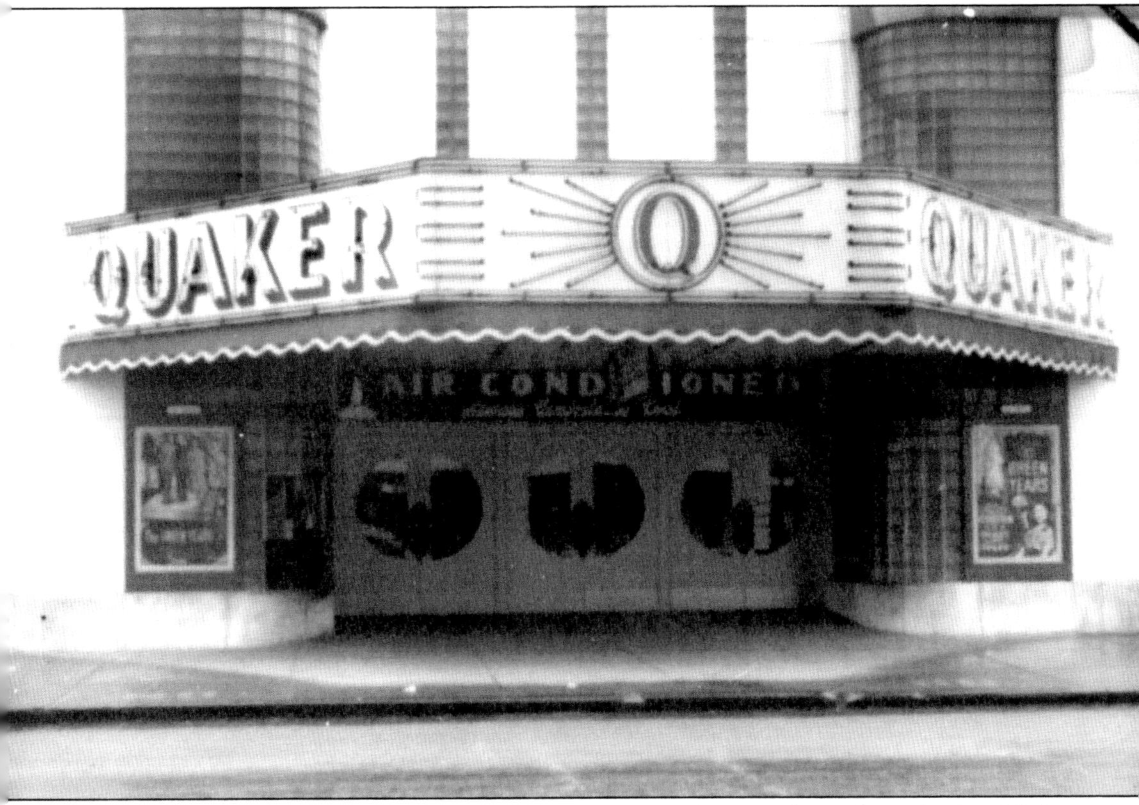

The Quaker Theater opened in 1940. Still in operation today, it is located at158 West High Avenue, offering movies for $3.

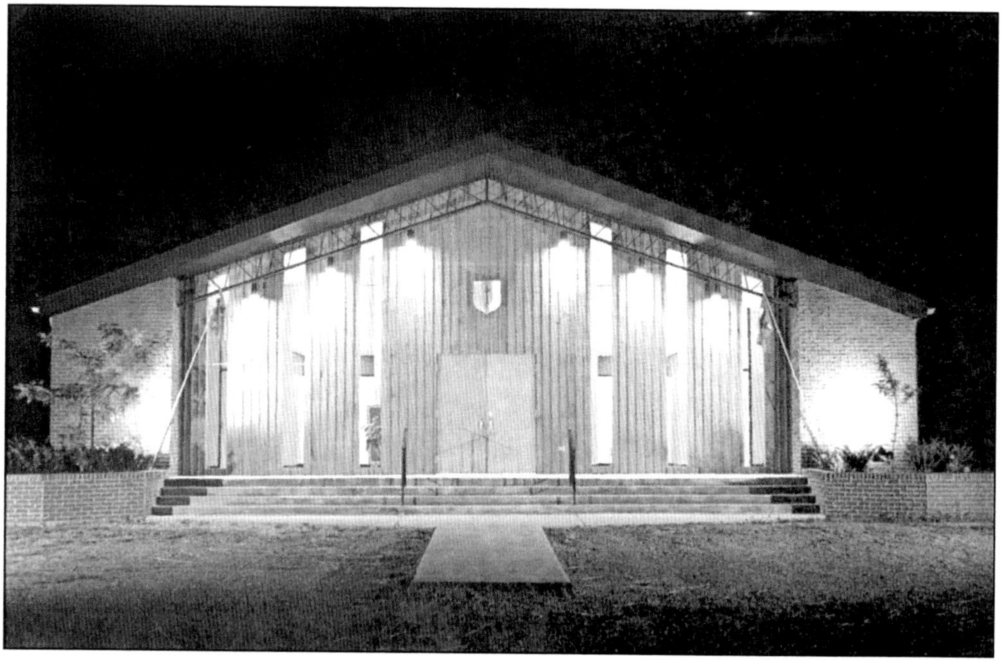

The Players Club of New Philadelphia perform two plays per year. Dover began a Little Theater movement, finally choosing a site in New Philadelphia to present productions.

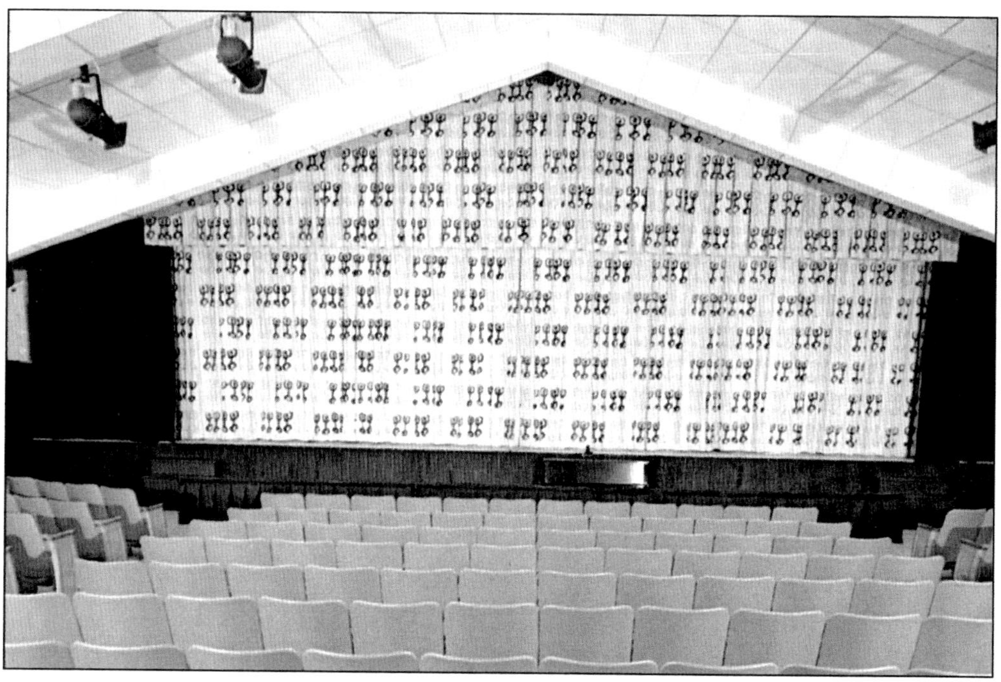

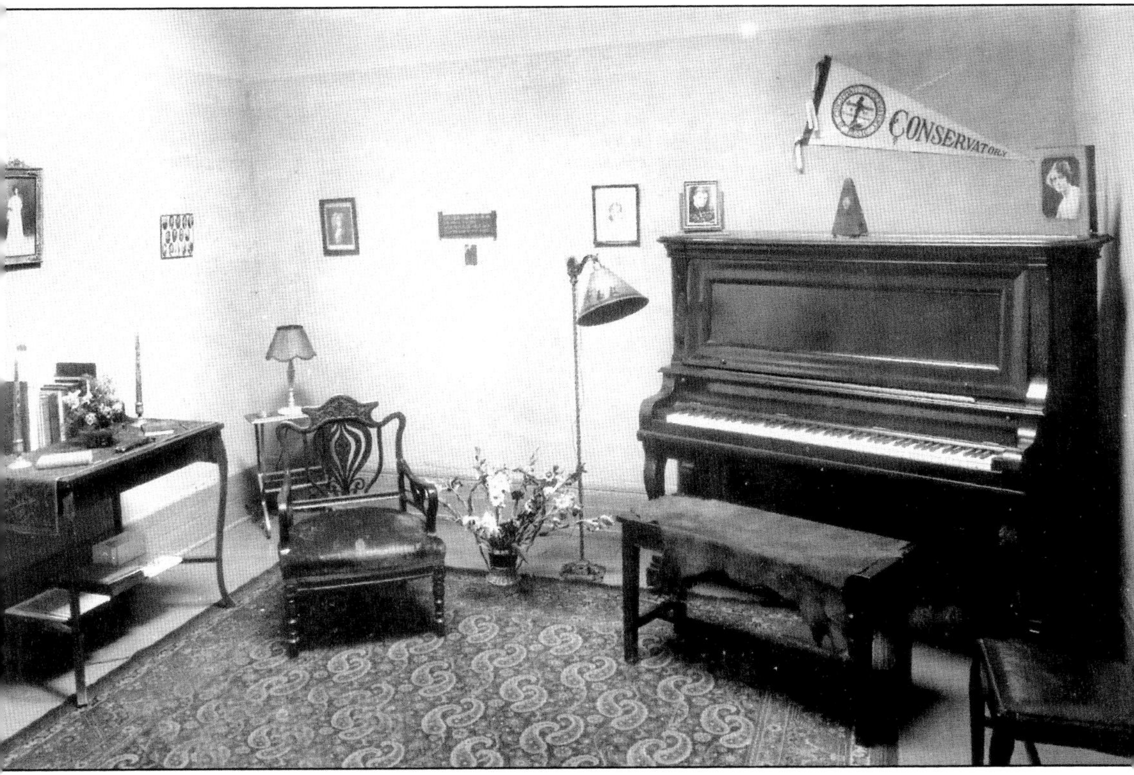

In the 1930s, the New Philadelphia Concert Orchestra was formed. In 1936, the organization officially became known as the Tuscarawas County Philharmonic Society. It staged its first outdoor concert at the New Philadelphia Concert Shell at Tuscora Park on August 2, 1936. Today, the orchestra, known as the Tuscarawas Philharmonic Orchestra, still performs each year in the concert shell. Eric Benjamin is the director.

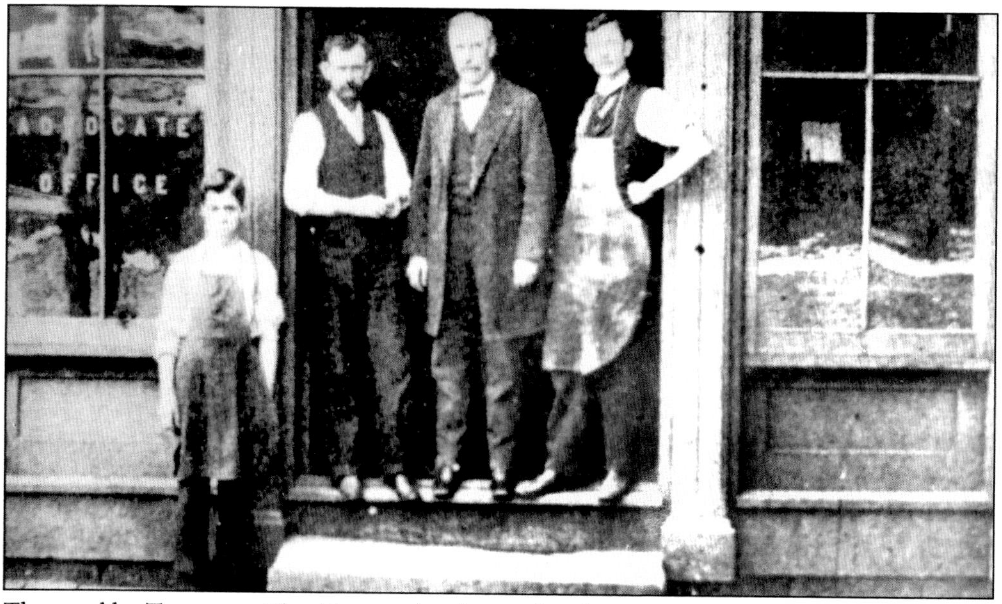

The weekly *Tuscarawas Chronicle* was the first and only newspaper published in Tuscarawas County for many years. Its first edition was dated August 24, 1819. It was a four-column, 11 by 18 inch folio with a $2 per year subscription. The publisher and editor was James Patrick of Belfast, Ireland. It became the *Advocate* in 1834 when Samuel Douglas bought the business. Two years later, Mr. Patrick repurchased the paper, publishing it until the spring of 1846. He sold the paper to his son Andrew while he went on to become a Tuscarawas County Common Pleas judge. Ownership of the *Advocate* changed many times. In 1865, McIlvane and Pittinger purchased it and appointed J.L. McIlvaine the sole publisher and editor.

Montag and Walter started *Der Deittsche Beobachter* in New Philadelphia in May 1869. In 1872, the name of the firm became Walter and Minnig. It was the only German newspaper and had strong Democratic political views. In September 1842, the first *Lutheran Standard* was issued from the basement of the Lutheran Church. Reverend E. Greenwold, pastor, was the editor. It was published for only two years, issuing its last publication on October 18, 1844.

During the latter half of the 19th century, 16 other newspapers appeared. Many succumbed to competition or to a dearth of subscribers. They included: *Ohio Democrat and Times* and the *Tribune* (both purchased by the *Daily Times*) and the *Iron Valley Reporter* (founded by Watson and Hull). In 1968, the *Daily Times* merged with the *Daily Reporter* to form the *Times Reporter.* In 1986, the *Times Reporter* acquired the *Evening Chronicle* of Uhrichsville-Dennison. In 1987, the paper was sold to Ingersoll Publications and operated under the umbrella of Community Newspapers Inc. until the Ingersoll Company filed for bankruptcy in 1990. The *Journal Register* purchased the conglomerate of Ingersoll newspapers. In 2000, the paper was once again sold and acquired by Copley Press Inc. of Copley, Ohio.

In 1949, Agnes Reeves, daughter of New Philadelphia business magnate Jeremiah E. Reeves, filed for ownership of radio frequency 1450 kHz. As a tribute to her father, Ms. Greer requested her father's initials as the radio station call letters—WJER. On February 21, 1950, WJER began broadcasting operations in the present studio facility at 656 Boulevard. WJER-FM 101.7 took to the airwaves in February 1969. Gary Petricola operates the station.

WTUZ-FM 99.9 premiered on Tuscarawas Valley radios on May 1, 1990. Station offices are located at 2424 East High Avenue with its transmitter on a hill in suburban Goshen. The station has been rated number one in the Arbitron surveys since its beginning and is owned by Ed Shumacher. WTUZ's most infamous broadcaster was Bob Jacobs, who was on the airwaves for almost 30 years.

Nine

Fire Departments and Major Fires

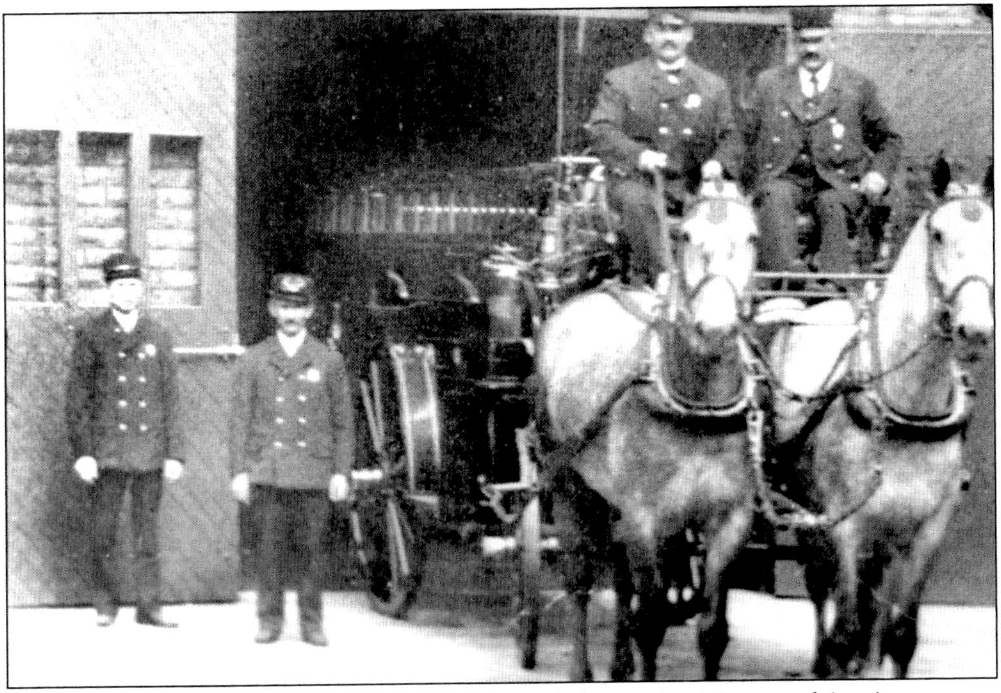

The first fire company was organized in 1859, and the Engine House and its cisterns were constructed on the courthouse lot in July 1860. When the Hook and Ladder Co. No. 1 of New Philadelphia organized, a hook and ladder truck and ladders were purchased. Then, a hand engine was purchased. In 1870, the Engine House had to be removed to build a new Courthouse at the site. Eagle Hall was constructed and would house the fire department, and the old Engine House was moved to the rear of the building. It is believed that the old hand pump was sent to the south side of New Philadelphia. In 1872, a steam fire engine was purchased and was used until 1883. On August 6, 1873, the city council ordered the Engine Company to recognize a hose company known as the Young American Hose Company as part of the fire department. George Knisely became Chief on July 1, 1906 and continued until 1926.

Also formed at this time was the engine company known as "The Relief Fire Engine Co. No. 1 of New Philadelphia," the second independently operated fire company. This station was located on the south side on Commercial Avenue. On April 3, 1877, the Relief Engine Company discontinued, and on March 7, the council resolved to pay the draymen to draw the engine to and from a fire. The building remains today and is owned by a church. It was two stories high, the first floor used for the apparatus in front and stalls for the horses in the rear. The second floor was used for living quarters for the firemen. Currently, the department is staffed with 22 firefighters, 15 of whom are paramedics. All firefighters are cross-trained for fire suppression and emergency medical services. The station is located at 108 Second Street SE and is staffed 24 hours a day, 7 days a week. Chief is Robert James Snyder II.

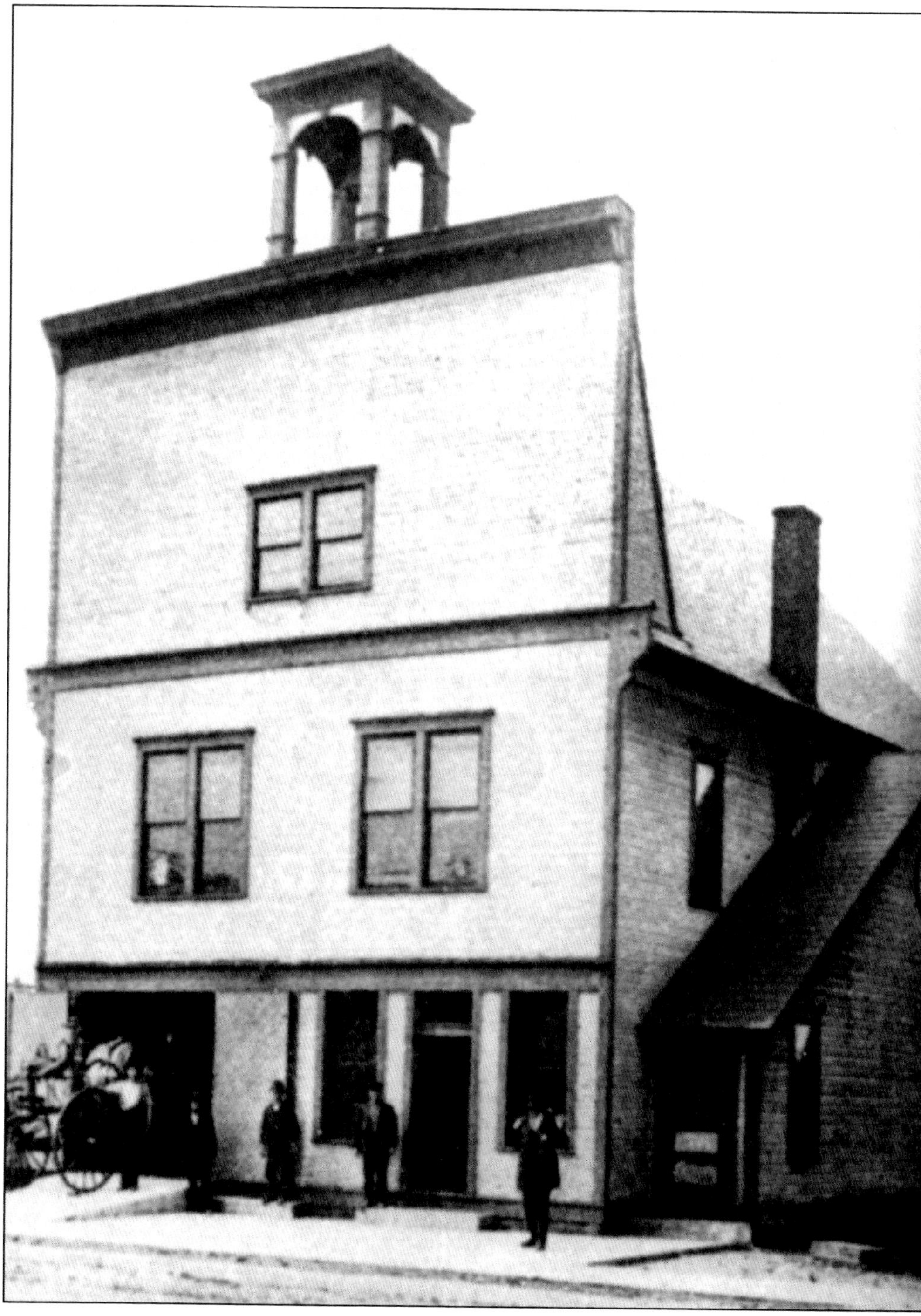

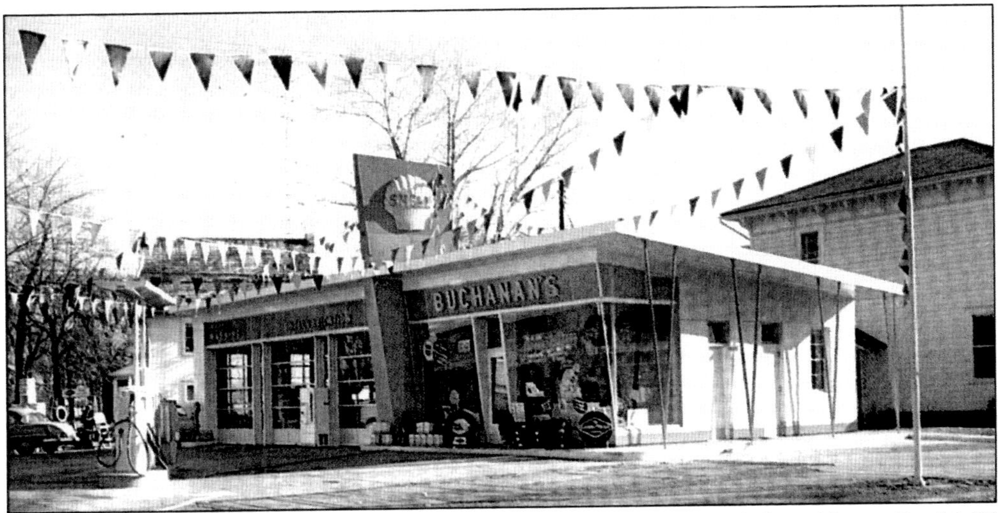

The first major fire was on Good Friday, March 25, 1910. It destroyed the Ridgway Feed Mill located on Allen Lane SW between South Broadway and First Drive SW.

Other major fires that have occurred over the years include: the Ridgway Feed Mill, completely destroyed on March 25, 1910; the Spicer Manufacturing, completely destroyed on May 10, 1916; the Union Country Club, completely destroyed on May 20, 1916; a woman and her son were the first recorded fire-related deaths in New Philadelphia on December 2, 1945; Walton's Auto Parts (South Broadway) with $35,000 damages on April 6, 1947; New Philadelphia Provision, completely destroyed on July 29, 1948; Cummins Diesel (1202 Kelly Street NW), completely destroyed on July 2, 1953; and Buchanan's Shell Station above (400 E. High Avenue), completely destroyed on February 15, 1958.

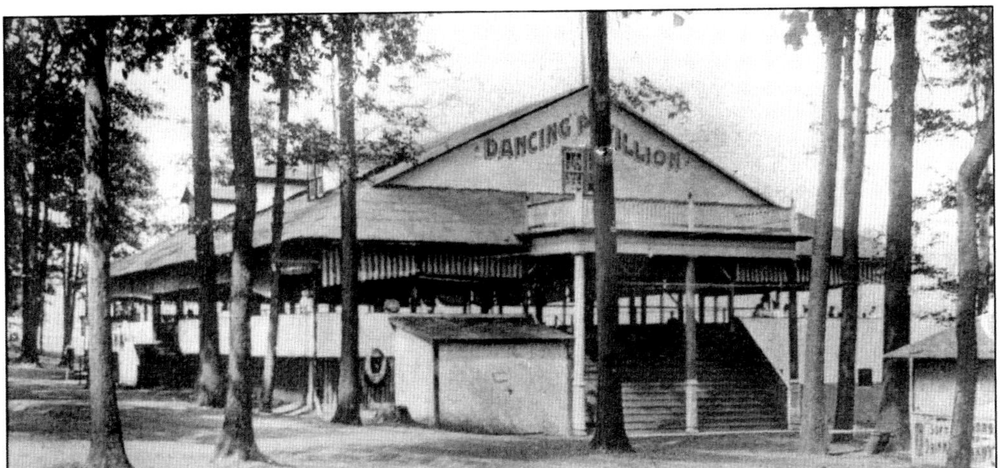

Major fires since 1958 include: the Tuscora Park roller rink, offices, and penny arcade, completely destroyed on January 10, 1961; Odd Fellows Hall (145-149 South Broadway), completely destroyed on January 6, 1968; the home of John Cookson on Third Street NW, completely destroyed on January 8, 1968; the Emmanuel Lutheran Church (corner of E. High Avenue and Second Street SE), destroyed on August 9, 1970; the Goshen Dairy barn (139 Second Street NW), destroyed on March 1972; the Front Avenue Elementary (248 Front Avenue SW), gutted on October 23, 1976; and the Apartment House (214 South Broadway) destroyed on January 4, 1979.

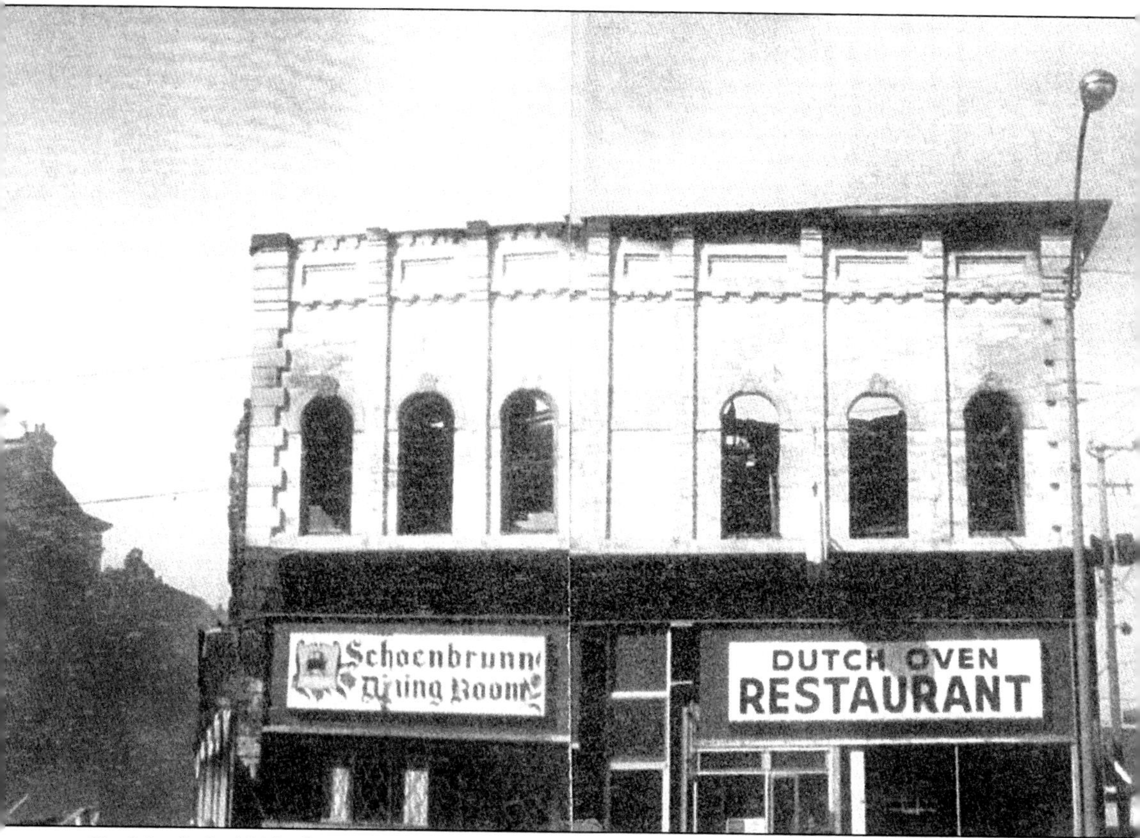

On March 3, 1983, the worst fire in the history of New Philadelphia occurred, destroying five businesses along the 100 block of East High Avenue and Court Street. The businesses were Marlin's Shoes, Bond's Shoes, Williams Furniture, Dutch Oven Restaurant (above), and Tedrick's Barber Shop. All were destroyed for a loss of $1,043,000.

On March 4, 1990, the New Philadelphia High School fire gutted several rooms causing the High School and Junior High to close. High School students were moved to Buckeye Career Center and Kent State University. Junior High students attended school at several area churches.

The majority of these major fires occurred within blocks of the New Philadelphia Fire Department. The overwhelming devastation is not due to the fire fighters skills, but the fact that most of these buildings were built between the early 1800s and early 1900s when the city was just beginning.

Ten

Public Buildings, Monuments, and Historic Streets

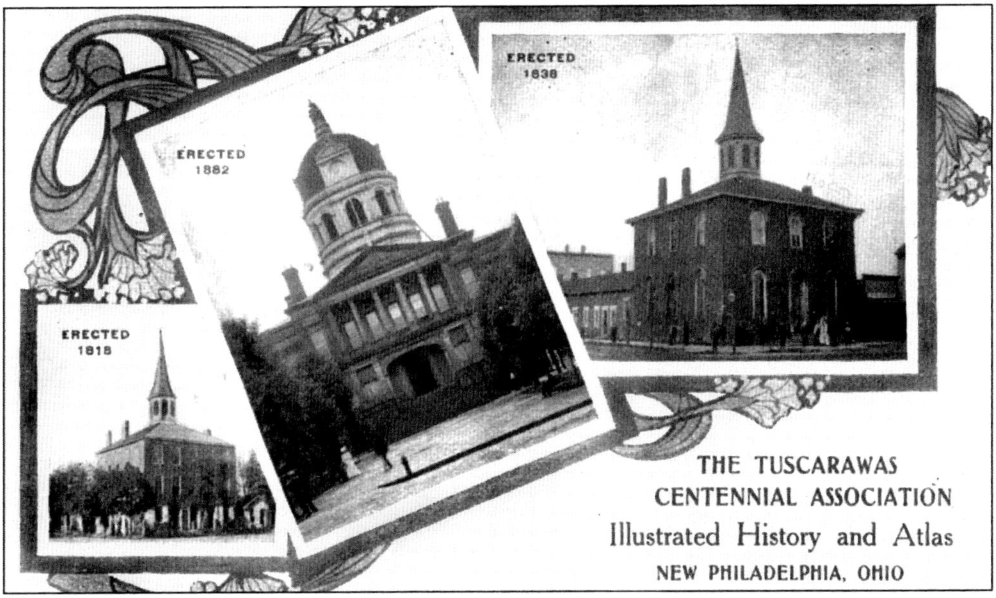

On March 15, 1808, Tuscarawas County became the 27th county to be officially recognized by the State of Ohio, and on June 28, 1808, county commissioners authorized the construction of a two-story structure with a jail on the first floor and county offices on the second. A contract for this log building, which also served as a church and school, was given to Peter Minnich for $1,500. It was 30 foot by 40 foot and was constructed on lots donated by John Knisely.

In 1818, the county had outgrown the building, and the commissioners advertised for a new building. It was not completed for seven years, so the 1825 commissioners rented an upstairs room in the Masonic Lodge No. 59 for $12 per year. The Courthouse was completed at a cost of $7,468. Its architecture resembled the original state capital building in Chillicothe. The courtroom and the clerk and auditor offices were on the first floor. The second floor had a separate room for juries. On December 7, 1825, Sheriff Blake took charge of the new structure. The courtroom occupied the entire first floor after renovations in 1837 following fire damage. A weathervane in the shape of a fish on top of a ball on a long red rod, known as the "weatherfish," sat atop the Courthouse. Louis Zellner salvaged the weatherfish from the Courthouse upon construction of the third courthouse. Large holes discovered in the weathervane ball are believed to be bullet holes from guns fired by Civil War veterans during their returning-home parade and celebration. Zellner placed the weatherfish on top of the H and A Drug Store located in a new block of businesses on West High Avenue. The weatherfish was finally taken down after storm damage, and today, the Michael Johnson family carefully stores the weatherfish.

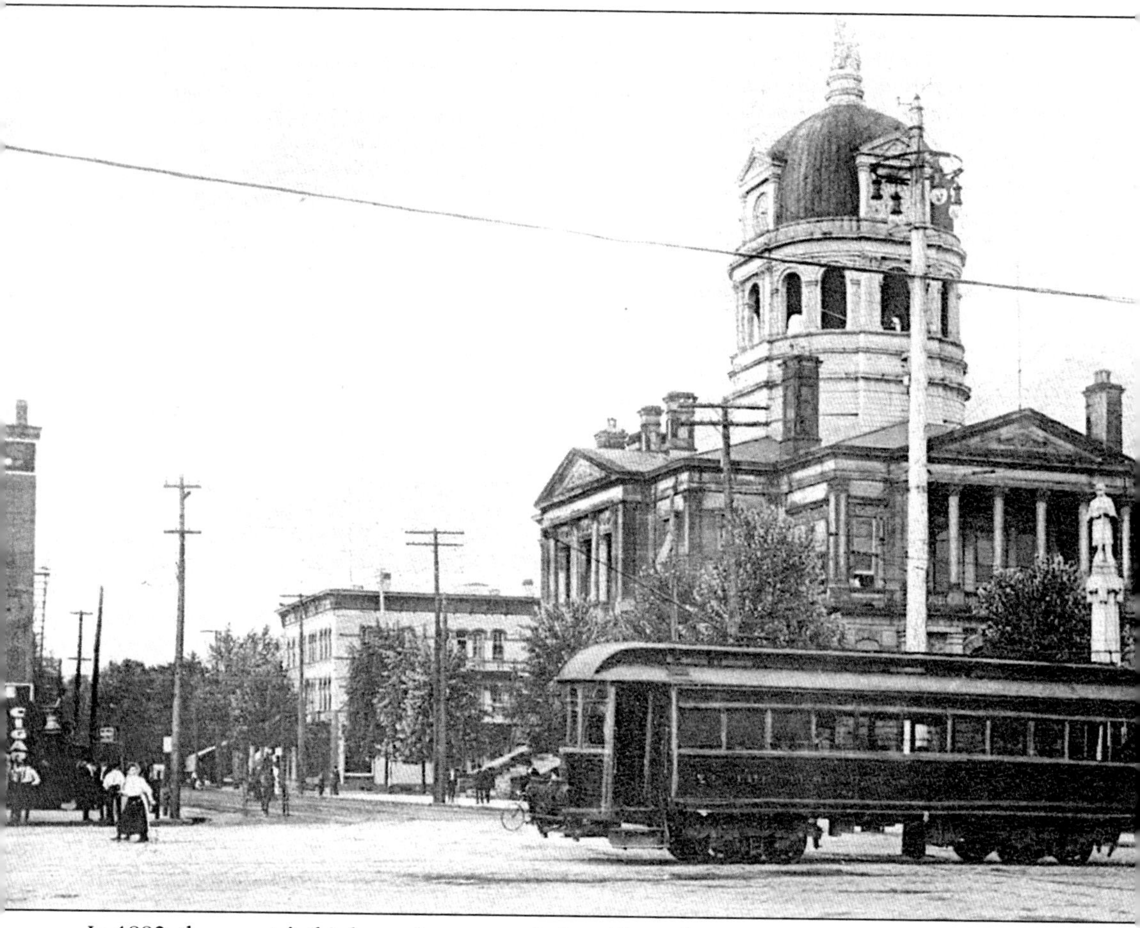

In 1882, the county's third courthouse was designed by architect Thomas Boyd and built by T.B. Townsend of Zanesville for $98,860. Townsend purchased the old building from the county for $900 and used the bricks under the new building. On October 25, 1882, over 10,000 people attended the cornerstone-laying ceremony after a two-mile-long parade that converged on the Public Square. Special railroad track were built to the site of the Courthouse to carry stone for the building from a Medina quarry. The building was 96 foot by 112 foot with 38 rooms on three floors and an attic.

A dome was constructed atop this Courthouse with a 10-foot-wide statue, the Three Ladies of Justice, made from zinc or lead-like metal weighing more than 699 pounds. It was removed for safety reasons in 1959. The ladies' heads are displayed in the commissioners' boardroom. Topping the dome today is a cupola, which was lifted into place by a helicopter on July 26, 1973. Currently, the Courthouse houses the Common Pleas courtrooms and administrative offices. The ground floor houses the County Law Library and Board of Elections.

The 1882 Courthouse is on the National Register of Historic Buildings and houses an 1888 Seth Thomas clock with solid brass gears. It is 8 foot tall and has a 225-pound solid cast iron pendulum. The faces on the outside are 6 foot in diameter made of glass one inch thick. The clock has to be wound once a week with the help of a small motor, and a hammer rings the bell.

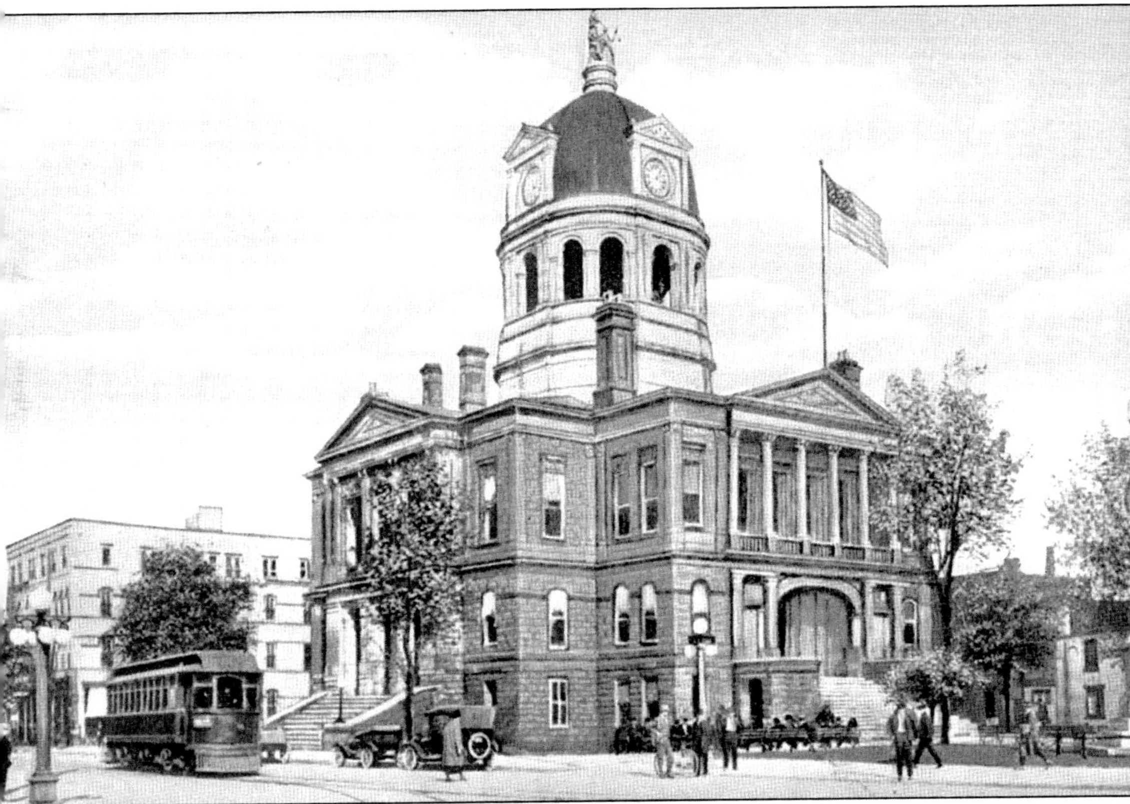

During 1995 and 1996, renovations were made to the 1882 Courthouse with design help from Fisher and Associates Architects Inc. to restore the building to its original splendor. The wood trim was stripped to its original black walnut color, the ceramic tile floors were cleaned and repaired, the ceilings were raised to the original 14 foot height, and the walls were painted in historic Victorian color schemes. A canvas mural depicting lady justice complete with scales and sword was discovered beneath a lowered ceiling. It was restored and framed and is on display in one of the courtrooms. Murals on the rotunda walls were renewed depicting historical scenes in the county, including a steel mill on the east wall, ox-drawn farm equipment and gasoline powered equipment on the west wall, pioneers arriving in covered wagons on the south wall, and cabins that housed the pioneers on the north wall. The rotunda also features four painted portraits that were finally labeled during the renovation: Colonel Mathias Bartilson, former Tuscarawas County prosecuting attorney and a Civil War colonel on the south wall; Robert Hunter Nugen, former superintendent to the Ohio-Erie Canal, member of the US House of Representatives, as well as a delegate to the Democratic National Convention in 1860 on the east wall; George W. McIlvaine, former mayor of New Philadelphia, Tuscarawas County Common Pleas judge and Ohio Supreme Court Justice on the north wall; and Charles H. Mitchener, former judge and co-founder of local newspaper the *Ohio Democrat* on the west wall.

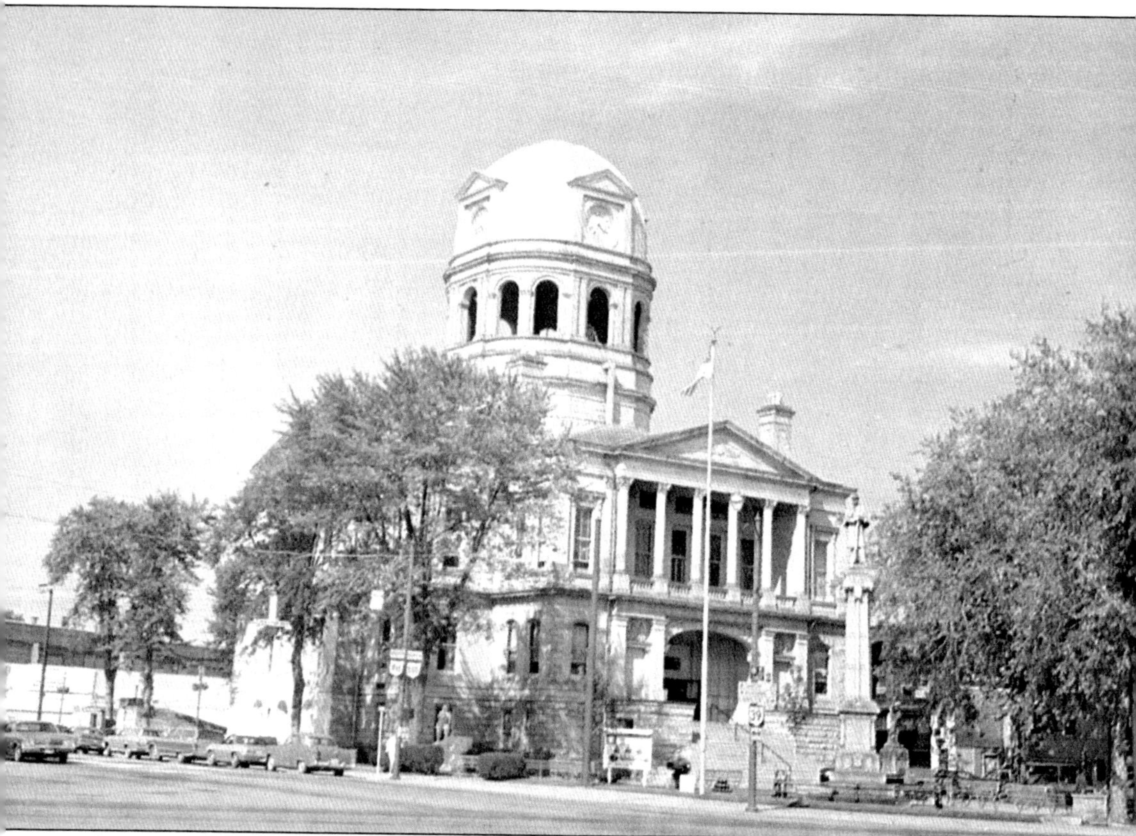

On October 27, 1900, the Tuscarawas County Office Building, adjacent to the Courthouse, was dedicated and opened to the public. The building was designed by MKC Associates Inc. and has a total of 54,500 square feet. The county obtained the land after a fire destroyed the existing building on the lot.

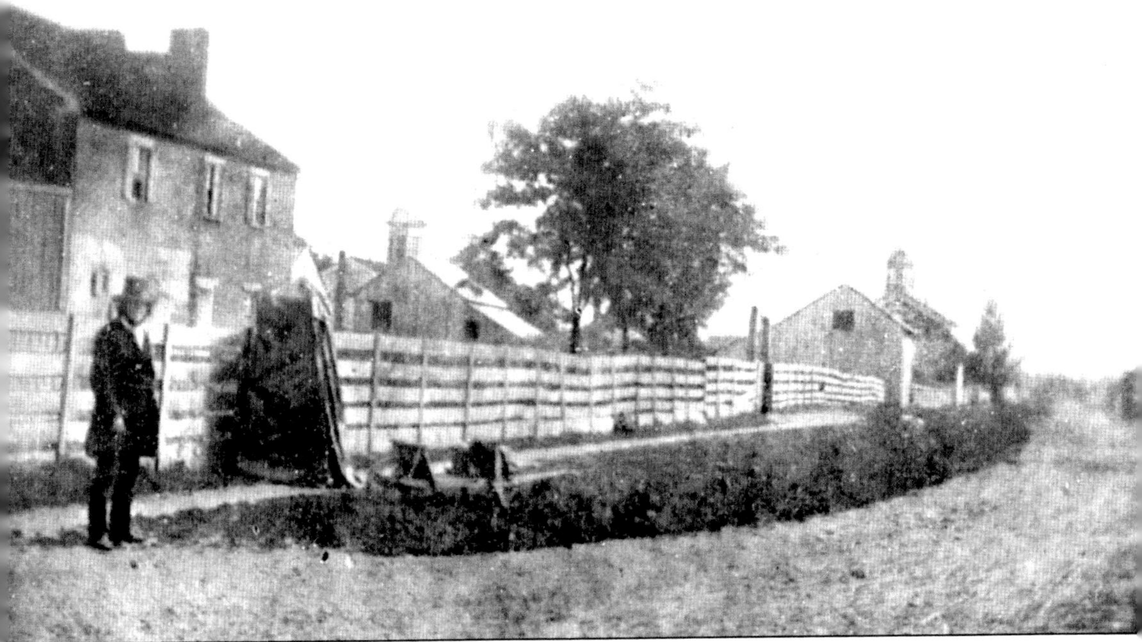

The first jail in New Philadelphia was a log structure built shortly after the county was founded in 1807. The second county jail was built on the corner of Second Street and Fair Avenue (now a parking lot) in 1870. The jail housed the sheriff and his wife on the second floor for many years. The jail was used until the 1990s when a new structure was built on Reiser Avenue.

The Funston Hanging, at the corner of Tuscarawas and West High Avenues (Allentown), was the only public execution in Tuscarawas County. On September 8, 1825, William Cartmell, a post-boy on the Freeport-Coshocton route, was murdered at the village later named Post Boy. Cartmell's companion William Johnson discovered the crime and found a young man rifling through the mail. The stranger fled, and later, Johnson was accused. In a desperate effort to be cleared, he called all young men of Tuscarawas County to assemble at New Philadelphia. From the group, Johnson singled out John Funston and accused him. During the two-day trial in November, Funston had three defense attorneys and pled innocent, but was found guilty and was sentenced to die. On December 29th, Funston tried to hang himself in his cell with his suspenders, but they broke. Later that evening, he made a confession to James Patrick, publisher of the *Chronicle*, saying he intended to kill and rob a Coshocton merchant and cattle drover that always carried a large sum of money and who had planned to take that road. The merchant had been delayed on his trip, and Funston killed Cartmell by mistake. He was executed by hanging on December 30, 1825. William Blake of Blake's Mill was sheriff during the Funston Hanging.

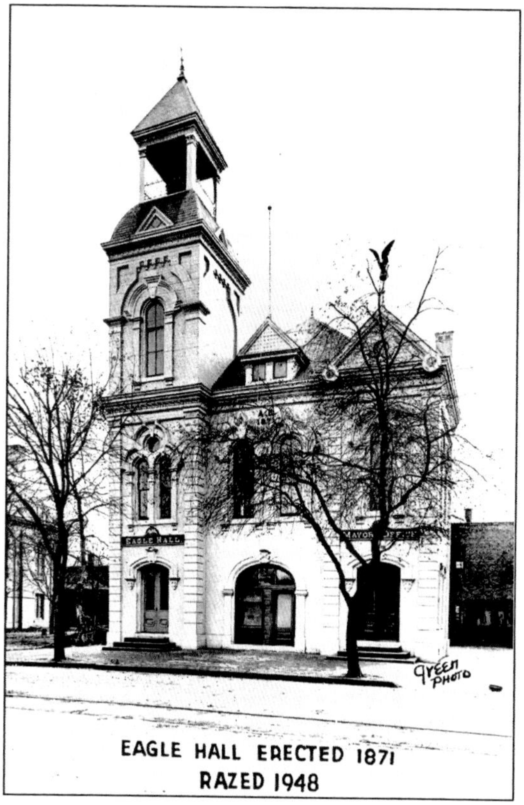

Eagle Hall was a large brick structure, standing on the southwest corner of High and Third Streets. It was built in 1871 by the Council of New Philadelphia at a cost of $22,000. The first floor contained the mayor's office, the fire department, and cells for offenders of the peace and dignity of the law. The second floor was a spacious public hall. To the rear of the building was the Fire Department. The structure was razed in 1941. A new municipal hall was constructed in 1950. The beautiful new Municipal Memorial City Hall was constructed at a cost of $150,000. The keys were handed to Mayor Fred Schneider during a council meeting on April 14, 1952.

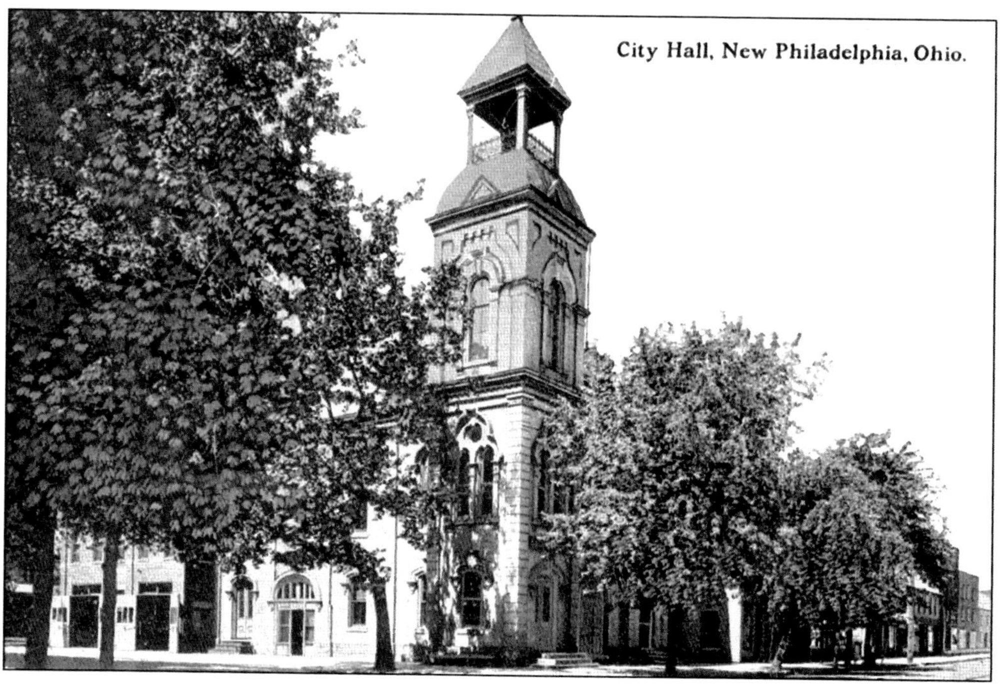

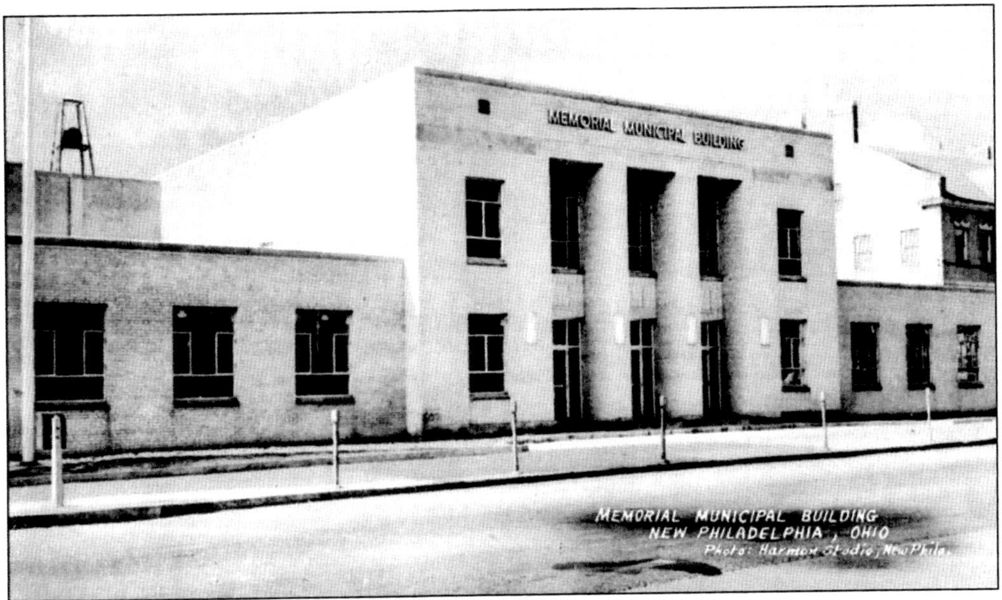

Built in the late 1920s, the distinguished Elks building stood as a center of social activity in New Philadelphia until city officials bought it in March 2000. Purchased for $700,000, the former social hall was slated to be a new Municipal Court. Plans fell through, and the council decided to convert it into a city hall. Total cost of the project, including the purchase of the building at $700,000 and the engineering plans were estimated to be about $2.5 million. The new building is now known as the John Knisely Municipal Centre. The original front entrance remains for cosmetic purposes only. Offices located in this facility include the Health Department, Auditor's Office, Water Billings Office, Income Tax Department, Mayor's Office, Safety Director, Clerk of Council, Prosecutor's Office, as well as Council Chambers with a seating capacity of 70. The third floor serves as a historical and archive room, additional storage space, and potential inter-department growth.

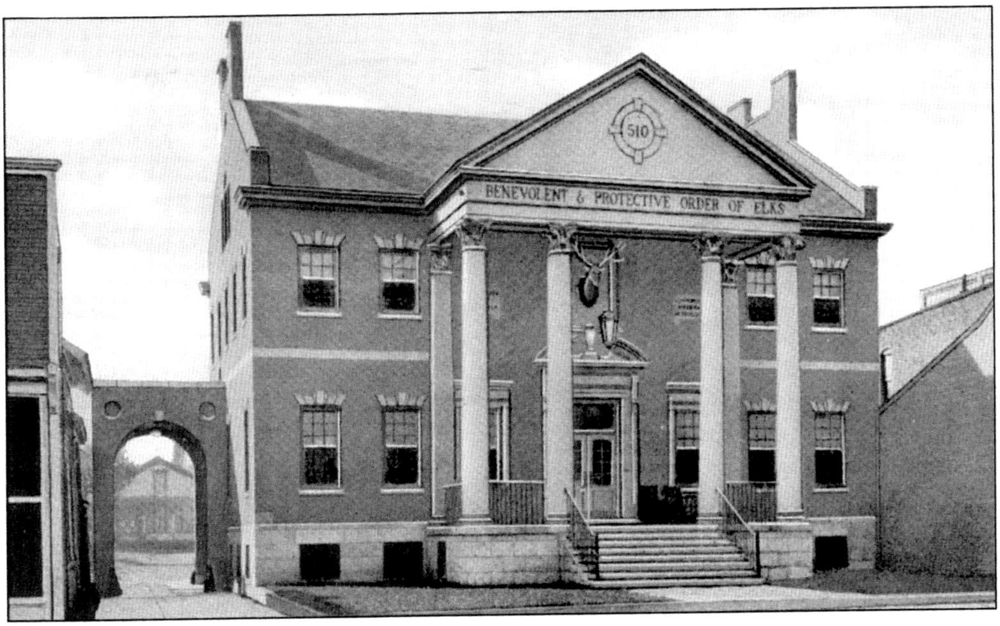

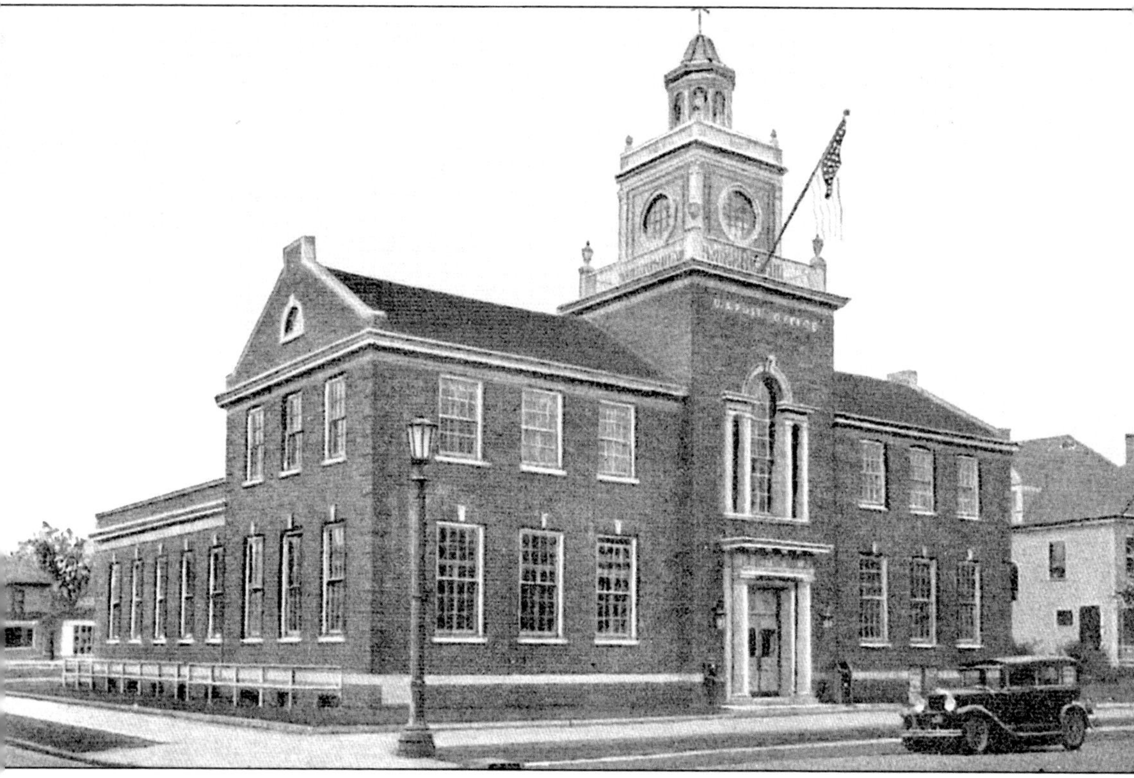

The first route of the rural free mail delivery out of New Philadelphia was started in 1902. New Philadelphia's Post Office, located on the corner of North Broadway and Fair Avenue NE, was built in 1929, modeled after Independence Hall in Philadelphia. The exterior walls are tapestry brick trimmed with limestone. Dominant features of the exterior are the multiple-paned windows and the cupola, which surmounts the entrance tower. Edwin B. Morris of Washington DC designed it.

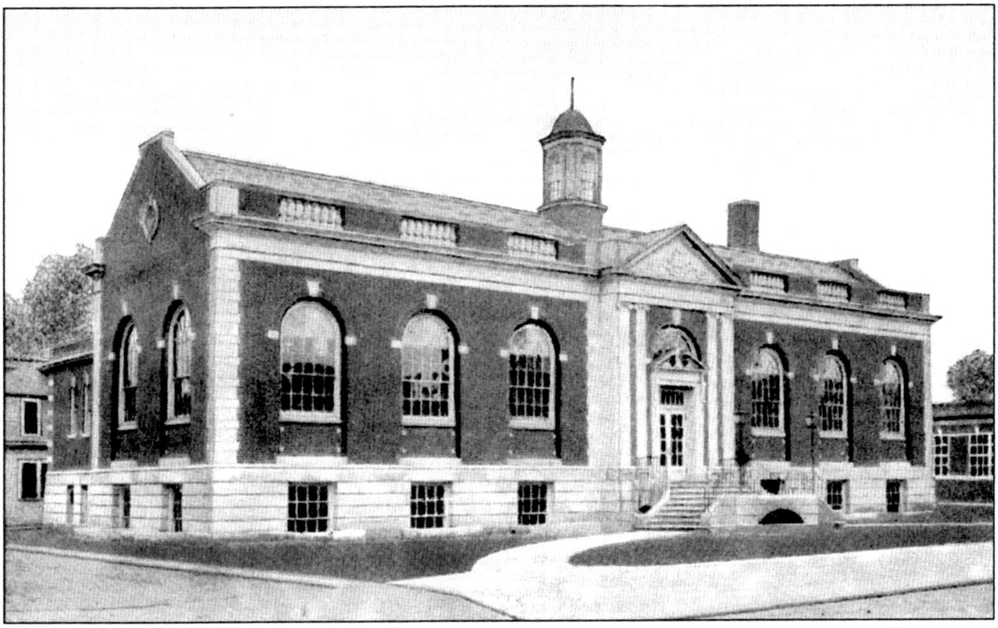

The Tuscarawas County Public Library is red brick with Indiana limestone corresponding to the general outline of the Post Office beside it. It was dedicated on February 7, 1937. In 1909, the Union Library Association deeded all of its books and furniture to the New Philadelphia Board of Education and the administration of a library then located in the Odd Fellows Building. In 1936, construction of a new building on the corner of West Fair Street and First Drive was completed in 1936. The library remained under the jurisdiction of the New Philadelphia Board of Education until 1948. The Board of Library Trustees petitioned the Tuscarawas County Commissioners to create a Tuscarawas County Public Library District, which was done with school board approval. In doing so, the library was removed from the jurisdiction of the New Philadelphia Board of Education.

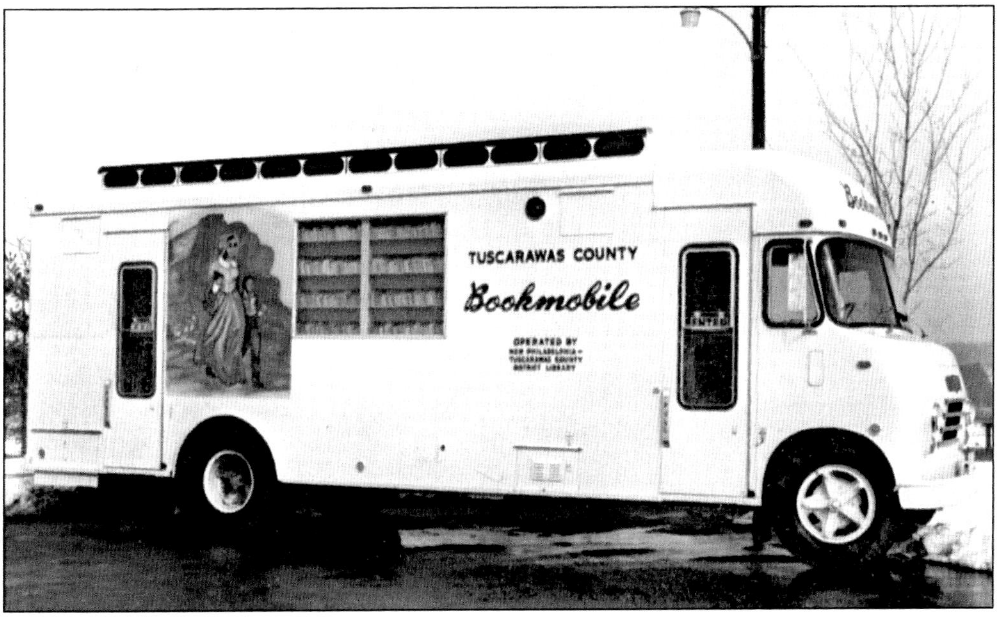

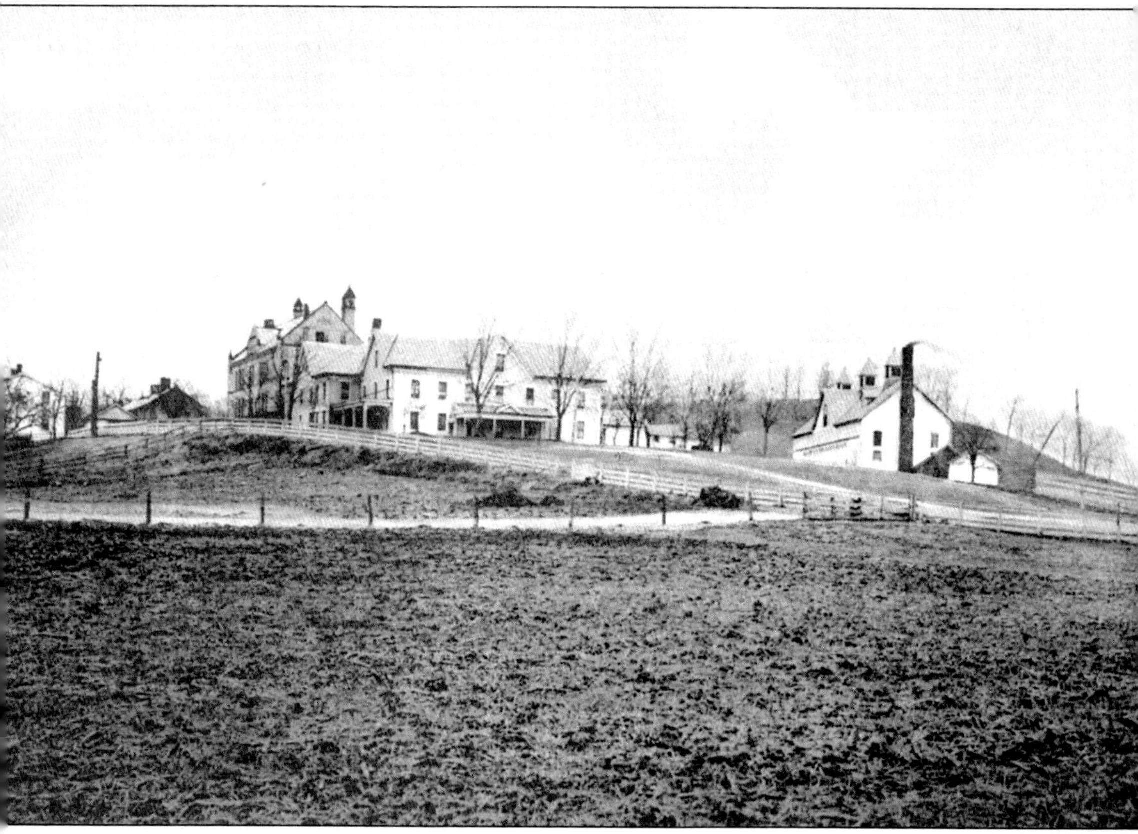

Approximately three miles southeast of New Philadelphia sits a two-story, 100-room fireproof building of deep, buff wire-cut brick built in 1929. The portico of the center section of the Tuscarawas County Infirmary was adorned with tall white columns. The 416-acre tract included a portion of the original area of Schoenbrunn. It provided care for those who had no relatives and could no longer take care of themselves. The name of the facility was changed to Colonial Manor in 1990.

Located next to the Tuscarawas County Infirmary, the Sanatorium was a low T-shaped building with isolation rooms for approximately 40 patients. The one-story building was built of wire-cut buff brick. Today, only one building of the Infirmary exists, extensively remodeled, known as the Tuscarawas County Attention Center on University Drive.

The Tuscarawas County Children's Home was located on South Tuscarawas Avenue for nearly a decade in the residence of Augustus Wilhelm. Wilhelm sold the home and farm to the county in 1881 for $25,000 for the establishment of an orphanage. The residence was a two-story square brick structure. Later, an addition was added, and the farm served the community for 74 years. The number of children housed in the institution was more than 100 reaching a peak of 150 during the 1933 depression. George W. Kelly, 723 East High Avenue, served as superintendent.

Starlight Enterprises Inc. (SEI), at 638 Commercial Avenue, is part of the Tuscarawas County Board of Mental Retardation and Development Disabilities where more than 180 employees do subcontract packaging, assembly, mailings, janitorial services, signage, engraving, woodworking, and more for area businesses. SEI's non-profit corporation formed in 1975, offering training programs to its employees in the hope that area businesses will employ them.

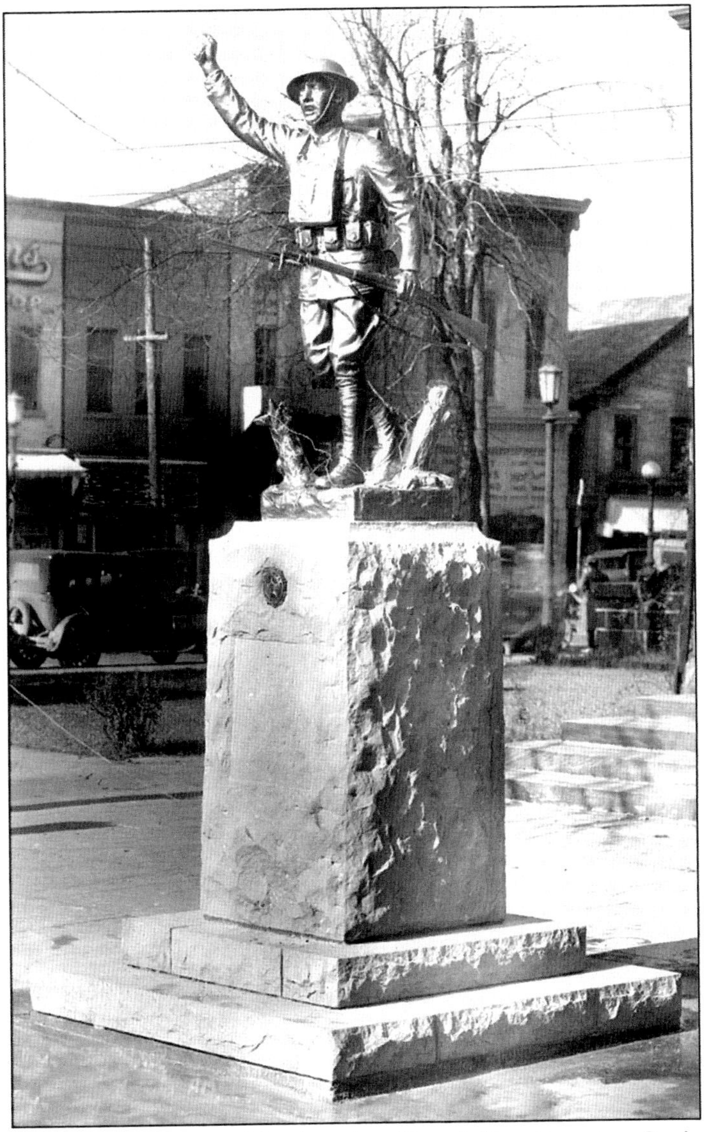

The World War I statue, the Spirit of the American Dough-Boy (American Legion Monument), was dedicated on Armed Forces Day (Memorial Day) in 1929. The Dough Boy is a life-sized, helmeted American soldier in bronze in the act of throwing a grenade. The monument stands 15 feet high, including the square stone base. Mrs. Clyde Stewart and Mrs. John Ellwood unveiled the monument, erected by the Mothers of Boys in Service. The dedication was delayed for over six months because the original monument was broken in shipment, and a new one had to be recast. James Knapp designed the landscaping around the memorial.

The WWII and Korean Conflict monument sits on the west side of the courthouse and commemorates the WWII and Korean Conflict. The Vietnam Veterans Memorial is located directly in front of the entrance to the County Office Building. This memorial commemorates the Vietnam War and those killed during service, listing all those from this county that were killed during service. There is a separate wall for each division of service. The Desert Storm Memorial is the newest monument and is closest to East High Avenue. It commemorates the Desert Storm conflict, also known as the Gulf War.

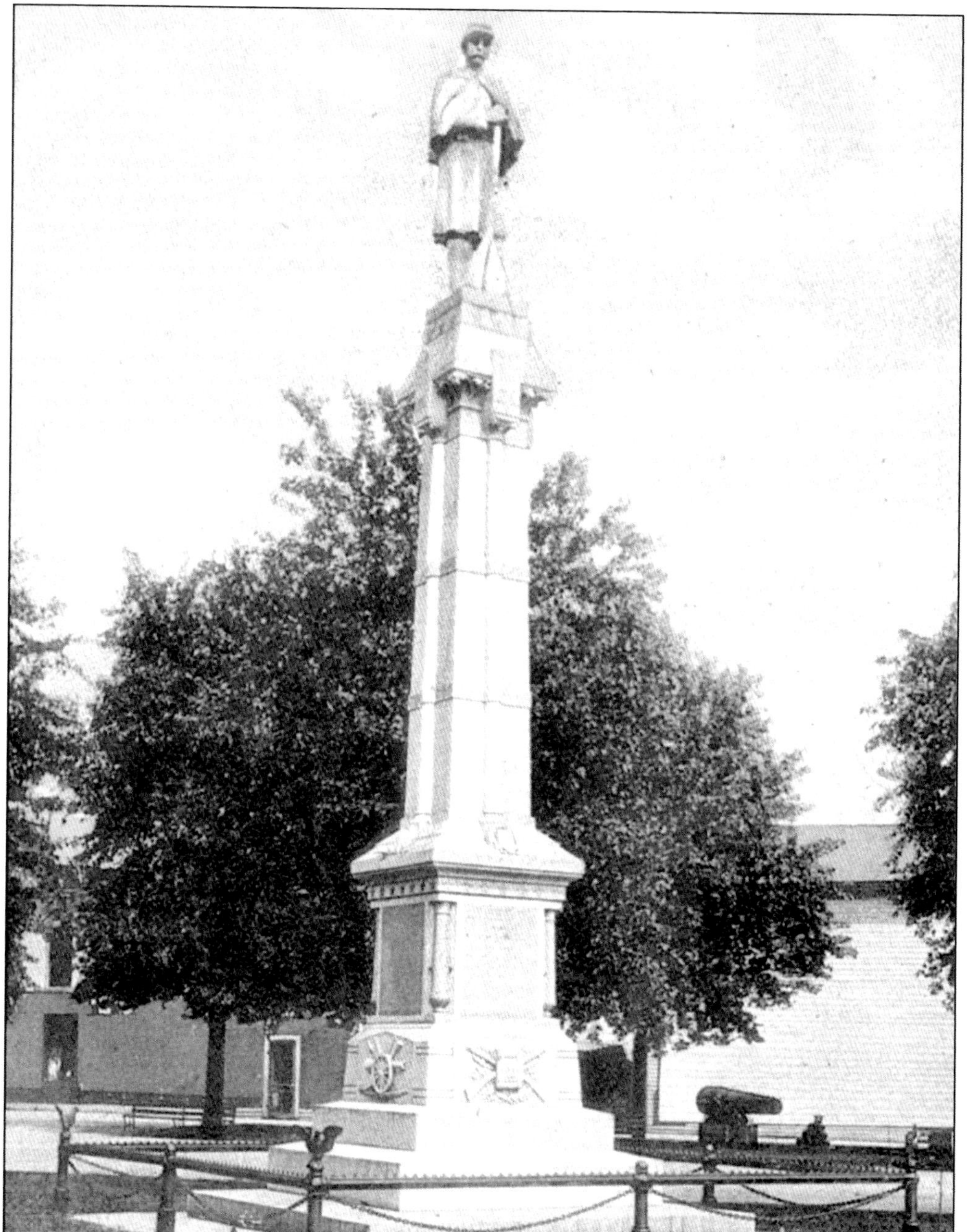

Erected in 1887, the granite Soldier's Monument, "The Sentinel," is a life-sized figure of a Union infantryman. It has a 12-foot square base and stands 35 feet tall. Major Henry Kaldenbaugh served in the 51st infantry division in the Civil War. He left a bequest in his will for the construction of the monument to honor GAR (Union) soldiers of the Civil War. Tuscarawas County had 3,357 men serve during the Civil War. Congressman William McKinley (who later became president of the United States) delivered the dedicatory address on May 19, 1887. Mayor of New Philadelphia, Daniel Korns who had been a captain in the 80th Ohio Regiment, presided at the monument dedication.

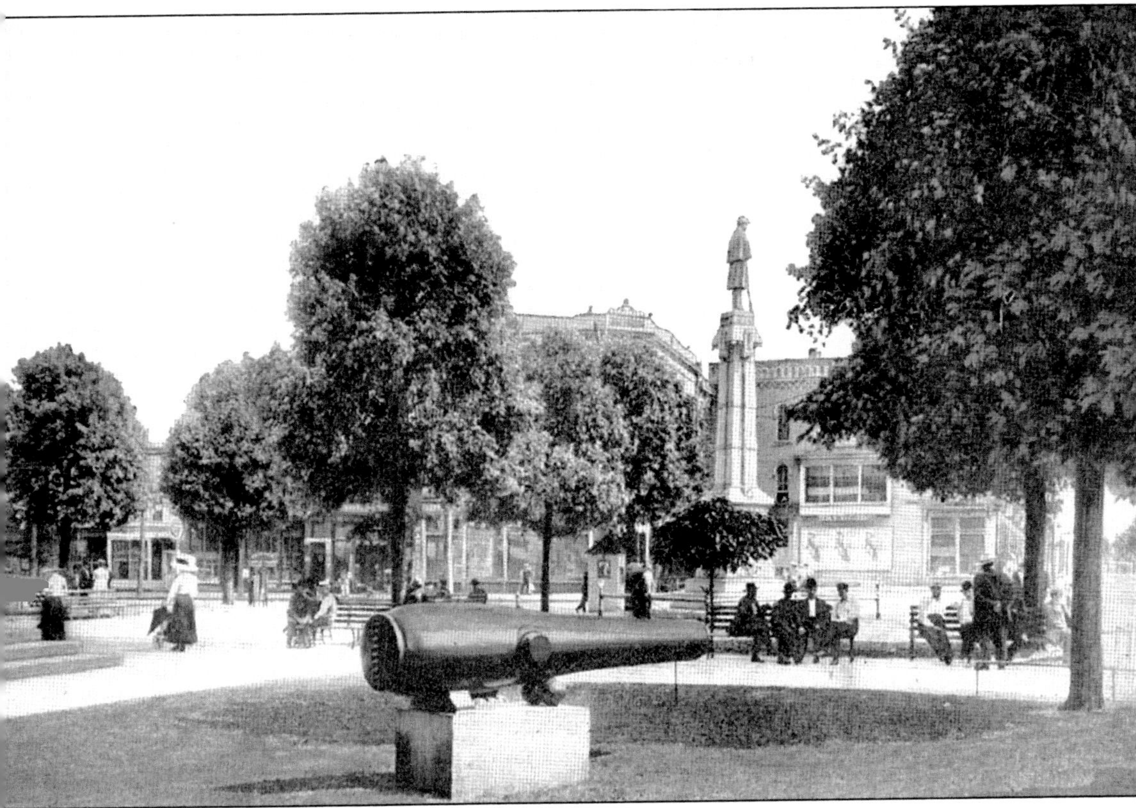

The Cannons and Cannon Balls are original and were used during the Civil War. There are round knobs on the cannon, allowing it to sit on the "cradle." When in the cradle, they were used to point the cannons to different elevations and move it in different directions.

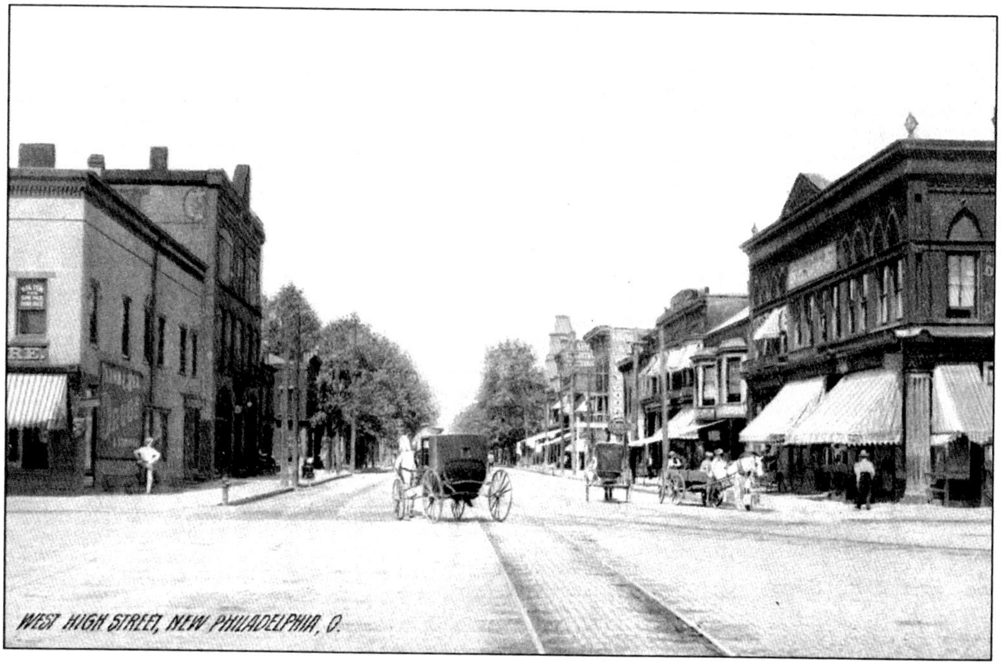

These postcards show two views of historic West High Avenue.

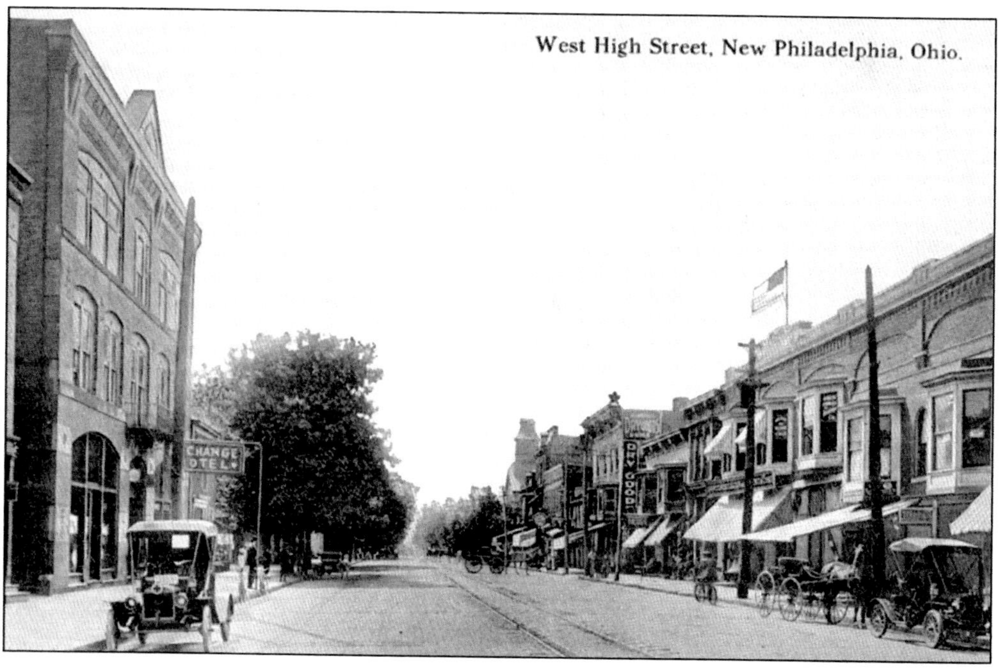

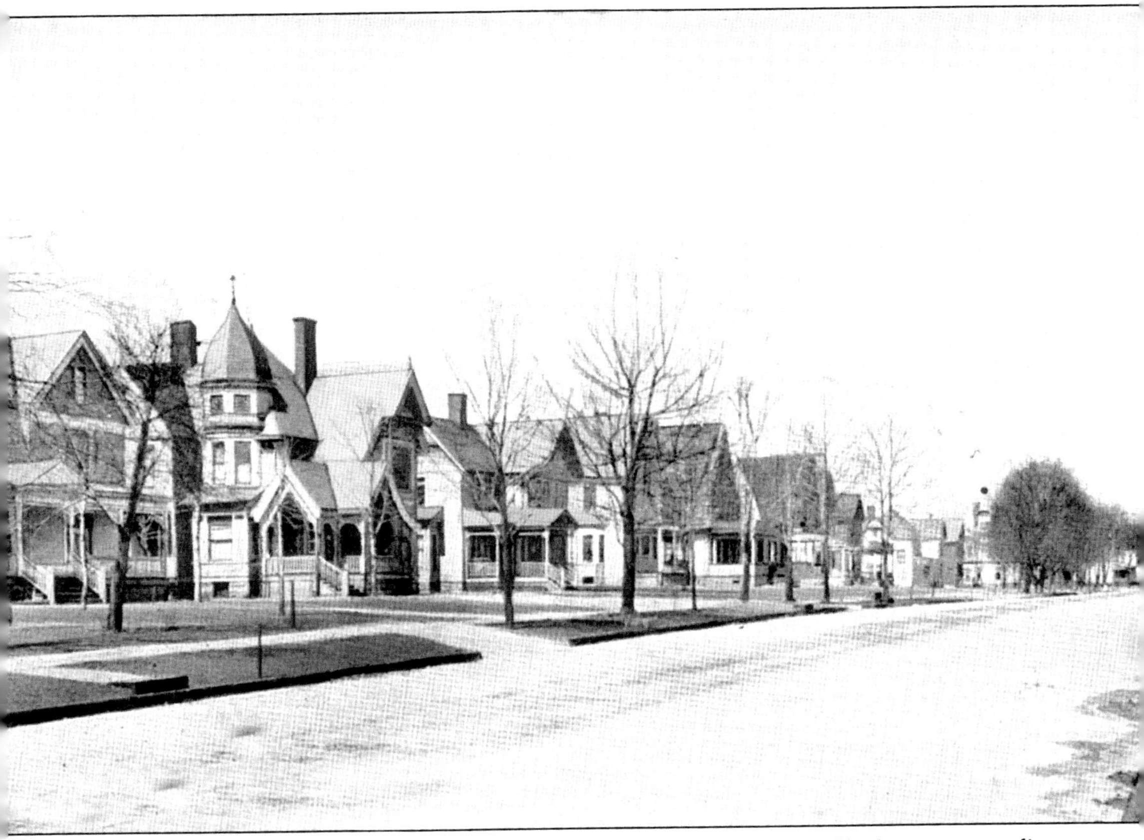

The Donahey residence on North Broadway opposite Tuscora Park affords a commanding view of the city and surrounding countryside. It originally sat on 15 acres (now part of the Donahey addition).

Alvin Victor "Vic" Donahey, the first governor of Ohio to serve three consecutive terms beginning in 1922, was known as the foremost vote getter of his day. A candidate for elective office 11 times, he was defeated only once, in a landslide of the opposition party. His majority in the election for the United States Senate set a record that still stands today. Vic attended school at New Philadelphia High, but quit in his junior year to learn the printing trade. He bought a print shop of his own at the age of 20.

Donahey served as clerk of the Goshen Township Board of Trustees. In 1905, he was elected county auditor and served for two terms. He also was a member of the Board of Education. In 1911, he was elected a delegate to the Fourth Ohio Constitutional Convention, which met the following year. By political convention time in 1912, he had attracted the attention of party leaders who caused him to be nominated for state auditor where he served two four-year terms. Nicknames given to him during his career included "Honest Vic," "Watchdog of the Treasury," and "Veto Vic." Vic moved to Columbus in 1929. He later served one term as Senator for Ohio from 1934 to 1940. Vic Donahey died in April 1946 and is buried at New Philadelphia.

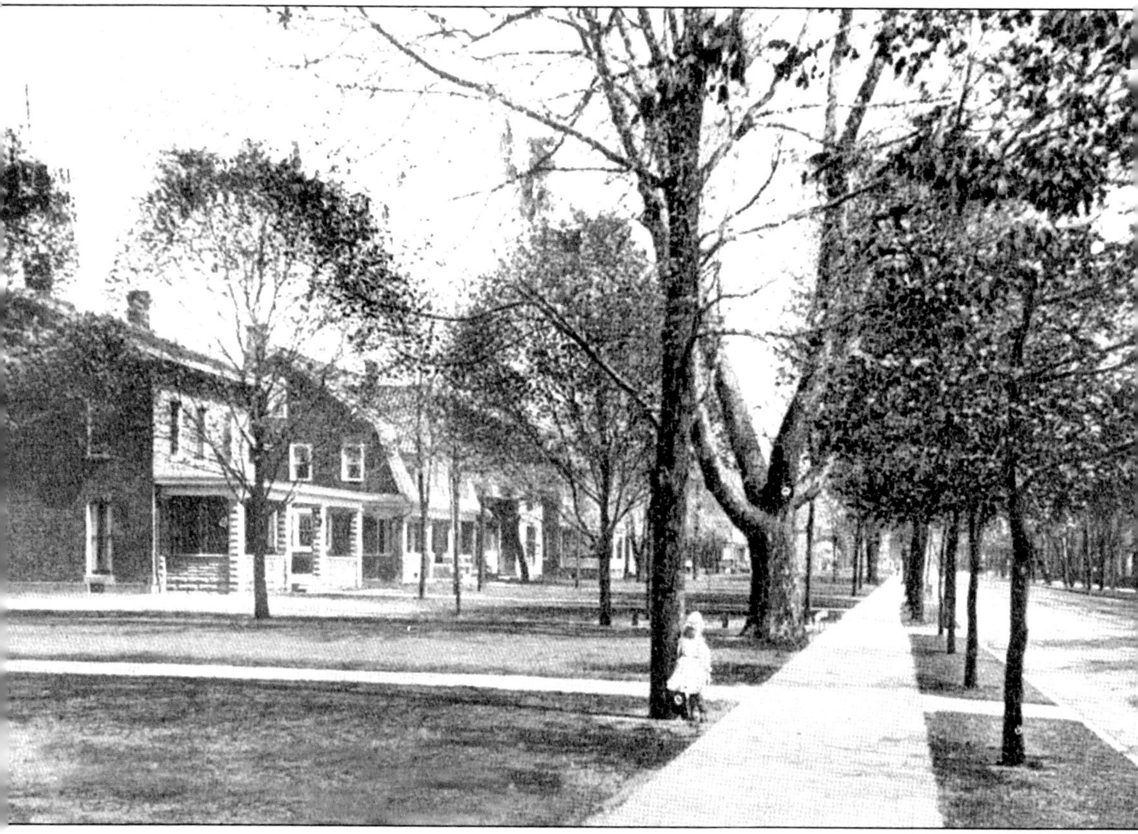

This postcard shows a view of the tree lined street and the lovely homes of East Avenue.

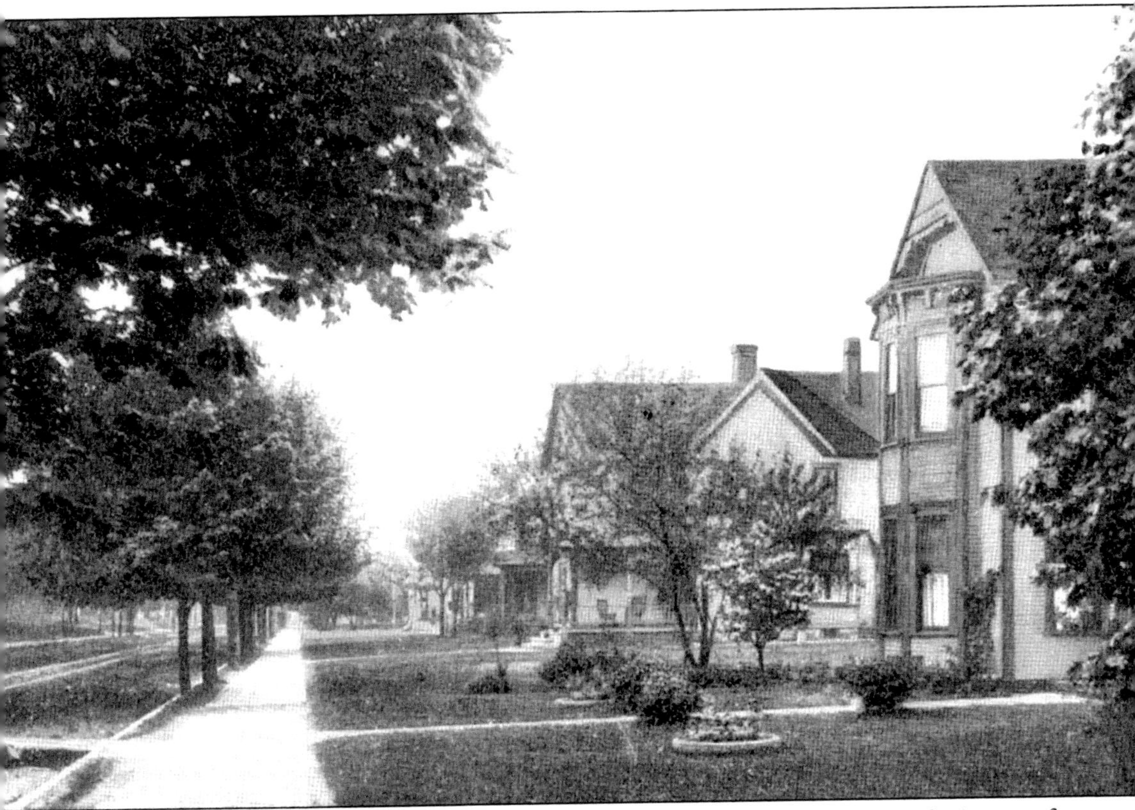

The beautifully landscaped yards and large homes are displayed in this postcard picture of Tuscarawas Avenue.

Many of these historic homes are owned by members of the "Heritage Homes Society." These well-kept and historically renovated homes are often referred to as "painted ladies."

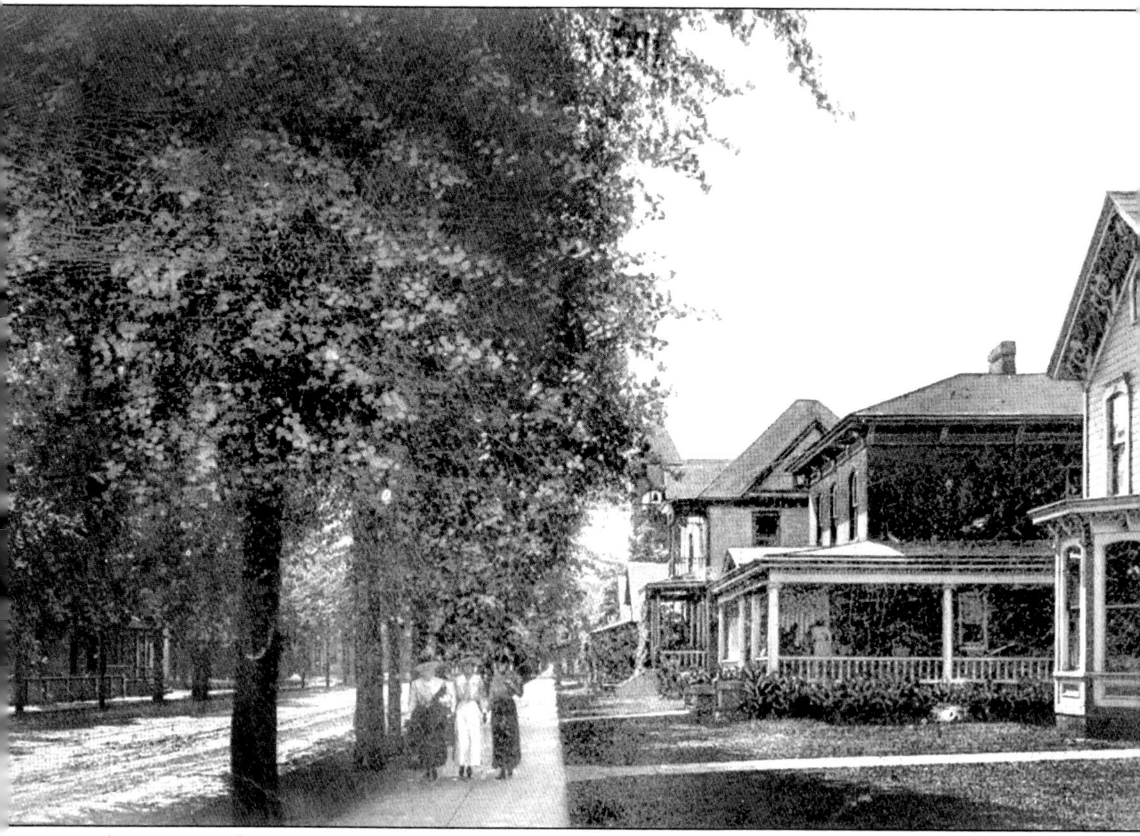

This image of West Fair Street shows off the large porches and neighborhood that invites evening strolls.

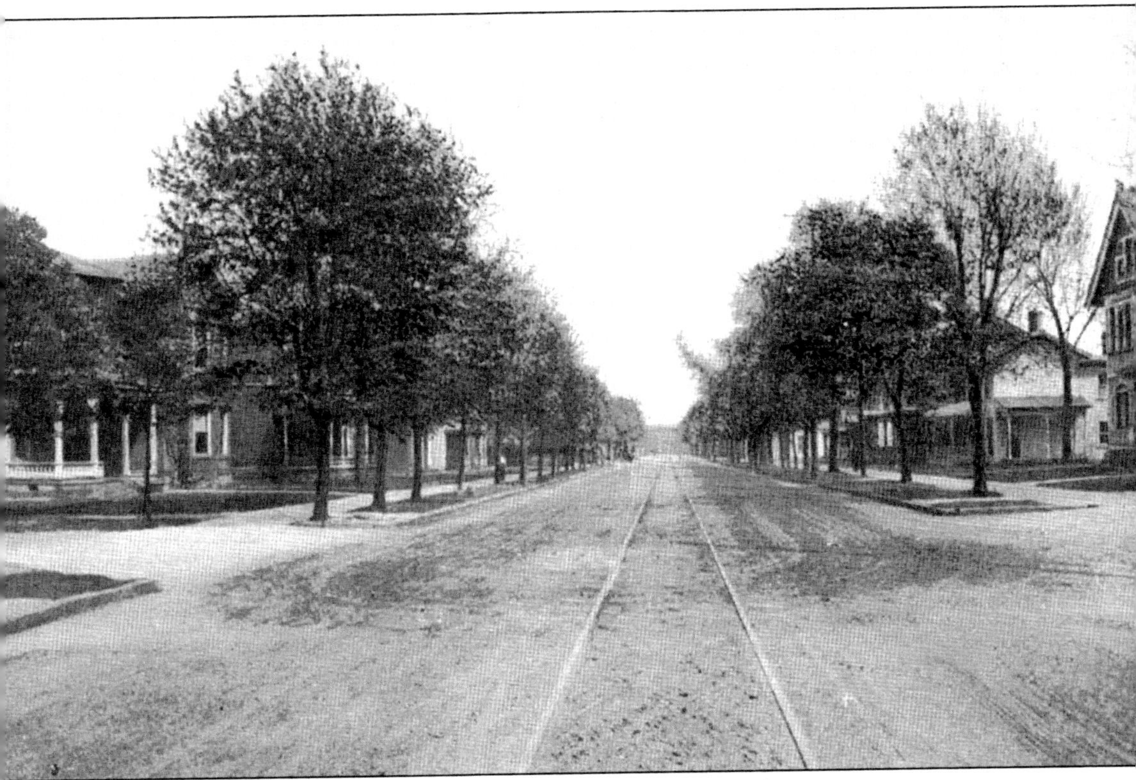

Notice the trolley tracks still lining West High Street in this postcard picture.

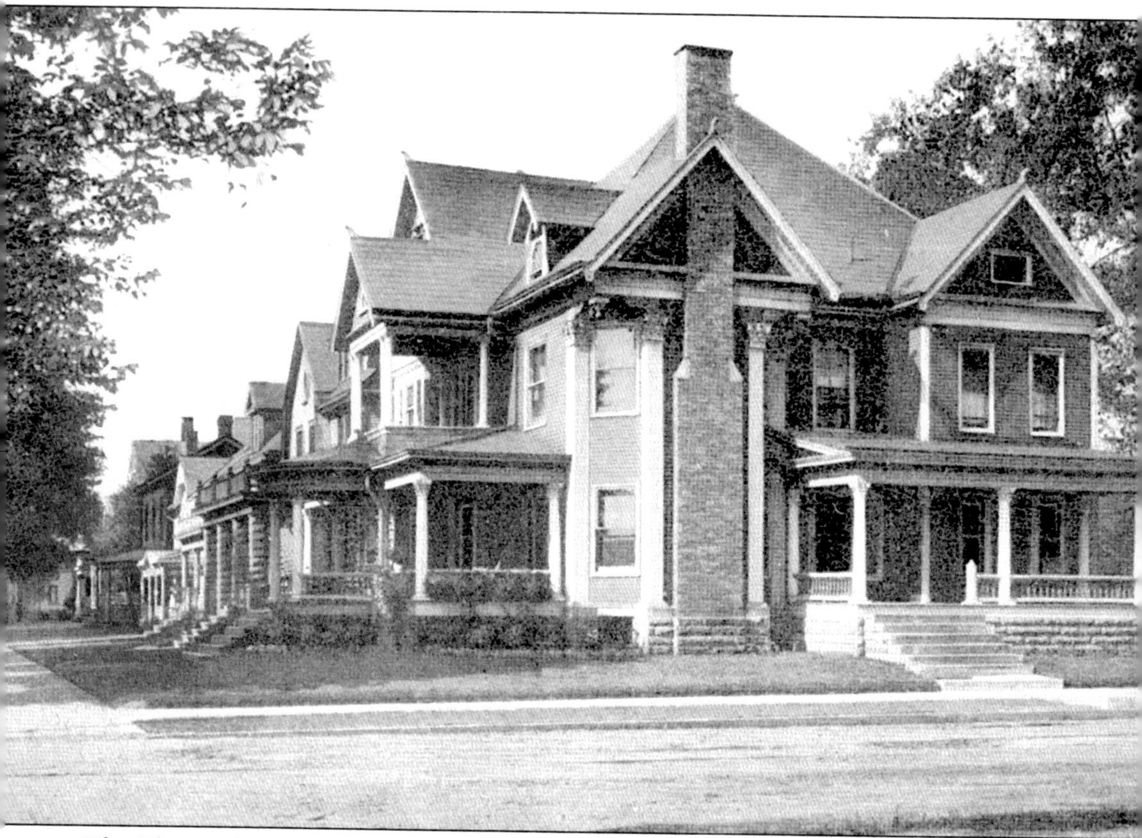

The Thomas Sargent (member of the first city council in 1833) home located at 325 North Broadway is a well-preserved example of the type of residence common in New Philadelphia nearly a century ago. Among its classic details are interesting fanlights in the gables and a single fanlight over the front entrance.

Abraham Knisely built his home at 202 Eighth Street NE. The original part of the old house was approximately 20 by 36 feet. Extensive remodeling, the addition of other rooms, and the siding covering the log structure have almost completely obliterated the outlines of the original home. Its location at an angle to the present street indicates that it was built before the town was platted.

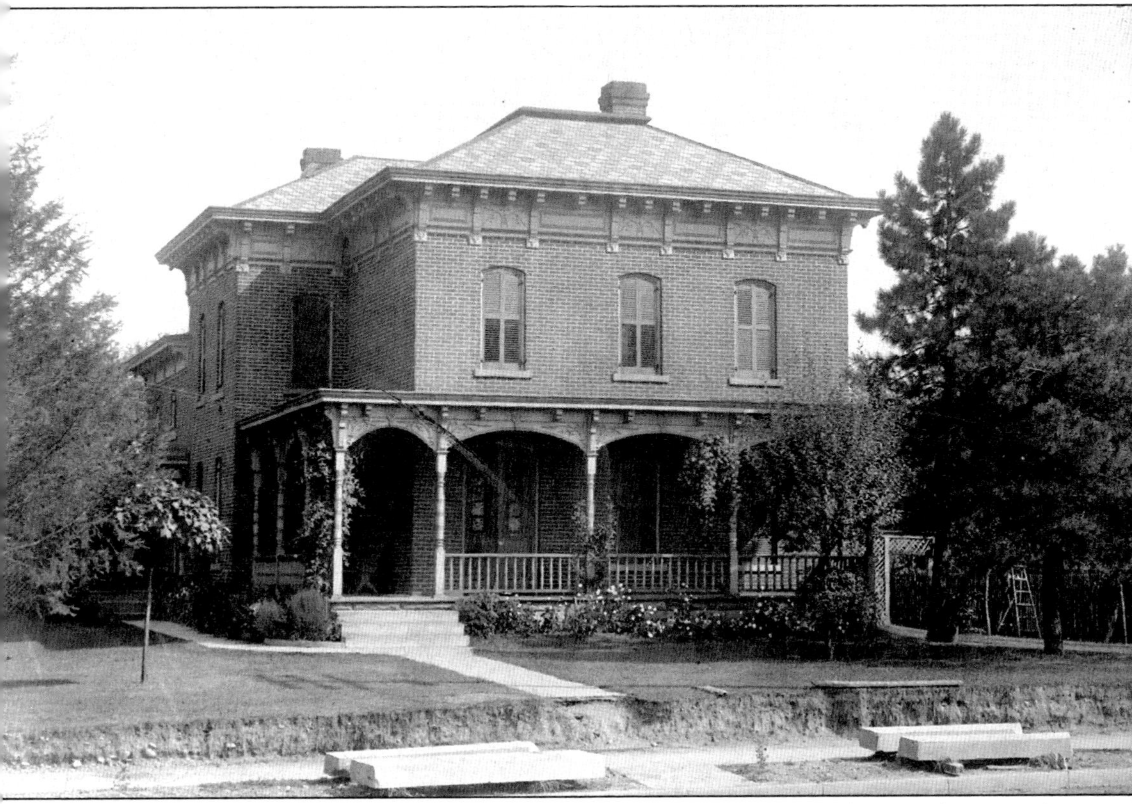

Located at 308 South Broadway is the former home of John A. Bingham, who served as United States Minister to Japan from 1873 to 1884, two decades after the country had been opened to the outside world.

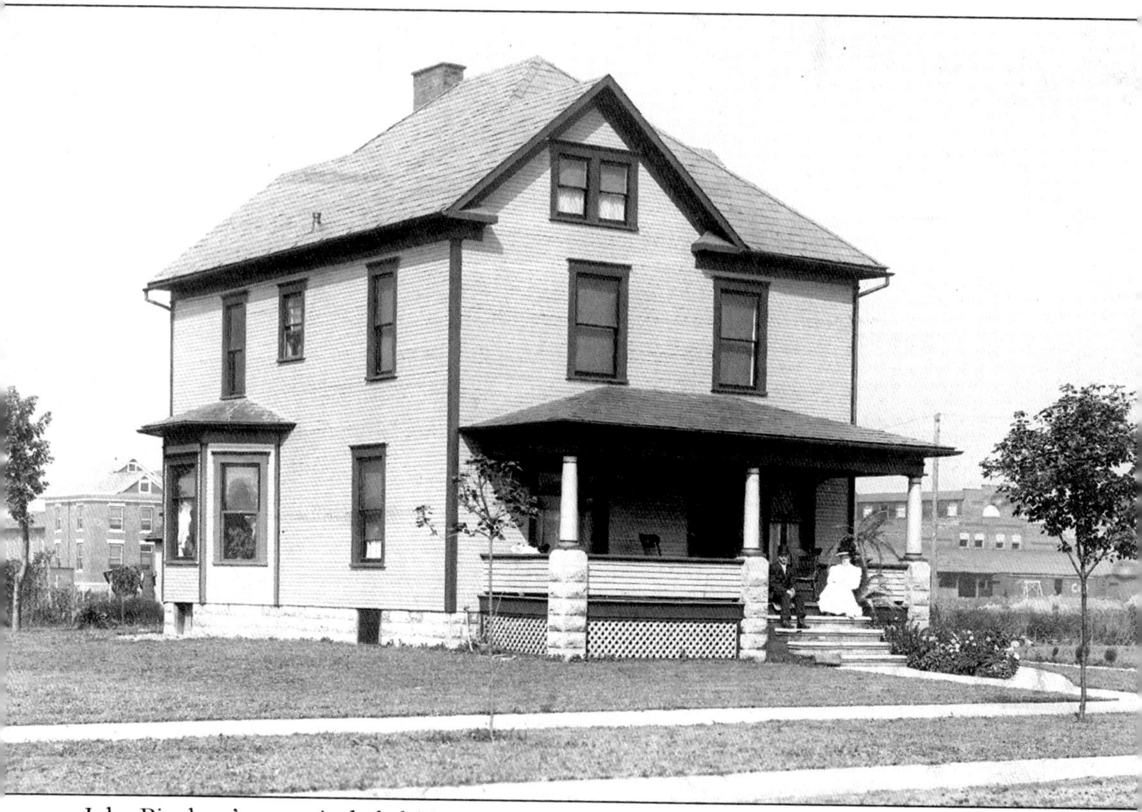

John Bingham's career included 16 years as a member of Congress, sponsorship of the Fourteenth Amendment (freedom of slaves), and service as defense counsel in the impeachment proceedings brought against President Andrew Johnson. Bingham occupied the residence for a time during the late 1840s.

BIBLIOGRAPHY

Grossenbacher, Jeanne. *A History of Public Education in our Town of New Philadelphia, Ohio.* Strasburg, Ohio: Gordon Printing Inc., 1987.

Hagloch, Henry C. *The History of Tuscarawas County, Ohio to 1956.* 2nd ed., Strasburg, Ohio: Gordon Printing Inc.

Kirk, Eleanor M. *Vic, 81 Active Years.* Self-published, 1984.

Lamneck, John H. *The County Squire, the Romance of a Law Abiding Citizen.* Boston: Christopher Publishing House, 1960.

Lohrman, H.P. and Raplph H. Romig. *A History of Tuscarawas County Ohio Valley of the Tuscarawas.* 1st printing, Ulrichsville, Ohio: Ohio Hills Publishers, 1972; 2nd printing, Strasburg, Ohio: Gordon Printing Inc., 1975; and 3rd printing, Dover, Ohio: R.W. Whitemyer Co. Lithographers, 1986.

Meese, Pede. *A History of the New Philadelphia Fire Department.* Strasburg, Ohio: Gordon Printing Inc., 2004.

Miller, Fred. *Images of America: Tuscarawas County.* Chicago: Arcadia Publishing, 2000.

Miller, Max T. *Straight from the Kitchen Table.* Beloit, Ohio: Amos Communications, Inc., 2001.

Tuscarawas County Chapter of Ohio Retired Teachers Association. *History of the Schools in Tuscarawas County Ohio.* Strasburg, Ohio: Gordon Printing, Inc., 1993.

Tuscarawas County Genealogical Society. *Historical Atlas, Tuscarawas County Ohio.* Strasburg, Ohio: Gordon Printing Inc., 1973.

Tuscarawas County Historical Society. *The Chronicler.* Strasburg, Ohio, Gordon Printing.

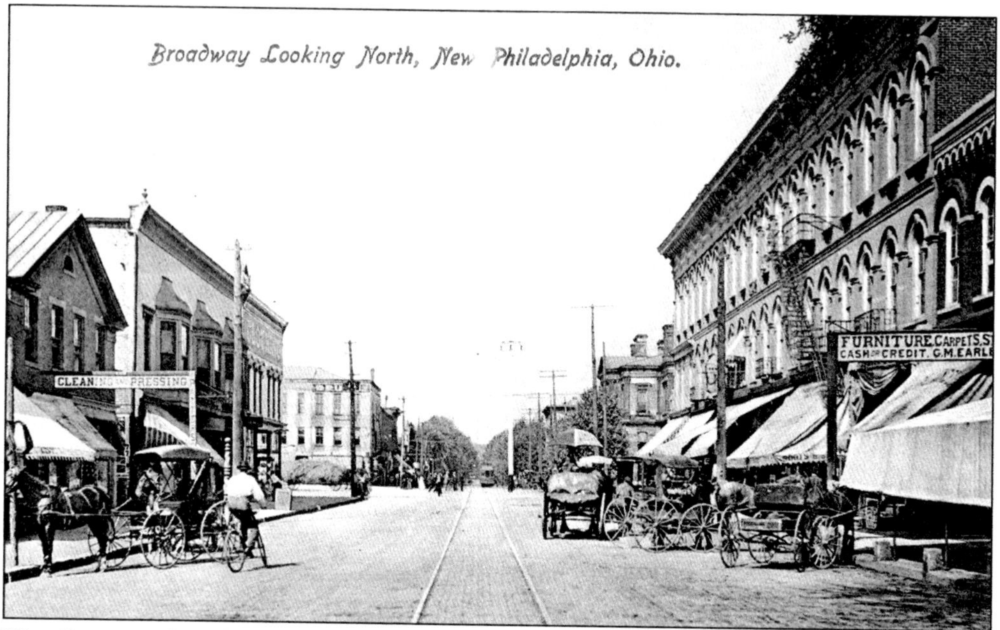

Wes Green, orphaned at a very early age, came to New Philadelphia on November 22, 1867. He tried his hand at farming, turned to the coalmines, and then worked for a paper mill, the railroad, and lastly a steel mill. In 1897, he built his first camera and began taking pictures of groups on Sundays for 16¢ each. The proceeds were used to add to Green's equipment. Publisher William E. Seibert asked Wes to join him at his business at 143 North Broadway to assist with the school picture business. Wes worked for Mr. Seibert for 7 years. In the summers, he operated picture galleries around the eastern part of Ohio. Green purchased his first picture camera from Al Rummell. Wes continued the later part of his career at 1044 West High Avenue. In 1942, Wes estimated that in the 40 years he had been a photographer, he had taken 6,000,000 pictures. Many of the post cards in this book were taken by "Green the Photographer." Wes was truly a pioneering master in his field.